PREACH THE WORD

Expository Preaching from the Book of Ephesians

JOHN R. MUMAW

Foreword by Myron Augsburger

HERALD PRESS
Scottdale, Pennsylvania
Kitchener, Ontario
1987

Library of Congress Cataloging-in-Publication Data

Mumaw, John R. (John Rudy), 1904-
    Preach the word.

        Bibliography: p.
        1. Bible.   N.T.   Ephesians—Sermons—Outlines,
syllabi, etc.   2. Bible.   N.T.   Ephesians—Homiletical
use.   3. Preaching.   I.   Title.
BS2695.4.M86   1987   251   87-23763
ISBN 0-8361-3452-4

Scripture references are from the *Holy Bible: New
International Version.* Copyright © 1973, 1978, 1984 by
the International Bible Society. Used by permission of
Zondervan Bible Publishers.

PREACH THE WORD
Copyright © 1987 by Herald Press, Scottdale, Pa. 15683
        Published simultaneously in Canada by Herald Press,
        Kitchener, Ont. N2G 4M5. All rights reserved.
Library of Congress Catalog Card Number: 87-23763
International Standard Book Number: 0-8361-3452-4
Printed in the United States of America
Design by Gwen M. Stamm

87 88 89 90 91 92 93 94 95 96 12 11 10 9 8 7 6 5 4 3 2 1

*To my former students in homiletics
and to all who preach the Word*

Contents

Foreword

It is refreshing to pick up a book on preaching that is such a strong statement for the expository method. John R. Mumaw has given us such a statement in *Preach the Word*. In fact, the book is both a commentary on the epistle of Ephesians as well as a homiletical exercise.

For many of us who were students of homiletics under Brother Mumaw, as we called him, reading this manuscript has been a review of his teaching. I had the distinct feel of being in his class again; hearing his forceful emphasis on exposition, on careful exegesis, on clarifying a theme for a given passage, on careful and clear structure, on illustrations that serve as windows but don't dominate or displace the biblical content, and on the movement of a sermon toward a chosen objective. The interfacing of homiletical instruction with the outlines of Ephesians is a helpful exercise for the pastor who reads this book.

It is important that a book on preaching serves to restore the prophetic role of the pastor. In far too many cases the preacher has been regarded as an authority figure more than a preacher/teacher/prophet. This is due, perhaps, to small congregations assigning the pastor a broad range of duties or vesting the full responsibility for a disciplined church in the pastor. Combining the administrative role with the proclaiming role has limited the hearer from perceiving the preacher as prophet. Consequently, the saying "don't preach at me" expresses a common negative attitude. We should cultivate, instead, an openness and a desire to hear the Word expounded. We need to restore the prophetic role as a part of the worship experience, as hearing the Word of the Lord.

In this book the author places a strong, and in my judgment correct, emphasis on careful study and preparation of the sermon. He emphasizes the role of the Spirit in the pastor's study, where the preacher engages the Word in a more authentic process of discernment. At times the spirit of the occasion, construed as the Holy Spirit, might actually be the human spirit quickened by adrenalin! One who preaches the Word knows the difference between the anointing of the Holy Spirit and the stimulus of group atmosphere, though this may be positive and supportive.

The outlines of the Epistle of Ephesians present well the author's homiletical style and exposition. Of course he does not expect others to preach from his outlines, but to develop those which fit the thought and personality of the given pastor. For some, these outlines are too much and persons will want to work with smaller sections or briefer outlines (as in the Summary points on page 60). For others, the choice of focus or style of shaping the points will be quite different. The important thing that the author has done is to hold us to the Word, to the text.

Years ago Bishop Quayle said, "Preaching is not so much preparing a sermon and delivering it as preparing the preacher and delivering him [her]." The total life speaks, not just the words we utter. When one steps into the pulpit, it is not simply to give a lecture on some segment of acquired knowledge, but it is to be a spokesperson for God. Biblical preaching happens not by simply quoting Scripture but by the meaning of the Scripture striking hearts anew at that moment.

One dilemma of preaching is the awareness that change happens, as the author points out, by participation. This means a mental interchange in which participants lay claim to a truth or insight as their own. One may assume that this happens most readily in discussion groups, but it is not necessarily so because persons may be more involved in the exchange of ideas or in what they may add to the dialogue than in assimilating new insights into their current lifestyle. Such change-by-participation can happen in preaching when the preacher creates vicarious dialogue—an exercise in which the preacher enters into the thinking of the audience without the negative effect of putting anyone on the spot. This may happen in either the preaching setting or in a group discussion.

In a day of the mass media and urban lifestyles, when many voices are heard as commercials, we need the revitalization of the prophetic ministry. Amidst a multiplicity of voices, persons need to be able to "Go unto the house of the Lord" and hear the Word proclaimed by a person who has done careful and diligent study and who, while applying the truth to contemporary issues, does so with the integrity of exegeting God's Word. As the author says, "We need preachers who herald the message of redemption with conviction, who speak with the authority of God's truth, and who deliver it in the power of the Holy Spirit."

—Myron S. Augsburger, Pastor
Washington Community Fellowship

Author's Preface

> When I came to you, brothers, I did not come with eloquence or superior wisdom as I proclaimed to you the testimony about God. For I resolved to know nothing while I was with you except Jesus Christ and him crucified. I came to you in weakness and fear, and with much trembling. My message and my preaching were not with wise and persuasive words, but with a demonstration of the Spirit's power, so that your faith might not rest on men's wisdom, but on God's power.
>
> (Paul in 1 Corinthians 2:1-5)

This unique testimony is of one who addressed a church with serious cases of carnality. He realized that dealing with sin requires more than human effort. His preaching was shaped by an awareness of need for divine wisdom and power. The pulpit is no place for personal display of education, talent, and human skills at the expense of divine revelation. It is not by human wisdom, nor by power of personality, nor by any supposed superiority of speech that people are convinced of divine truth.

These warnings do not relieve the preacher from responsibility to identify a purpose and to plan structure for the delivery of truth.

The emphasis is upon the use of Scripture to shape a biblical message which the Holy Spirit can use to convey the will of God. Expository preaching is designed to fulfill that purpose. It specializes in making clear the teaching and content of the Bible. It brings the message of definite units of God's Word to the people.

Forty years ago I was given the privilege of serving a small congregation as its pastor. After some months of regular expository preaching, a layman expressed his appreciation for this method of preaching. He compared it with the topical method and said, "I can now follow the sermon while relating it to the passage in my open Bible. When I go home, I reread the passage and relive what I heard from the pulpit."

On another occasion, while serving an intermediate assignment, I introduced expository preaching in a series of Sunday evening messages. A member of the congregation expressed his evaluation of this different approach by saying, "By this method we are told what the Bible says."

I want to express my gratitude for the encouraging responses from persons like these who have helped to "make my day" again and again. I owe a debt of thanks to students in my courses in preaching. They have helped me refine my methods. They gave me further confidence in expository preaching when I witnessed their growth in applying these principles. And above all, I thank God for his grace in classroom procedures and in pulpit performances.

—John R. Mumaw

Introduction

The hope of the author is that a study of this book will serve to stimulate direct biblical preaching. Two things are intended. One is to help preachers discover the advantage of disciplines involved in exposition. Another is to provide models in outlining sermons for pulpit use. The outlines may be used as they appear, but it is expected that each preacher will make adaptations.

The book of Ephesians concentrates interest in the church as a body of believers. The present study demonstrates versatility of content within a somewhat standard form of thought development. It represents an evangelical use of the Scriptures without dictating precise details of interpretation.

Two other features are included to stimulate improvements in preaching. The first section of each chapter pertains to homiletical principles that serve to strengthen the preparation and construction of sermons. The last section of each chapter speaks to general factors related to the preaching content and its effectiveness.

The value of expository preaching becomes more evident with growing expertise in the use of this method. It forces the preacher to make clear statements of biblical truth, which requires in-depth study of the Bible. Consequently, one will preach with greater authority and urgency. From the viewpoint of the audience it facilitates lay literacy of the Scriptures and provides a broader base of truth for Christian commitments. It also stimulates more intelligent Bible reading.

Expository preaching increases pulpit influence. As a pre-eminent force of influence in the church, it is important to achieve the highest level of preaching effect. It is a matter of informing the intellect of our people with spiritual truth. They need to be convinced of ethical principles for daily living. Their hearts must be moved to deeper religious devotion, especially in their attitude toward the Scriptures. That will help to shape their Christian convictions for religious duty. And what is more essential than to have experiences in worship that influence the will to act in personal commitment to the will of God?

Dr. H. Clair Amstutz once said, "The combination of an informed mind and a caring heart makes the ministry of the church effective." Let me add that the combination of a trained mind and a compassionate heart makes the pulpit ministry a valid witness.

PART I

Getting Started

CHAPTER 1

Why Preach?

We Have an Opportunity.
We Have a Revelation.
We Have an Interpretation.
We Have an Obligation.
We Have a Purpose.
We Have an Anointing.
We Have a New Calling.

The current wave of protest against preaching is subsiding. It was not unusual in the sixties to have people berating the pulpit. Although that was nothing new, it nevertheless made a rather severe impact upon the practice of preaching. It forced the church to face the realities of mediocre performance. Recently, more is being said in favor of the pulpit and its influence in molding the lives of people in the pew.

One of the factors that in times past brought the pulpit into disrepute was a failure to recognize the constant need for renewal and improvement of preaching. Another was the general decay of life in the church. And what is even more serious was the apparent laxity in the preacher. We may never take it for granted that people will listen because it is announced as a sermon. We may never assume because it pertains to the Bible that it will attract attention. We may never rely upon the force of tradition to keep preaching alive. This is a discipline that requires constant improvement and repeated adjustment.

We Have an Opportunity

"How shall they hear without a preacher?"[1] The Christian ministry involves proclamation. The special ministry of preaching identifies a role compounded of mission (apostleship), prophetic declaration (prophet), evangelism (evangelist), and pastoral-teaching service (pastor-teacher).

In any attempt to measure the influence of the pulpit we will discover a fluctuating line of effect. It is evident, however, that if it is evaluated on the basis of its manifold functions, the total impact will be seen as a positive force in human history. One who enters the preaching arena today will have an opportunity to help shape the course of contemporary human affairs. It will certainly give shape to the forms of Christian witness. The church offers a channel of influence in its pulpit that has no equal in political or social careers. Preaching has always been a major function of the church both as a recruitment agency and as a fortifying nurture of its faith.

The life of the church has long been influenced by its preaching. It has been, and is, a means of determining the way people think about life and godliness. Even though what the preacher says alters only slightly the direction of thought in one person there is an accumulative effect when it is multiplied by one hundred. And there are times when the pulpit becomes the switchboard that controls human destiny. What really counts is measured by what happens when the gathered church is scattered.

Sermons have a great deal to do with influencing the way a congregation functions during the week. If the people are to be a saving and healing agency in the community, they must have not only the means of salvation at hand, but also the method of healing human hurts. Good preaching equips members for ministry to human needs. As Sweazey says, "A church's best forms of service are likely to get their inspiration, aims, and promotion from the pulpit. And the best sermons are likely to be extensions of all the church is doing."[2] Thus we affirm that the role of preaching has tremendous importance in the total life and work of the church.

Preaching can best be understood in relation to worship. It stimulates response to the knowledge of God. It is different from a public speech in that it is designed to bring about a commitment to divine revelation. It is one element of experience with God. "All the deep human needs that make worship necessary make preaching necessary."[3] A dynamic pulpit ministry is a powerful instrument in bringing about vital encounters with God. In the Pauline tradition of preaching the Word, the minister represents the mind of Christ for human reaction. The sermon is designed to expose the meanings of Scripture whereby faith is solicited and nurtured. We preach to support people's intention to worship God.

Another aspect of preaching is the fellowship it promotes. Christianity is not like many world religions which emphasize solitary temple meditation. The Christian faith involves brotherhood. The sermon is addressed to a group where love and faith are transformed into fellowship. In that setting a message from God is delivered to persons in relationship with each other. What is more significant is the fact that communication takes place through a person. The message is expressed in words but the meaning of those words is enhanced by the human voice and a convincing eye. Sermons reach the hearts of hearers when they express divine truth with the warmth of a lively personality.

Preaching is a characteristic function of Christianity. Without it the church would fail in its mission. It conveys and explains the saving truths of the gospel. It serves to nurture a growing faith. It tells who Christ is and what he has done to redeem fallen humanity. Sermons are designed to report the saving acts of God and to invite people to faith. They extend the meanings of faith into the life of Christian discipleship. The pulpit is the place to highlight the kingdom of God and to proclaim its priority in the everyday life of the Christian.

We Have a Revelation

There are two words in the New Testament that together identify the major portion of ministerial responsibility. Both of them refer to the exercise of speech for the impartation of divine truth. One is *euangelizō*, which means "to preach the gospel." It is proclamation of the "good news." This suggests the need of humanity and the provision God has made. In light of human need, including all the sin and sorrow of lost people, we declare the fact that God has lovingly and graciously arranged humanity's redemption. This brings us to the recognition of divine revelation. It has been made known that God is ready to forgive the penitent sinner and to receive him or her into the kingdom. When we preach we stand between human need and divine grace as messengers of the good news of redemption.

The other word is *kērussō*, which means "to proclaim from a throne." God has acted and he has spoken. He has authorized the declaration of peace as having been delivered on behalf of a Ruler. "He has prepared his throne for judgment."

Preaching thereby becomes a message from the throne. The message is delivered on the authorization of heaven's highest court. It is presented to the conscience of each person for human obedience. It is directed to persons' wills for response. And God's message calling for action has in it an insistent demand because it comes from a King.

When Paul called upon Timothy to "preach the Word," he was asking him to *speak the truth of God with authority.* The Word is the written truth God has made known. It needs to be understood, exposed, and applied. The Christian ministry assumes that God has expressed himself progressively throughout Old Testament history, and supremely and finally in Jesus Christ. God has revealed his character and expressed his will through the life of Jesus, his teachings, his crucifixion, his resurrection, and his ascension—even his present mediatorial work.

Preachers are stewards of the *mysteries of God* and must give an honest accounting for their use of divine revelation. This refers to meanings that are not discovered by intellectual research. They proclaim truth that has been made known to those who have been initiated into the kingdom of God by faith in Jesus Christ. It means that the preaching of the Word is an activity that moves into the realm of the supernatural. Someone has well said that the words of Jesus are more supernatural than the things he did. When we use revealed truth in our preaching we are handling elements of the supernatural. Touching human need with healing and uplifting power requires proclamation of revealed truth. What we preach is not something a mere human has discovered. It is the truth God has made known.

We Have an Interpretation

Every sermon is an interpretation of some portion of Scripture. Interpretation is basic to biblical preaching. What is declared from the pulpit is an explanation of the meaning of the Scriptures. Regardless of the type of sermon construction, the message should always represent what God has said in his Word.

Originality in preaching is expressed in the form, not in the *ideas*. Audiences expect preachers to be original. They are not therefore called upon to derive their thoughts from some subjective intellectual process. The content of their messages is drawn from divine revelation even though the expression of those ideas may differ. Herein lies the preacher's originality: the way revealed truth is put together. A preacher may follow certain principles of homiletics and apply specific structural guidelines, but the total expression of that person's thought patterns and personality traits will give the sermon a unique literary flavor and make the message that person's own product.

From this discussion it should be understood the preacher has no aspiration to undertake the *creation of new truth*. There is no use to aim at giving expression to ideas that have never been heard before. Only God can create something absolutely new. Whatever originality a preacher expresses is relative and personal. It is the selection and arrangement of ideas which enables the preacher to achieve relative originality. The audience may say, "We never heard it said that way before."

When we declare that in preaching we have an interpretation, we are asserting that we have gone through the process of exegesis and have arranged ideas in a way that can be understood by the audience. The human dynamic engaged in the task of exposition and delivery is the source of originality. It is this power of interpretation and of ingenius expression that keeps the pulpit performance fresh and effective.

We Have an Obligation

The obligation to preach is derived from both the experience of truth and the authority it possesses. Paul said, "Woe is me if I do not preach the gospel." He saw in its message "the power of God unto salvation."[4] He was convinced of its effect. On another occasion he said he preached in "much assurance." He was persuaded to believe it would effect change in the lives of people who heard it.

The *contrast* observed between the way Jesus handled the Scripture and the way the scribes of his day taught[5] is significant to our understanding of obligation. The scribes used their position as reason for people to accept their messages. Jesus ignored the authority of office and rested his case on the intrinsic value of the truth itself. What he preached and what he taught had in it demands upon private life and social relationships that can be achieved only through regeneration. Nevertheless, he presented the message as representing the realities and demands of the kingdom of God.

We have this same message to proclaim to our generation. Its power to redeem rests not in the calling to preach but in the Word we preach. Knowing that the Scriptures are the key to human redemption and renewal, we are under obligation to proclaim its truth. The preacher becomes an authentic voice that calls people into encounter with God.

We Have a Purpose

A major function of the church is accomplished through preaching. The church is engaged in the multitudinous task of *meeting the needs of the whole person.* The pulpit holds a firm position in dispensing spiritual resources for its members to cope with the critical issues of life. The sermon is no panacea for all the complex ills of society. But preaching is an effective means in the church to fulfill significant purposes in its spiritual ministry.

Preaching opens the Bible for *popular understanding.* The preacher stands between the biblical message and the needs of the people. People must know what God has to say to them. And God wants an agent of communication to make known his gracious will. In this mediating stance the preacher is confronted with a prevailing challenge.

Preaching is focused on the *saving acts of God.* We proclaim what God has done to redeem the fallen race. This theme constitutes a major emphasis in the evangelical message. This supersedes the urge to give advice in handling moral and social issues. What God has done in Christ to provide the means of producing new persons living in the Spirit is more important than the call to make minor adjustments in human relationships. Sweazey has so aptly said, "The sermons and instructions about sermons in the New Testament make it clear that the basic theme of preaching is the declaration of what God has done through Jesus Christ, with the call for personal acceptance and repentance."[6] Let it not be supposed, however, that we have no obligation to preach about the manner of life the Christian is called to follow. The proclamation of salvation without touching on the meaning of discipleship is a misunderstanding of the intent of the gospel.

Preaching is designed to initiate *a genuine encounter with Jesus Christ.* The purpose of the church is to bring people into a vital relationship with a living Person. Discipleship implies having a personal relationship with Christ as Lord. It is the business of the sermon not only to tell what Christ did in his atoning work but also to proclaim what he is ready to do (and is doing) now. Preaching is an enabling force that creates in people an awareness of the real presence of Christ. The Word we preach not only says something, it *does* something. It penetrates the inner life of the hearer and sustains the depository of truth for effective living. It may not happen with ecstatic experience, but it has a way of fastening itself in times of growing illumination and with accumulating certainty.

There is a broadly accepted view that the sermon should perform a *teaching function.* Ozora Davis insists that healing, exhortation, admonition, confirmation, and edification are all valid elements of the sermon. Preaching accomplishes a variety of purposes. It may be addressed to people outside the church for evangelistic purposes, to new converts in the church as preparation for church membership, and to members of the Christian community to improve their knowledge of the Christian faith. Preaching can exhort to holiness and instruct believers in the way of life.

Another expectation of the pulpit is *encouragement.* People are constantly seeking for strength to do their daily duties. It is not only an opportunity for the church to give encouragement to its people, but it is an essential function in its ministry to the congregation. Preaching is a major channel of influence through which people get help for the critical issues they encounter in vocational activities. Preaching is one way God has to heal the brokenhearted and to lift the burdens of life.

There are many authentic opportunities for preachers. Preaching opens the way to influence decision-making in important issues. It prophetically addresses the evils in our society. It provides a forum to deal with living concerns. There is really no end to the spiritual interests we can touch in preaching.

We Have an Anointing

The Holy Spirit enables us to render service to the kingdom of God. The Spirit provides the capacity to discern truth. This constitutes the anointing which all believers receive for the performance of duty. And preaching is no exception to receive this basic resource for action.

The anointing is from *Christ.*[7] It is a consecration to holiness. As Christ was anointed to his office, so are we. The believer shares in his life and mission and therefore is engaged in promoting the benefits of his kingdom.

The anointing is with *truth.*[8] The final strength of the Christian lies not in that person's own effort, but in the truth by which he or she is inspired. As the agent of illumination the Holy Spirit ratifies the proclamation as the Word of God.

The anointing is done by the *Holy Spirit.*[9] The Holy Spirit is the Christian's reliable Helper, Comforter, and Guide. The Spirit's communications are intended to uphold us in all our activities. The Spirit instills the mind of Christ and enables the Christian to walk in the power of the resurrection. Having such powerful resources in the Spirit gives ample motivation to put them into use in preaching. The Spirit gives confidence, freedom, and courage to proclaim the Word.

We Have a New Calling

Our times have produced a public mind that challenges the effectiveness of preaching. We must therefore take into consideration contemporary objections to the claims of the pulpit. These have in part come from the influences of the so-called "global revolution."

Established authorities (including the church) have come under vigorous attack. Appeals for reform have focused attention on social injustice and economic oppression. This has produced a "liberation theology." Religious leaders have picked up these concerns to the neglect of biblical proclamation.

Fortunately, many people of the general public are now turning again to the church for answers to their current problems of survival. They are beginning to see in the Scriptures ways of developing positive elements of human relationships.

"Christians know from both Scripture and experience that human fulfillment is impossible outside the context of some authority. Freedom unlimited is an illusion. The mind is free only under the authority of righteousness. It is under Christ's yoke that we find the rest he promises, not in discarding it."[10] We expect the church to use the instrument of the Word, with its intrinsic authority, to meet the contemporary needs of searching souls. At a time when many in the church are capitulating to the prevailing secular culture, the prophetic duty of the preacher is to promote the universal principles of divine truth. We need to reaffirm what Stott calls the "Christian Counter-Culture"[11] by declaring the validity of the Sermon on the Mount for today's Christian living.

This constitutes a call to biblical preaching. It rests on the holy conviction that *the Bible has priority over human resources.* We are called to "preach the Word." The best method by which to fulfill that mandate is to preach expository sermons. By this we mean bringing out what is in the text and exposing its meaning for today.

> The work of the preacher, as he *expounds the written Word* to his congregation, must ever be the supreme method of God's communication. If our lot is cast in an age with little more than amused contempt for preaching, that in no way affects its importance or its preeminence in the purpose of God. Christ came preaching. From the day of Pentecost, the apostles spent themselves in preaching. Great movements in the church have normally been initiated and developed by preaching. Revival has invariably come by preaching. By preaching, it may confidently be anticipated, it will come again.[12]

Preaching has always been a prominent action in the church. It is a form of spiritual exercise designed to inform the intellect with spiritual truth. It serves to convince the judgment of ethical principles contained in the Scriptures. Preaching is intended to move the hearts of hearers to religious devotion. It is expected that, as a result of hearing a sermon, persons will have developed conviction in their own hearts for the performance of religious duty. Preaching has not completed its function until it has moved the will to act in personal commitment.

CHAPTER 2

Expository Preaching

The Nature of Expository Preaching
The Aim of Expository Preaching
The Primacy of Expository Preaching
Advantages of Expository Preaching

I am convinced of the value of expository preaching. When I began my ministry of the Word in 1928, the use of the topical method was a natural application of the academic approaches that had influenced my thinking. But it was not long until the textual method seemed more appropriate. Too often, however, it was using the text as a mere introductory element to my topic. Later, I became more sensitive to the limitations such a selection of Scripture imposed upon me. I began developing the sermon structure from the elements of truth contained in the text itself. Finally, I came to see the advantage of using the full-blown method of exposition. And this remodeled my pulpit proclamation. Since then, I have covered most of the New Testament in expository preaching.

The Nature of Expository Preaching

An expository sermon is based on a biblical passage of some length beyond that of a textual message. The theme and major divisions are drawn from the content of the text. Depending on the length of the Scripture passage, subpoints to the main divisions may also be found within the text. In any case the thought of the sermon is developed from the chosen portion of Scripture without "importing" major ideas from other portions of Scripture. It is unified by the trend of thought that corresponds with the aim adopted for its use.

The expository sermon is more than a running commentary. It is something different from an exegesis of the passage. It has its ideas focused on a single theme, omitting what does not contribute to the development of the prominent thought. The theme formulated from the passage itself serves as the basis for selecting the sermon material. Another controlling factor is the preacher's purpose for the particular occasion.

The Aim of Expository Preaching

Any effort to improve pulpit influence must consider the *method* of preaching. This includes expository preaching. We must reach for help in making expository preaching most useful and more improved when it is used.

"The principle task of the preacher is to proclaim the truth as set forth in the Scriptures."[1] Expository preaching fulfills the primary purpose of pulpit proclamation. It is distinguished from other types of preaching by its manner of treatment.

The aim in expository preaching is to make clear the content and teachings of the Bible. Specifically, a single sermon developed by this method exposes the meaning of a certain portion of Scripture. In most cases it goes beyond that to make application of the exposed truth to Christian life. It not only offers a key to the meaning of Scripture; it also identifies the relation of biblical truth to current human need.

An expository sermon is designed to tell what a given portion of Scripture means for the contemporary church. The leading ideas of the passage are expressed in terms of today's cultural understanding. The major divisions come from the text under consideration. Details are used as subpoints insofar as they relate to the theme. This involves a process of selection which leaves thoughts unrelated to the theme for another time.

Selection is indispensable. We choose such materials as will yield important ideas for the purpose of the message. Some of the material will need explanation to show the point of relevance in the sermon.

The Primacy of Expository Preaching

With the heavy demands on the preacher's time and energy, there must be some justification for expository preaching. Is there any guarantee that its use will promote biblical teachings? Merrill F. Unger says, "The glory of the Christian pulpit is a borrowed glow." There must be some way for preaching to reflect the glory of God. Advocates of the expository method assume that "preaching the Word" (cf. 2 Timothy 4:2) can best be accomplished by exposing biblical meanings in some effective manner. The "glow" that emanates from the Scriptures derives its strength from the Word of truth. Therefore, we want to use the best method by which the biblical message can be delivered with conviction and authority.

Expository preaching can be made an effective instrument in communicating divine revelation. It has in it the potential of an effective spiritual influence because:

1. It systematically expounds the Word of God.

2. It exalts the use of Scripture to counteract the influence of secularism.

3. It promotes spiritual insights with direct support from Scripture.

4. It delivers an authoritative declaration of God's will.

5. It engages the Word of truth as an effective base for the Spirit's message.

6. It helps to make a passage of Scripture cling to the listener's mind and heart.

7. It diversifies spiritual values that meet hidden human needs.

8. It offers opportunity to cover overall messages inherent in an entire book.

9. It develops spiritual maturity in people who are thereby effectively rooted and grounded in the Word.

10. It broadens the base for commitment to doctrinal beliefs.

11. It provides a wholesome biblical diet that prevents disproportionate emphases.

12. It covers a wide variety of problems and life situations for the pulpit agenda.

In the earlier years of my ministry I was asked to serve as an interim pastor of a congregation that was seriously and adversely affected by a civic disturbance in the community. The local minister became involved in the crossfire and found himself in an awkward position for leadership.

In an attempt to rebuild church attendance and Christian faithfulness, I introduced a series of expository sermons in the Sunday evening services. The attendance increased from week to week and a genuine interest developed in the study of the Bible. The community supported the program and expressed appreciation for the approach. One man said to me, "Why don't other preachers tell us what the Bible says?"

The obvious conclusion is that many people want to know "what the Bible says." Although an attraction to biblical preaching does not rest entirely on the use of the expository method, there are at least some advantages in exposing people to the truth through expositions.

I have found in this method the satisfaction of knowing that my message is biblical in content and therefore gives some assurance that it has a real potential for "feeding the flock of God." It has led me to a broader use of scriptural material which offers a wider coverage of truth. This helps me promote in the congregation a wholesome balance of doctrinal and practical beliefs. It opened up to me a greater sensitivity to the timelessness of biblical truth. I discovered in working through a series of messages from consecutive verses and chapters that what appeared on the surface to be somewhat unrelated to current life did have relevance to contemporary situations. I simply needed to make applications of eternal principles to present needs. Often a careful study of the context yielded a clue to a line of thought that was useful in constructing the sermon.

A commitment to expository preaching has its own "price tag." It takes time, energy, and perseverance. The exercise of faith in the Scriptures is not the least of requirements. The judicious use of tools can be very rewarding in terms of biblical insights. It calls for an objective approach with an open mind to new understandings. And the whole process must be subject to the guidance of the Holy Spirit.

The following chapters are intended to clarify the procedure with explanations and demonstrations.

Advantages of Expository Preaching

I have found a number of advantages in using the expository method. This is not to say it is the only viable method of preaching. And it does not mean that every sermon must be developed over a standardized pattern.

The following statements are intended to suggest a preference for using this method as a general practice. The comparisons have been made with topical and textual sermons.

1. It guards against the snare of using a text as a mere starting point for a topical discussion.

2. It generates a broad base for biblical instruction or nurture of the congregation.

3. It exposes the unity and coherence of Scripture even by the use of a single passage—more so in a series of messages based on an entire book.

4. It encourages the discovery of a divine plan and purpose in revealed truth.

5. It avoids the temptation to dodge certain truths because of difficulty in interpretation or because it touches an issue with delicate current implications.

6. It produces a literate congregation and encourages reference to the Bible in hand.

7. It calls people to a simple faith and obedience to the Word.

8. It promotes the evident effect of the authority and power of the Word.

9. It sharpens the cutting edge of the effect of Scripture upon the faith and practice of the hearers.

10. It is a reliable means of identifying ethical issues and of judging the thoughts and attitudes of the heart. (See Hebrews 4:12.)

11. It is compatible with the work of the Holy Spirit in teaching the things of God.

12. It is a means of increasing the store of biblical knowledge.

13. The word study it demands expands awareness of the wealth of scriptural truth.

14. With this method the gospel is proclaimed with much

assurance. (See 1 Thessalonians 1:5-6.)

15. It is a potential opportunity to "correctly handle the word of truth." (See 2 Timothy 2:15.)

16. It explores the wealth of inspiring scriptural themes opening up new vistas of truth that otherwise might be unnoticed.

In expository preaching the Bible is the center of interest and the basis for religious authority. Its aim is to elucidate a portion of Scripture and thereby clarify Christian privileges and moral duty. It is intended to make clear what the will of God is from the content and teachings of the Bible. This has particular relevance to the New Testament where biblical revelation has its application to the historic and contemporary church. It is therefore an effective means of explaining the meaning of Scripture.

As a method of preaching it forces the speaker to clarify statements of biblical truth. It leads both the pastor and members of the congregation to a deeper study of the Scriptures. In most cases it lays a broader foundation for Christian character.

CHAPTER 3

The Book of Ephesians

Preliminary Considerations

The reading and study of this epistle will be enriched by keeping in mind its setting in the first century. At the same time it will be important to remember that the essence of the Christian message remains the same through all the succeeding ages and changing cultures. Whereas the writer addressed the church at Ephesus with firm convictions about prevailing social conditions of its time, the epistle represents an uncompromising position about the meaning of the gospel and its application to living in modern times.

The book of Ephesians is an answer to several religious influences. Judaism promoted salvation by works of the Law. Greek philosophy sought to achieve salvation by intellectual processes. The mystery religions held by cults stressed processes of nature as illustrated by those who were worshiping the goddess Diana. Into this arena of religious and philosophical quests and confusions, Paul came to offer the claims and challenges of Christianity to the best of minds in his time.

Paul presents Christianity as a way of salvation by divine provision, as over against the various forms of human attainment. He saw the church as a fulfillment of divine promise and purpose. He tells what we can and must believe to be saved (chapters 1—3) and then shows how to live and behave in personal and corporate living (chapters 4—6).

The book contains the basic elements of the Christian faith and its moral standards. It is definitely a record of divine revelation. A Jewish professor very aptly said, "My religion (Judaism) is a religion of hands doing the works of the law as a means of getting right with God. Your religion (Christianity) is a religion of the heart, believing that someone else (Jesus Christ) has done for you what you could never do for yourself to make you right with God."

The book of Ephesians has profound and mature thoughts about the role of Christ and his church in God's great purposes. The writer's aim is "(1) to confirm Christians in their faith, (2) to widen their spiritual horizons, and (3) to draw them closer in their bonds of Christianity and brotherhood."[1] This message to the Ephesians identifies the moral demands for the church: (1) to promote unity among its members, (2) to renounce pagan ways, (3) to build up Christian homes, and (4) to put on the whole armor of God. John A. Makaye describes the book as unveiling "the nature of God's order."

In this series of studies we trace the glorious thread of truth about the church and its mission in a brotherhood of worship and love. The glory of the church embodies the eternal purpose of God. He has a purpose of love for all who receive his Son. His will is made clear for the community of faith.

In this epistle we see how the church encounters hostile forces which can be subdued only by the power of God. It explains how the church is to execute God's purpose in a common fellowship and unity of belief. In all of this, Christ is held central in every aspect of the church's life and work.

There is no intention in these studies to ignore the elements of spiritual experience in personal faith, but the emphasis is on corporate life within the church. This accounts for the frequent application of salvation truth to the body of believers. In many instances the benefits of spiritual blessings to the church are traced from personal faith to the contribution it makes to the community of faith.

An Overview of Ephesians

One pattern of expository preaching is to cover an entire book in a series of messages. That is the design of this presentation. Each sermon, however, can stand on its own. Since the nature and composition of biblical material can be full of ideas, one should limit the length of passages to be treated according to more or less defined units of thought.

There are two major "tracks" one could follow in this particular epistle. There are treatments in Ephesians that focus on individual experience of divine blessings. There is good justification for that approach. Easily developed, that is the usual approach.

I have chosen to pick up another line of thought. There is strong evidence that this epistle was addressed to the community of faith, having in mind also the individual contributions that effect church life. These messages are therefore directed toward improving the life of the church. This epistle more than any other expresses concern for the corporate body of believers.

In order to understand the thrust of individual sections one must see the whole message. This is a part of the process of interpretation—namely, to get acquainted with not only the immediate context of the passage, but also to see the trend of thought through the entire book.

The outline that follows is a condensed combination of outlines prepared for the separate divisions. Whereas each forms the basis of an individual sermon in the series, they are all related to the major thrust in the larger context (the entire epistle).

Insight into the overall purpose or theme of a book will influence how one outlines the individual parts. For instance, this outline is influenced by an emphasis upon the church's role in mission to the internal needs of the body of Christ. It also focuses on the benefits of church activity in the lives of individual members.

These outlines concentrate on the corporate experience; secondary attention is given to individual blessedness. Here the major emphasis is on benefits of divine grace bestowed both on the individual and the corporate body. Although there are passages that focus on the benefits of grace to the individual Christian the overall impact highlights the mission of the community of faith. For that reason we find it entirely appropriate to use the heading,

The Church and Its Mission

Introduction

The church was initiated by Jesus Christ.

The church was established by the Holy Spirit.

The church was perpetuated by spiritual leadership.

A. *The church* provides opportunities for **worship.** (chapter 1)
   1. **Worship** honors and adores the *Godhead.* (1:3-14)
      a. We bless *God* for his providential care.
      b. We bless *Christ* for his redemptive care.
      c. We bless the *Holy Spirit* for his "sealing" care.
   2. **Worship** responds to *spiritual realities.* (1:15-23)
      a. Worship is enhanced by *spiritual insight and illumination.*
      b. Worship is induced by *spiritual experience and power.*
      c. Worship is affirmed by *spiritual authority and fullness.*
B. *The church* provides opportunities for **fellowship.** (chapter 2)
   1. **Fellowship** includes the assets of *brotherhood.* (2:4-7)
      a. *Brotherhood* gives support in suffering and service.
      b. *Brotherhood* bears mutual burdens.
      c. *Brotherhood* shares admonitions and testimonies.
      d. *Brotherhood* encourages confession and forgiveness.
   2. **Fellowship** includes the benefits of *reconciliation.* (2:8-18)
      a. *Reconciliation* resolves prevailing estrangements.
      b. *Reconciliation* resolves conflicting tensions.
   3. **Fellowship** includes the strength of *togetherness.* (2:19-22)
      a. People are brought *together* in faith and life.
      b. People are born *together* in a single household.
      c. People are built *together* on the same foundation.
      d. People are fit *together* in a growing temple.
      e. People are put *together* with divine habitation.
C. *The church* provides a channel for **revelation** (chapter 3)
   1. It has received the **revelation** of the Christian *mystery.* (3:1-13)
      a. The *mystery* came by the dispensation of grace.
      b. The *mystery* is found in the gospel of grace.
      c. The *mystery* was authorized through the gift of grace.
      d. The *mystery* is displayed as a dispensation of grace.
      e. The *mystery* is realized through the appropriation of grace.
   2. It proclaims that **revelation** as the *will of God.* (3:14)
      a. *God's will* for the church is to be an instrument of power.
      b. *God's will* for the church is to be the habitation of deity.
      c. *God's will* for the church is to be the model of love.
      d. *God's will* for the church is to express the glory of God.

D. *The church* provides a stewardship of **truth.** (chapter 4)
　1. **Truth** is preserved by *teaching* it. (4:1-7)
　　a. It *teaches* fidelity to the body of Christ.
　　b. It *teaches* the presence of God through the Spirit.
　　c. It *teaches* Christ as the only way of salvation.
　　d. It *teaches* the lordship of Christ.
　　e. It *teaches* grace as the gift of Christ.
　2. **Truth** is perpetuated by spiritual *leadership.* (4:8-16)
　　a. *Leadership* is composed of gifts.
　　b. *Leadership* is exercised by distribution of gifts.
　　c. *Leadership* is designed to prepare believers for ministry.
　3. **Truth** is proclaimed to regulate *moral behavior.* (4:17-32)
　　a. *Morality* is expressed by refraining from worldly practices.
　　b. *Morality* is expressed in adopting Christian ideals.
　　c. *Morality* is expressed in disciplined lives.
E. *The church* expresses the **will of God.** (chapter 5)
　1. The church expresses the **will of God** in *sexual morality.*
　　a. *Sexual morality* is achieved by personal disciplines. (5:1-6)
　　　(1) Immoralities are ruled out (act).
　　　(2) Indecencies are unbecoming (word).
　　　(3) Perversions stand under divine judgment (disposition).
　　b. *Sexual morality* is sustained by creative activity. (5:7-16)
　　　(1) Christian conduct reproves immoral conduct.
　　　(2) Fruitful living exposes evil practices.
　　　(3) Circumspect walk repudiates social sins.
　2. The church expresses the **will of God** in *Spirit fullness.*
　　a. It is dominated by the *Spirit's power.*
　　b. It is controlled by the *Spirit's will.*
　　c. It is swayed by the *Spirit's leading.*
　3. The church expresses the **will of God** in *domestic harmony.*
　　a. It identifies the role of the wife in *submission.*
　　b. It identifies the role of the husband in *love.*
　　c. It identifies the union with mutual *respect.*
F. *The church* renders service in **the name of Christ.** (chapter 6)
　1. The **name of Christ** is upheld in *household order.* (6:1-9)
　　a. The *household* order identifies parent-child relations.
　　b. The *household* order identifies employer-employee relations.
　2. The **name of Christ** is upheld in *Christian conflicts.*
　　a. The *conflict* requires the whole armor of God.
　　b. The *conflict* requires spiritual strength.
　　c. The *conflict* requires preparation through prayer.

CHAPTER 4

The Church

The church emerged as an event of promise.
The church emerged as a fulfillment of prophecy.
The church emerged with the provision of a presence.
The church emerged with an initiation of power.
The church emerged in demonstration of a purpose.

Before we proceed to a sermonic study of the church in Ephesians, we need to consider how the church emerged. Pentecost marked the beginning. It was the day of arrival for the Holy Spirit. In the words of G. Campbell Morgan, "On the day of Pentecost, the Spirit of God came into relationship with the whole of humanity." It was indeed a memorable occasion full of meaning.

Jesus had finished his teaching ministry. He had endured the cross and left the tomb empty. The apostles had received their last instructions and the clouds received Christ out of their sight. He left one "command" for immediate obedience: they should not leave Jerusalem but wait for the "promise."

The Church Emerged as an Event of Promise

During the days of Christ's ministry (and on various occasions), the apostles were promised another Person to be with them. He would minister to their needs along with Christ after his ascension to the Father. What he had told them about the Holy Spirit and his work was so important that he later referred to it as "the" promise.

On the day of Pentecost (ten days after the ascension) the apostles and other believers were faithfully waiting. It took faith to gather for prayer day after day with no more evidence than a "promise." Having chosen the location in Jerusalem for their waiting room, they "all continued with one accord in prayer and supplication." It does not say they prayed for the coming of the Spirit; that was not appropriate. Jesus had made the promise. In light of the resurrection and the subsequent ascension, there was no real occasion to doubt that something would happen; the Holy Spirit would come. The praying is not described except that it was their major occupation while waiting.

This ten-day prayer meeting in the upper room produced a humility of mind and yearning of heart that prepared them for the coming of the Spirit. It must have been a time of unhurried confession, searching, and expectant supplication. The Spirit came. It was the one time in history when the event of Pentecost could occur. All that happened in the church since then has taken place in a living and continuing relationship with the Spirit. There is no more waiting. There has been no other Pentecost. The Spirit of God came to stay as long as the church remains.

The Church Emerged as a Fulfillment of Prophecy

Peter used the occasion of the large gathering at Pentecost to preach. It was a powerful sermon. He introduced it by answering the sharp inquiry of the meaning to what happened. The violent wind, the flames of fire, and the diversity of languages were all the object of curiosity and wonder. Peter insisted this was a fulfillment of prophecy. He related the whole event to the words of prophet Joel who had said,

> In the last days, God says, I will pour out my Spirit on all people. Your sons and daughters will prophesy, your young men will see visions, your old men will dream dreams.
> Even on my servants, both men and women, I will pour out my Spirit in those days, and they will prophesy.

I will show wonders in the heaven above and signs on the earth below,
blood and fire and billows of smoke.
The sun will be turned to darkness and the moon to blood before the
coming of the great and glorious day of the Lord. And everyone who
calls on the name of the Lord will be saved.[1]

The charge that the apostles were drunk was untrue. Instead of
being filled with new wine they were filled with the Spirit. This was
in line with the prophet's prediction that God would pour out his
Spirit in a new age. He saw, through this prophetic vision, a time
when a great movement would begin. The presence of the Spirit of
God would be universal. There was to be a new demonstration of
power.

During the age of the Spirit significant dreams, visions, and
prophecies should occur. And now Peter told his critical crowd that
"this is that" which was predicted to come. On that day of Pentecost
they all witnessed what God had planned for the Christian church. A
new reality of divine presence and power had appeared.

The Church Emerged with the Provision of a Presence

The story of Pentecost represents the occasion of a new life.
What people heard, what they saw, and what they felt was evidence
of a majestic presence. This was now what Jesus had promised—the
appearance of another presence. The apostles were told that Jesus
would retire from the scene and another Person would come into
their company. And now they heard the sound of the wind that
blows where it likes and they saw the evidence of the "Spirit of burning." A great fusion of human spirits had taken place. The new presence of deity was unmistakable. The events of Pentecost had
initiated the era of the Holy Spirit.

Never before had the Spirit of God come to earth to stay. Never
before had the Spirit touched a whole company of people at one
time. Never before had the Spirit come to permanently indwell a
person. With this a new dispensation began. The disciples now
possessed a newfound courage.

The fearlessness of Peter was clear evidence that he was a
changed person. He proclaimed boldly a message that cut across the
grain of opposition and unbelief. This first effect of Pentecost was

the spark of bold aggression. The disciples were filled with daring.

The church received its initial glory through proclamation of the gospel. In addition to the announcement that the great day of redemption had come, the dawn of a new age was proclaimed. The Holy Spirit had come to make the church his perpetual residence. Believers were now living in a new creation. This Jesus who was regarded a criminal was indeed the Messiah. The call to repentance was unmistakable. All who repented and were baptized received the Holy Spirit.

Jesus promised that after he went back to heaven the Spirit would teach believers many things about the truth. This had already begun at Pentecost. The presence of the Spirit enabled the disciples to see in the Scriptures meanings they had never understood before. They not only found an interpretation of Scripture, they discovered a power to communicate the message it contains.

The distinguishing mark of the church is the presence of the Holy Spirit. Without the Spirit no assembly of people can be the church. The reality of a corporate Christian experience is guaranteed by the gift of the Spirit. The real test of the church lies in the presence or absence of the Spirit.

The Church Emerged with an Initiation of Power

The unusual phenomena that accompanied the arrival of the Spirit were symbolic of divine power. The sound of a rushing, violent wind was from heaven. Tongues, like flames of fire, touched down upon all the believers. And they, being filled with the Holy Spirit, were given ability to speak in different languages.

Jesus had told the disciples that after the Holy Spirit came upon them they would receive a new power. They would be enabled to do things that seemed impossible. Then they would be witnesses to him in all parts of the world. The staggering task of preaching the gospel "to all creatures" would be accomplished. The tangible evidences in the wind, fire, and speech gave a strong impulse to the apostolic efforts of that day.

The power bestowed upon the believers on the day of Pentecost was conferred for the discharge of new responsibilities. As Frank Stagg says, "this presence of God in power in the Christian community is a turning point in the life of the community, taking its place among the most significant events of the sacred story."[2]

The resurrection of Christ was the climax of redemption, but Pentecost was the great initial event of the church. The resurrection victory and the ascension prepared the way for the dramatic outpouring. The Holy Spirit became the dynamo of energy to perpetuate the Christian community.

Immediately the power was engaged to communicate the gospel. It convicted men and women of sin, of righteousness, and of judgment. Thousands were converted. People of great diversity in culture and beliefs were united in faith and practice. J. Oswald Sanders says, "Had Pentecost been omitted from the divine counsels, it would have been like perfecting a costly machine, and then failing to supply it with the necessary motive power." Pentecost provided the facility for perpetual power to the church. It put into motion the "machinery" which God had perfected for human salvation.

The Church Emerged in Demonstration of a Purpose

God had in mind for a long time to establish the Christian church. Prophets who spoke of coming events did not understand this. The church was a mystery whose meaning was unknown to Israel. What was included in the predictions, however, identified the purpose of God to offer salvation freely to all people. There should be a day of universal blessing. A decision made in heaven before the creation of the world determined the source and nature of redemption. As Paul wrote to the Ephesians, the church was chosen to receive its blessings in Christ. On the day of Pentecost God's long intention came to pass.

This, then, was the occasion for the formation of the church. With the descent of the Holy Spirit, the church became an organic reality. It was formed spontaneously and existed without civil authorization. The Spirit's presence and power were the factors which achieved the divine purpose.

The assembly of believers was transformed into the body of Christ. The community of saints became a temple for the habitation of the Holy Spirit. The many followers of Christ were related in a living union with him.

On the day of Pentecost the coming of the Spirit changed the character of the waiting disciples into a group of aggressive witnesses. It transformed a group of dislodged people into a corporate whole. It formed out of unlikely Roman citizens the church of the living God. God created a "new body" with all the essentials of the church present—a new institution for praise, prayer, and prophecy. None of these functions could be fulfilled without the abiding and enabling of the Holy Spirit.

The Holy Spirit is the key to effectiveness in the life of the church. The Spirit's presence makes valid the claims of redemption. The Spirit's power puts the force into the witness of faith. The Spirit's illumination makes authoritative the use of Scriptures. The Spirit's guidance gives direction to the work of the church.

PART II

Ephesians 1

CHAPTER 5

Sermon Introductions

Guidelines
Outline: The Church in Position of Blessing
Ephesians 1:1-2 (Sermon 1)
Word Meanings Essential to Interpretation
Finding the Message in Preaching

Guidelines for Sermon Introductions

In an approach to sermon delivery it is important to establish a valid connection between the speaker and the audience. It becomes a matter of filling in the gap between the preacher's purpose and the condition of the listeners.

The first step in the preaching procedure is to gain the attention and the interest of the congregation. By some means the introduction must focus the concern of the audience on the message to be delivered. This may be done by indicating the significance of the sermon to the immediate situation and it should somehow establish the direction of thought to be pursued in the discussion.

There are several limiting factors. The introduction should be brief. Avoid expounding material that properly belongs to the main discussion. It should be to the point without detailed explanation. It must be appropriate to the theme of the message. Prepare the way for audience participation in hearing the Word of the Lord.

First, a few words of caution. The introduction should never promise more than the speaker is prepared to deliver. One should avoid any remarks that may arouse hostility in the audience. It is unfortunate to have the thoughts of listeners diverted from the Scriptures by some silly joke or misleading comment. The introduction should excite people into consideration of the spiritual issues at hand.

There are many ways by which a sermon can be introduced. In consideration of the chosen text some background information can help listeners understand the concern expressed in it. Frequently there are terms (words or phrases) that require definition. It may also be helpful to clarify concepts to be used in the discussion.

The introduction should clear the way for the speaker to move from the known (in the audience) to the unknown (in the speaker's proposal). The introduction can also lead the audience's thought processes from the natural to the spiritual.

Among the variety of short expressions to introduce the message are the following: personal experience, recent news item, statement of a problem, a series of pertinent questions about the text, some motto related to the subject, a dramatic incident, a relevant quotation, reference to the season, a vivid word picture descriptive of some truth related to the text, a proverb, a prayer, or a recent observation. Whether one or more of these suggestions is used, it must lead into the focus of the message.

The introduction of an expository sermon should reflect the nature of truth in the text. One way is to give an overview (one or two salient points) of the message it introduces. Another way is to announce the theme of the message accompanied by a few remarks to indicate its purpose. In a series of messages drawn from the same book (such as we are studying here), it is good to make brief reference to what has gone before. Focus on the progression of thought leading up to the current passage.

Do not overlook the importance of defining key words that appear in the text. Some clarification of grammatical factors can do much to communicate difficult concepts expressed in the passage. Often the text itself poses a problem to be solved. The introduction can serve to indicate how the speaker proposes to find that solution.

Observe the first passage of chapter one. It is a salutation of only two verses with only one sentence. It strongly resembles a textual outline. In this case, however, the elements of truth carry depth of meaning and follow a progression of thought that lends itself to the expository method.

This passage is packed full of major ideas. As you can see, the phrases have three main divisions. The structure represents unity and coherence of thought. The main points and their supporting subpoints are taken directly from the passage under consideration. The next line of thoughts conveys ideas drawn from meanings inherent in the modifying words and phrases. They are equally biblical, but are expressions of truth derived from a general knowledge drawn from other portions of Scripture.

The passage is obviously intended to introduce the epistle to the Ephesians. It is a salutation that follows the normal Pauline address to the intended readers. In this series of sermons it serves the purpose of introducing the entire series.

In preparing an introduction to the individual sermon at hand, one must look at the content of the passage to find a suitable approach. For that reason it should emphasize its significance to current living. Focus on acceptance of the theme. Note the nature of the introduction attached to the outline that follows:

1. It identifies the background of a church in a pagan setting.

2. It moves directly into an application to today's church to avoid moral corruption.

3. The description of the church at Ephesus is used to move quickly into the content of the passage.

Sermon 1
The Church in Position of Blessing
Ephesians 1:1-2

Introduction

The church needs divine guidance to cope with the pagan influences that surround it. This epistle addressed to the church at Ephesus has effective guidelines for our own time. Christian people in that city were in a spiritual position properly designated to be "in Christ Jesus." The same principle applies to the church today.

This phrase *in Christ* serves as a keynote for the entire epistle. We are introduced to a description of a faithful church in Christ Jesus. Just as they needed spiritual help to escape the moral corruption of their time, so we need guidance to overcome the pagan influences of our time.

The Ephesian Christians were addressed as "saints," that is, holy ones. They also had the significant title, "faithful." Their faith was characterized by faithfulness in their calling to Christian witness. They were serving God with fidelity. They relied upon God.

We turn to the text to find guidance for our contemporary church. Here is a divine message to show the way.

Theme: The salutation introduces a divine ***message.***
  A. The *message* was addressed with divine **authorization.**
    1. **Authorization** was identified by *apostleship.*
      a. *Apostleship* identifies relationship to Christ.
      b. *Apostleship* signifies an official assignment.
    2. **Authorization** was given by divine *will.*
      a. *God's will* indicates a holy purpose.
      b. *God's will* designates Christian action.
  B. The *message* was addressed to the **Christian church.**
    1. The **church** was composed of *saints.*
      a. *Saints* are set apart by God's sanctification.
      b. *Saints* are set apart for God's service.
    2. The **church** was composed of faithful *people.*
      a. The *people* were faithful in believing.
      b. The *people* were faithful in devotion.
    3. The **church** was composed of people *in Christ.*
      a. Being *in Christ* indicates union with him.
      b. Being *in Christ* indicates a position for blessing.
  C. ***The message*** was opened by **Christian greetings.**
    1. The **greetings** conveyed the benefits of *grace.*
      a. *Grace* is the unmerited favor of God.
      b. *Grace* is divine loving-kindness in action.
    2. The **greetings** conveyed the benefits of *peace.*
      a. *Peace* indicates being in harmony with God.
      b. *Peace* indicates having spiritual wholeness.
      c. *Peace* indicates having assurance of salvation.
    3. The **greetings** are conveyed from God, the *Father.*
      a. *Fatherhood* implies sonship.
      b. *Fatherhood* implies providential care.
    4. The **greetings** are conveyed from the *Lord* Jesus Christ.
      a. *Lordship* identifies the place of loyalty.
      b. *Lordship* identifies the sequel of redemption.

Conclusion

The salutation sets the tone of divine authority and compassion for the entire Ephesian epistle. God and Christ appear in conjoint action to enrich the church with grace and peace. The benefits of spiritual blessing are designed for the corporate body of believers who are faithful in their saintly calling.

Word Meanings Essential to Interpretation

An *apostle* is an accredited messenger of Christ.

Will of God emphasizes the divine aspect of an assignment. It represents authorization for Christian action and indicates divine purpose.

Saints in the New Testament is a word that puts an emphasis upon being set apart for God's service. It also conveys an element of spiritual maturity as the church is called to be holy (2 Corinthians 1:2). Its membership is composed of "holy ones."

Ephesus. Some manuscripts do not have this designation. It does occur, however, in others. It may be that Paul intended the letter to be read also to other congregations in the area.

Faithful in Christ Jesus is a descriptive term that indicates a continuous consecrated activity. They had a wholehearted devotion to Christ.

In Christ is a key phrase that identifies a close relationship. It designates the spiritual location where God's benevolence is received. It is a designation based on union with Christ.

Peace refers to the believer's union and harmony with God—a true spiritual wholeness and prosperity. It is a common experience of assurance of salvation.

Finding the Message in Preaching

The preacher's function is to serve as a spokesperson for God. The Bible is the preacher's major resource, the source for learning what God wants proclaimed. The introduction to expository preaching in chapter 2 contains a dozen reasons why this method is "an effective instrument in communicating divine revelation." At the close of the chapter are numerous reasons why this method is to be preferred as the general practice in preaching.

There are various ways to discover the message for today. The goal is to draw truth from the Word of God. That procedure has two main facets for exploration: (1) the meaning of Scripture and (2) the needs of people.

The first pertains to a careful study of a passage of Scripture. (The procedure is outlined in more details in later chapters.) The authority of the message comes from the Word. The preacher can thus address the identified issues with confidence. One can do this with cardinal affirmations of Scripture to answer the burning questions which people have to decide.

The second aspect of this exploration pertains to the audience. One should cultivate a sensitive awareness of the needs of people. This is how one finds relevance for the message. It is an essential factor in any attempt to communicate. To be able to proclaim the gospel effectively one must discover the meanings and attitudes already established in the minds of the people.

In one sense the task is to fill in the gap between what persons already know and have accepted, and the Word of truth we want to communicate. Part of preparation is gathering the assumptions and questions of the people and bringing the meanings and mandates of Scripture to apply to the known issues. As Andrew Blackwood once said, "A preacher enters the pulpit to meet a need, not to explain a passage."

Having discovered a need, Scripture can be brought to bear upon it. Many basic human needs are common to all:

1. Resolve problems of guilt.
2. Find relief from pains of sorrow or disappointment.
3. Gain reassurance from fear or anxiety.
4. Establish security in Christ and divine providence.
5. Overcome feelings of loneliness.
6. Handle feelings of failure and defeat.
7. Resolve feelings of anger.
8. Overcome doubts and insecurity.
9. Find peace in the midst of tensions.
10. Overcome injurious habits.

Preaching is not limited to the resolution of problems. People need to be reaffirmed in many areas. Among them are:

1. The practice of discipleship.
2. The sanctity of marriage.
3. The implications of stewardship.
4. The support of brotherhood.
5. The practice of nonresistance.
6. The separation of church and state.
7. The observance of ordinances.
8. The principles of nonconformity.
9. Christian nurture in the home.
10. The privileges of prayer.

Some forces weaken the life and testimony of the church. A positive approach to prevention usually works best.

1. Christianity as a counterculture.
2. Christian unity that averts internal divisions.
3. The validity of biblical ethics.
4. Stewardship—answer to materialism.
5. Commitment to evangelical faith.
6. The simple lifestyle that challenges secular indulgences.
7. Principles of peace that overcome anger and retaliation.
8. The call to relationships: absolving individualism.
9. The Christian mission that supersedes social action.
10. Trust in God that goes beyond material securities.

Most preaching is done in a congregational setting. For that reason we should remember that people go to church to hear:

1. Reverent affirmation of great truths.
2. Messages that inspire a closer walk with God.
3. How faith can be made convincingly real.
4. Explanations of difficult issues in private life.
5. A prophetic voice on challenges of the times.
6. Biblical answers to contemporary issues.
7. How to hear the voice of the Spirit.
8. How to triumph over temptations.
9. How to die with grace and dignity.

CHAPTER 6

Purpose in Preaching

Guidelines to Purpose in Preaching

To make an expository sermon effective, the speaker needs to adopt a specific purpose in preaching that particular message. There is a subtle danger in assuming that explanations about the various elements of truth in a selected passage will somehow find their coherence without any special effort. Exposition demands rigorous study and careful construction to achieve unity. Good sermons are achieved by design.

The pattern of a sermon is determined by an adopted purpose. The purpose is determined by human needs. Preparing a sermon involves asking several questions: "What need can this message fulfill?" "What is to be accomplished in the hearts of the hearers?" "What difference can this message make in their daily living?" "What service can this sermon perform?"

The preacher may start with some need discovered during a pastoral visit. For instance, one might sense in a conversation that the member lacks appreciation for Christ. The passage in Ephesians under consideration in this chapter could meet that need.

The adoption of an identified purpose has a direct bearing upon the selection of material to be used in the sermon structure. It influences progression of thought. It calls for setting a goal to accomplish certain end results. One cannot do this effectively without the guidance of the Holy Spirit. The entire process is under the Spirit's influence. The sermon structure is intended to make a channel through which the Spirit can work.

One should thus adopt a purpose in the early stages of developing an outline. However, if during the process of analysis and exegesis (see the fuller discussion of these later) it becomes clear that the identified purpose does not fit the meaning of the passage under consideration, an adjustment is necessary. One can either adopt a revised purpose or select some other passage that reflects more accurately the chosen purpose.

In the case of this passage (Eph. 1:3-6), the Scripture serves well the intent to magnify the purpose and work of Christ.

A word of caution. If we had found that our purpose for the sermon was not supported in this passage, it would not be appropriate to superimpose our purpose upon the text. The theme must always be inherent in the Scripture itself. This is a limitation on using consecutive passages in a series of messages.

"A basic theme for preaching is the declaration of what God has done through Jesus Christ in his plan of redemption."[1] This also calls for human response. Salvation is based on repentance and a personal commitment to Christian discipleship. "The proclamation of salvation, apart from its implications for daily living, can be a pious sham."[2]

Preaching is intended to inform the intellect *and* the will. The message must be designed for results, connecting divine truth with real living.

Sermons can be used to kindle emotions. People can be led to feel deeply about what they believe. Sermons can also motivate the will to action.

The adoption of a purpose for a given sermon engages the principle of selection with a view to achieve clarity and unity. Select only those ideas that are pertinent to advancing the intended thrust of the message. Ideas which fail to advance the purpose will be eliminated. The entire process of analysis, arrangement, expansion, and delivery is controlled by the purpose. The chosen objective is thus enhanced by a sound foundation.

As the sermon takes shape, the discipline of setting emerging ideas and thoughts in order gives the preacher a sense of ownership. Enthusiasm for the message develops. As these ideas begin to affect the preacher's own life, application for the lives of others becomes obvious. A deep urge to preach develops.

The following suggestions identify ways in which this principle can be applied.

A. Elements of purpose applicable to each sermon:
   1. The sermon should inform the intellect.
   2. The sermon should kindle the imagination.
   3. The sermon should touch the emotions.
   4. The sermon should convict.
   5. The sermon should clarify ethical duty.
   6. The sermon should give impulse to the will.
   7. The sermon should illicit response in worship.
B. Elements of purpose open for adoption:
   1. Proclaim the power of God's forgiving love.
   2. Proclaim the potential of life's fullness.
   3. Proclaim the presence of the guiding Spirit.
   4. Proclaim the purpose of the divine will.
   5. Proclaim the practice of community.
   6. Proclaim the prospect of spiritual growth.
   7. Proclaim the preeminence of servanthood.
   8. Proclaim the pilgrimage to eternal habitation.
C. Elements of purpose that can meet specific human needs:
   1. Explain the nature and implications of faith.
   2. Express the real meanings of life and death.
   3. Establish priorities among human values.
   4. Confront the deep tragedies of life.
   5. Provide guidelines to solve human predicaments.
   6. Direct judgment against sin.
   7. Extend invitations to join the kingdom of God.

Sermon 2
The Church in the Plan of God
Ephesians 1:3-6

Introduction
The foundation of the church is "in Christ." Whereas the experience of being "hidden" in Christ has a direct application to the individual believer, this vision of God's benevolence is focused on the corporate body, the church. Here then is true adoration for God's goodness which he has invested in the community of faith. Divine blessings bestowed upon the church are humbly and gratefully acknowledged. Every spiritual blessing from the Father flows into the church by way of Christ.

Theme: The **church** is chosen in Christ.
  A. The **church** is chosen in Christ to be **blessed.** (v. 3)
   1. The church experiences **blessedness** in *spiritual realities.*
    a. *Spiritual realities* are expressed in righteousness.
    b. *Spiritual realities* are obtained in peace.
    c. *Spiritual realities* are possessed in joy.
   2. The church experiences **blessedness** in the *heavenlies.*
    a. The position of the church is *heavenly* in privilege.
    b. The position of the church is *heavenly* in possession.
    c. The position of the church is *heavenly* in practice.
   3. The church experiences **blessedness** in *Christ.*
    a. *Christ* is the source of eternal life.
    b. *Christ* is the sustainer of eternal life.
    c. *Christ* is the security of eternal life.
  B. The **church** is chosen in Christ to be **holy.** (v. 4)
   1. **Holiness** was predetermined for the *church.*
    a. Holiness for the *church* was designed in heaven.
    b. Holiness for the *church* was designed for earth.
   2. **Holiness** was predetermined for *believers.*
    a. *Believers* achieve holiness by divine grace.
    b. *Believers* express holiness by divine characteristics.
   3. **Holiness** was predetermined to be realized in *Christ.*
    a. *Christ* makes the church different within the world.
    b. *Christ* makes the church a witness to the world.
   4. **Holiness** was predetermined to include *blamelessness.*
    a. *Blamelessness* qualifies for worship.
    b. *Blamelessness* qualifies for service.

C. The *church* is chosen in Christ to be God's **heritage.** (v. 5)
  1. The church is treated with *filial care.*
    a. God *gave* to the church its Redeemer.
    b. God *gave* to the church its Shepherd.
    c. God *gave* to the church its Truth.
  2. The church is the object of divine *pleasure.*
    a. God takes *pleasure* in corporate worship.
    b. God takes *pleasure* in its missionary witness.
    c. God takes *pleasure* in its caring ministry.
  3. The church is the channel of *divine will.*
    a. God's *will* is demonstrated in the church.
    b. God's *will* is disseminated through the church.
D. The *church* is chosen in Christ to be **honored.** (v. 6)
  1. The church is **honored** with the *glory* of divine grace.
    a. The *glory* of divine grace is seen in forgiveness of sin.
    b. The *glory* of divine grace is seen in newness of life.
    c. The *glory* of divine grace is seen in fullness of joy.
  2. The church is **honored** by the gift of divine *love.*
    a. Divine *love* is realized by confession of Christ.
    b. Divine *love* is realized by faith in Christ.
    c. Divine *love* is realized by obedience to Christ.
  3. The church is **honored** in Christ by *adoption.*
    a. *Adoption* assures capability for spiritual insights.
    b. *Adoption* assures suitability for spiritual endowments.
    c. *Adoption* assures qualification for spiritual leadership.

Conclusion
The church is blessed and loved on the basis of divine intention.
The church is blessed and loved on the basis of human response.

Word Meanings Essential to Interpretation

v. 3 *Praise* (blessed be) means that God be well spoken of.
This ascribes honor and adoration with thanksgiving.
May God have credit for providing redemption.
Blessed us indicates that we have received spiritual well-being.
The benefits are from the heavenly realm.
Elements of truth and experience come from heaven.
Blessedness comes by virtue of being in Christ. (To be in Christ is the keynote for the entire epistle, an essential element to understand its message. It refers to a mutual relation between Christ and the church.)

Spiritual blessings (in Christ)

In virtue of our being in union with Christ we receive spiritual benefits.

(a) It denotes our position (standing with God).

(b) It defines our privileges (spiritual opportunities).

(c) It determines our practices (Christian behavior).

(d) It designates our prospect (to be God's heritage).

v. 4 *Chosen:* The "how" of redemption.

The choosing involved the Church, not individuals.

The choosing was effected in Christ.

Before creation refers to the eternal plan.

It pertains to God's original intention.

It was determined by divine will:

—that people should find God in Christ.

—that redemption should be "finished" by Christ.

It indicates the time of decision.

Holy and blameless refers to achievement in character, in designation and in consecration.

v. 5 *Predestination:* setting things in order on the basis of foreknowledge. It was predetermined how people would be adopted in his family: through Christ. Human choice brings to pass God's intention and provision.

Pleasure and will refer to:

(a) The plan of redemption was designed with expectations of pleasure in it.

(b) The plan was conditioned by divine purpose and good will.

(c) God's will was directed to the highest good.

v. 6 *Praise:* (a) expresses adoration and thanksgiving.

(b) expresses the deep gratitude in exultation.

Glorious grace refers to a sense of splendor in divine action. The favors of God display his excellence.

One he loves refers to the Son of his love (Col. 1:13). To experience the love of God requires being in Christ.

Comments on the Message (1:3-6)

The divisions of the first part of chapter 1 are drawn on the basis of the repeated phrase "the praise of his glory" (vv. 6, 12, and 14). This marks the three sections devoted to remarks about the relation of the triune God to the church. That accounts for the separate treatment of God the Father, Christ the Son, and the Holy Spirit.

It seems appropriate that special attention be given to each of these in relation to its bearing upon sermon construction. In each case, specific doctrines provide further background for the expositions.

God in Preaching

The outlines in this book emphasize structure. Technique is important, but it dare not displace doctrine. What we believe matters a great deal. As one author put it, "Theology is more important than methodology."

At the beginning of the epistle the light of truth is focused on God. It is essential that the preacher be aware of that. "Behind the concept and act of preaching there lies the doctrine of God, a conviction about his being, his action, his purpose. The kind of God we believe in determines the kind of sermons we preach."[3]

"God is love." We must keep that in mind while preparing to speak about him. This element of truth flavors both the approach (motivation) and the nature (quality) of any biblical proclamation. "God so loved that he gave his only Son" has been declared thousands of times. We must believe it and recommend it. As emphasized in this passage, he has acted to redeem humanity.

"God is light. In him is no darkness at all." When Jesus said, "I am the light of the world," he gave assurance to those whom he calls to preach that he is completely open to human need. When we address an audience there are various needs among the people. It is a satisfaction to know that God has the answer. Whether it be sadness, fear, doubt, or disbelief, the wisdom of heaven is available. Whether it be guilt or neglect, God is ready to forgive.

The character of God gives us confidence in biblical preaching. He is truthful and faithful. He will fulfill the promises we draw from the Scriptures. In this respect it can be said that God has spoken. We are the messengers. We simply tell others what he has said. To do that we must be faithful to preach the Word. Expository preaching is a reliable way of doing just that.

Here, then, is a fundamental conviction that the church is chosen in Christ, that God has made provisions for his people to be holy and that he intends to make the church his own heritage. What an honor to be so regarded!

There is yet another aspect to this trinitarian view of divine action in preaching. Through the centuries God has spoken through prophets and preachers in support of his plan for the ages. Even before the creation of the earth the course of history was known. Accordingly, the plan of redemption was devised and the church was projected as the instrument of his purpose in the world.

Christ himself is the supreme act of divine ministration. The incarnation brought the Son into the arena of human history. It initiated the full revelation of God in the cloak of humanity. Yet all that Christ accomplished was done in complete union with the Father. In his earthly state he taught with authority and acted in demonstration of spiritual power and social justice. His death and resurrection completed the work of redemption, making full satisfaction of divine judgment.

The coming of the Holy Spirit was an inauguration of the new covenant. He established the church and provided wisdom and power for its mission. He is engaged in managing the affairs of the kingdom. This is being done in its latter stages of preparation for the eternal reign of God. Then comes the glorious heavenly habitation for his children.

"We need to pray more persistently and expectantly for grace from the Holy Spirit of truth. A Christian understanding is not possible without the Spirit's enlightenment, nor is Christian assurance possible without the Spirit's witness. . . . The primary witness is that of God the Father to God the Son, through God the Holy Spirit."[4] This is fully substantiated in the words of Jesus who said, "When the Counselor comes, whom I will send to you from the Father, the Spirit of truth who goes out from the Father, he will testify about me; but you also must testify, for you have been with me from the beginning."[5]

This lays a heavy responsibility upon preachers of the Word. It can best be accomplished by delivering carefully planned expository sermons.

CHAPTER 7

Sermon Construction

Guidelines
Outline Structure
Outline: The Church in the Purpose of Christ
Ephesians 1:7-12 (Sermon 3)
Word Meanings Essential to Interpretation
Comments on the Sermon
The Purpose of the Incarnation

Guidelines for Sermon Construction

The task of preparing an outline for an expository sermon involves numerous techniques. In previous chapters we have looked at some of the major factors in the process. Accepting the necessity of structure puts one under obligation to observe details of procedure. The suggestions that follow should be helpful in producing an acceptable pattern for sermonizing. Although the focus here is on exposition, many of these are equally applicable in constructing outlines for other types of sermons.

During the process of preparing an outline keep in mind that:

1. The sermon must have a purpose
2. The sermon must have unity.

3. Clear-cut divisions must follow movement within the passage or be synthesized according to purpose.

4. There is no virtue in having a subtle structure.

5. Relevance to the contemporary scene is essential.

6. Concreteness in expression helps to project imagery.

7. Lucidity is a prime virtue in outlining.

8. Figures of speech must be identified and defined.

9. Only the results of exegesis should be used, not the process.

10. Allowance for flexibility and variety sustains interest.

11. Formulating the theme (proposition) must be done with care and purpose.

12. Coherence of thought must carry through the entire sermon.

13. Points of division are to be stated in the form of sentences.

14. A judicial use of "the art of omission" avoids overloading the sermon and the temptation to digress.

15. The aim is persuasion.

16. Meeting human need is more important than explaining the passage.

17. Showing what the passage means is to indicate what difference that truth makes today.

Outline Structure

In light of the above comments on sermon construction, observe the theme of the following sermon. The theme statement focuses on the words *Christ* and *purpose*. The main divisions of the outline carry the primary emphasis on *purpose*.

The first line of subpoints picks up the four elements related to the purpose in Christ: namely, redemption, wisdom, hope, and praise. These are each expanded with pertinent thoughts drawn from the text. The latter two appear near the close of the selected passage.

The discussion of these first-line thoughts is contained in the second line of subpoints. The explanations employ scriptural truths drawn from outside the text. Some of those explanatory ideas, however, are explicit in the text, while others are used by assumptions of their direct relationship.

The underscoring of words and phrases is intended to show

unity in the passage and in the sermon. It also shows how the theme has influenced the selection of ideas.

These divisions and subpoints are all framed in sentence form. This is an aid in thinking through the propositions. It also aids delivery when speaking from an outline.

Sermon 3
The Church in the Purpose of Christ
Ephesians 1:7-12

Introduction

In the previous section we observed the plan of the Father to call out a people for his own to the praise of his glorious grace. We are now ready to observe how the plan of redemption was accomplished.

Human nature is endowed with adequate capacity to receive divine benefits. This has opened the way for restoration from the fallen condition to a favorable relation to God. Salvation became a matter of human choice. The intention of God to establish the church as a community of faith is achieved through accepting by faith the accomplished work of Christ.

Theme: Christ accomplished redemption with *divine purpose.*
   A. The *divine purpose* is expressed in **redemption.**
      1. The means of **redemption** is the blood of *Christ.*
        a. The blood of *Christ* cleanses from sin.
        b. The blood of *Christ* purges the conscience.
        c. The blood of *Christ* affects behavior.
      2. The nature of **redemption** includes *forgiveness.*
        a. Forgiveness is granted without human merit.
        b. *Forgiveness* remits the punishment for sin.
        c. *Forgiveness* releases the guilt of sin.
      3. The measure of **redemption** is in the riches of *grace.*
        a. The riches of *grace* are an overflow of divine love.
        b. The riches of *grace* are adequate for human need.
        c. The riches of *grace* are available in Christ.
   B. The *divine purpose* is expressed in words of **wisdom.**
      1. **Wisdom** enables the church to know *God's will.*
        a. *God's will* is expressed in the plan of redemption.
        b. *God's will* is expressed in the purpose of redemption.
      2. **Wisdom** is revealed in the *mystery* of God's will.
        a. The *mystery* is now disclosed.
        b. The *mystery* is revealed in the initiated believer.

3. **Wisdom** is revealed in the *pleasure* of his will.
   a. His *pleasure* is to give the kingdom.
   b. His *pleasure* is purposed in Christ.
C. The *divine purpose* is expressed in **hope**.
   1. **Hope** is fixed on the *consummation* of the ages.
      a. The *consummation* will occur in due time.
      b. The *consummation* will complete this age.
   2. **Hope** is fixed on the *integration* of all things.
      a. All things will be *integrated* in Christ.
      b. Heaven and earth will be *integrated* for habitation.
   3. **Hope** is fixed on the *exaltation* of Christ.
      a. Christ will be *exalted* as Head over all.
      b. Christ will be *exalted* in final triumph over evil.
D. The *divine purpose* is expressed in **praise**.
   1. The **praise** of his glory is the *goal* of the church.
      a. The church is given the *vocation* of praise.
      b. The church will become God's *heritage*.
   2. The **praise** of his glory is the *purpose* of the church.
      a. God's *intention* for the church embraces salvation.
      b. God's *intention* for the church is union with Christ.
   3. The **praise** of his glory is the *fulfillment* of the church.
      a. The church is given the right to *eternal hope*.
      b. The church is given the right to *eternal glory*.

Word Meanings Essential to Interpretation (1:7-12)

. 7 *Redemption* is the condition of the church as God's rescued ones. The divine purpose is being accomplished:

(a) Through his blood. Christ's death is the ransom, the *medium* of redemption (Heb. 9:15, 22).

(b) in the forgiveness of sins. It is a benefit of redemption. This designates the *quality* of redemption.

(c) Through the riches of God's grace. This refers to the boundless resources of his free favor to the church. It is the *basis* of redemption.

. 8 *Wisdom* refers to the wealth of God's grace and the spiritual understanding of his purpose in redemption. It concurs with his plan. Believers are made "wise unto salvation" in the knowledge of God's will (cf. Colossians 1:9).

Understanding conveys the idea of prudence. "Wisdom deals with principles; prudence with action. In this way prudence may be called the child of wisdom" (Westcott). Prudence or the act of discernment is making practical application of the knowledge gained in Christ, the riches of God's grace in Christ.

v. 9   *The mystery of God's will* refers to the "secret" of his plan which was previously unknown. It is now revealed; that is, made known by revelation (cf. Eph. 3:3). It was a disclosure of the design of his grace for the church. This masterpiece of mercy was his good pleasure.

Being purposed in Christ is the key to understanding the role of redemption. What God intended to do through his saving grace was invested in the work of Christ.

v. 10   *The fulfillment of times* indicates a dispensation connected with the "mystery" of God's will. He acts according to his own will and time. His disposition toward these events is to act in mercy.

Consummation involves bringing together all things in Christ. It consists of bringing the redeemed elements together under the rule of God's anointed King. It will effect a perfect adjustment of the universal moral system to be reconstituted in Christ. At the consummation the church will be united under the King of kings, the Lord of all.

v. 11   *Chosen in him* means the church is appointed in the new dispensation to be to Christ what Israel was to God in the old. It refers to God's people.

Predestination signifies that all things will be brought together in Christ according to the original plan. The church, therefore, will have been given its eternal benefits through its Redeemer. Everything is to be worked out in conformity with the purpose of God's will. Rather than a comment on the nature of God, predestination is meant to affirm the efficacy of God's grace.

The *first to hope* in Christ received fulfillment of the promise of the Messiah as first declared to Israel. The messianic expectation was projected before the first advent of Christ. Now that hope is realized in the present relationship with Christ.

The *praise of his glory* looks forward to future blessedness. We have been gloriously saved with the anticipation of winning an adoring admiration as the bride of Christ. The church moves on toward the goal of its yet unfulfilled ultimate splendor.

Comments on the Sermon

What follows is the development of the material suggested in the preceding outline on Ephesians 1:7-12. This is submitted as a model of what can emerge from the proposed outline structure. It does not include any illustrations which can be inserted at appropriate places in the sermon at the time of delivery. More space will be devoted to the nature and purpose of illustrations later in the book. Both the introduction and the conclusion are suggestive. They may be revised in the light of particular circumstances on the occasion of delivery.

The intention is that this sermon will show how to use the sentences that form the outline. They can be used in many different ways. This material can be adapted if the speaker keeps in mind the basic principles of sermon development.

The Purpose of the Incarnation

The gospel of Christ is the perennial item on the preaching agenda. A primary aspect of the proclamation of Jesus Christ is the historical reality of his incarnation. Believing this doctrine is relevant to preaching the Christian faith. It is so vital to Christian experience that the content of preaching must utilize the significance of teachings about the purposes of Christ's coming into the world.

The incarnation was more than taking on human flesh. It was the union of human and divine essence. It also became the cornerstone of reality in the union between God and humanity. By means of human action Christ paid the ransom for man's redemption.

The incarnation revealed the mystery of God. "God was made visible in human flesh." In Christ we have the knowledge of God expressed in terms of humanity. In him the thoughts of God were expressed. He represented the feelings of God and demonstrated the divine character. His teachings declared the purposes of God to redeem mankind.

> Beyond all question the mystery of godliness is great: he appeared in a body, was vindicated by the Spirit, was seen by angels, was preached among the nations, was believed on in the world, was taken up in glory.[1]

The incarnation testifies to the glory of God.

> The Word became flesh and lived for a while among us. We have seen his glory, the glory of the one and only Son, who came from the Father, full of grace and truth.[2]

We see the splendor of his grace in the many favors he performed, in the many gifts he delivered, in the many blessings he bestowed, and in the many loving-kindnesses he shared.

The incarnation declared the will of God. He established a new order of obedience. The standard of human excellence was raised permanently. Christ represented the total of human virtue. His demonstration of divine love was a new expression of God's commandment. In his life he showed the essential human possibilities by giving a new significance to life.

> He said, "Here I am, I have come to do your will." He sets aside the first [covenant] to establish the second. By that will, we have been made holy through the sacrifice of the body of Jesus Christ once for all.[3]

The incarnation expressed the love *(agapē)* of God, the kind of love that specializes in giving. It cares for human life and copes with its needs. It is a love that shares eternal life.

> This is how God showed his love among us: He sent his one and only Son into the world that we might live through him. This is love; not that we loved God, but that he loved us and sent his Son as an atoning sacrifice for our sins.[4]

The incarnation revealed the nature of eternal life. The life of Christ expressed the nature of divine life. In him we see the character of God. In his teachings we see God's intention for humanity. He represents the true image of God and confirmed hope in immortality.

> This we proclaim concerning the Word of life. The life appeared; we have seen it and testify to it, and we proclaim to you the eternal life, which was with the Father and has appeared to us.[5]

The incarnation destroyed the work of the devil. Christ rendered Satan powerless to break the union of the divine and human. By this means God delivers believers from satanic influences. Christ was sent to change the prospect of human destiny and to recover the life of sinners.

> Since the children have flesh and blood, he [Christ] too shared in their humanity, so that by his death he might destroy him who holds the power of death—that is, the devil—and free all those who all their lives were held in slavery by their fear of death.... For this reason he had to be made like his brothers in every way, in order that he might become a merciful and faithful high priest in service to God, and that he might make atonement for the sins of the people.[6]

The incarnation provided the means of redemption. The merit of Christ's sacrifice is ascribed to his person. He came into the world equipped to redeem. Being the Son of God, his atonement was sufficient. Being the Son of Man, his atonement was applicable to human need. He was raised from the dead to become an effective Mediator between God and the redeemed.

> God sent his Son, born of a woman, born under law, to redeem those under law that we might receive the full rights of sons.... So you are no longer a slave, but a son; and since you are a son, God has made you also an heir.[7]

CHAPTER 8

Choosing a Text

Guidelines on Choosing the Text

In expository preaching there is always the responsibility of choosing an appropriate text. In the series we are following here, the consecutive passages have already been determined. As pointed out earlier, it is crucial to discover what purpose this passage can fulfill. But there are other approaches.

Those who follow a liturgical calendar have prescribed suggestions drawn from the changing seasons (Advent, pre-Pentecost, post-Pentecost, and open calendar). The advantage of this system is the recapitulation it offers to impress the story of biblical revelation.

Another form of the church's calendar is to follow a trinitarian structure. This involves a program that reflects a rehearsal of how God revealed himself progressively as Creator and Father, as Son of God made flesh, and in the person and work of the Holy Spirit. In this arrangement of messages from Ephesians, sermons 2, 3, and 4 follow this idea precisely. A series apart from Ephesians could include a broader selection of passages from other parts of the Bible. This suggests a topical approach (God, Christ, Holy Spirit) but the treatment of each sermon can be expository in structure.

There are other sources of motivation and suggestions such as current events (local, national, international), pastoral contacts (from visitation, personal study, individual requests), and personal convictions (from devotional reflections, personal observations, literary suggestions).

Sermon 4
The Church in the Promise of the Spirit
Ephesians 1:13-14

Introduction

What God planned for the church and what Christ purposed for it is made effective by the Holy Spirit. The center of interest now shifts to the third person of the Godhead. This short passage is packed full of meaning to be conveyed to the contemporary church. It represents a kind of conclusion to the discussion of the relation of the church to the triune God: Father, Son, and Holy Spirit.

The meaning of *in Christ* continues to be the key to Christian experience. This applies to individual participation in Christian realities. It also has benefits for the entire community of faith. While the Holy Spirit is projected as the active Agent to accomplish spiritual goals in the church, the relationship to Christ remains the primary aspect of its divine engagement.

Theme: The Holy Spirit is a divine assurance to the **church.**
  A. The **church** is assured of **life** in the Spirit.
    1. **Life** in the Spirit is *based* on the Word of truth.
      a. The Word of truth *contains* the promise of the Holy Spirit.
      b. The Word of truth *contains* the promise of eternal life.
    2. **Life** in the Spirit is *sustained* by the Word of truth.
      a. The Word of truth *sustains* life in Christ.
      b. The Word of truth *sustains* life in the Spirit.
    3. **Life** in the Spirit is *affirmed* by the Word of truth.
      a. The Word of truth *affirms* the saving grace of God.
      b. The Word of truth *affirms* saving faith in Christ.
      c. The Word of truth *affirms* the saving presence of the Spirit.

B. The ***church*** is assured of its **privileges** in the Spirit.
1. **Privileges** in the Spirit are *realized* by faith.
   a. Faith in Christ *establishes* communion with God.
   b. Faith in Christ *establishes* eternal life.
   c. Faith in Christ *establishes* the Spirit's indwelling.
2. **Privileges** in the Spirit are *sustained* by faith.
   a. Trusting Christ *sustains* the reality of forgiveness.
   b. Trusting Christ *sustains* the reality of victory over sin.
   c. Trusting Christ *sustains* the reality of the Spirit's presence.
C. The ***church*** is assured of its **identity** by the spirit.
1. The mark of **identity** validates one's experience of *eternal life*.
   a. *Eternal life* is validated by having been born again.
   b. *Eternal life* is validated by a new quality of living.
2. The mark of **identity** ratifies *divine sonship*.
   a. *Divine sonship* is made real by the Spirit.
   b. *Divine sonship* is made vital by the Spirit.
3. The mark of **identity** indicates a *purchased possession*.
   a. Being a *purchased possession* identifies ownership.
   b. Being a *purchases possession* identifies care.
4. The mark of **identity** guarantees *security*.
   a. The *security* of the believers is fixed by the Spirit.
   b. The *security* of the believers is conditioned by faith.
D. The ***church*** is assured of its **inheritance** by the Spirit.
1. The **inheritance** of the saints includes present *experience*.
   a. The *experience* of peace is a current possession.
   b. The *experience* of hope is a present anchor.
   c. The *experience* of power is a continuing resource.
2. The **inheritance** of the saints is assured of future *glory*.
   a. The present taste of glory will be *perfected*.
   b. The present touch of the Spirit's anointing will be *unlimited*.
   c. The present position in the heavenlies will lead to the *heaven of heavens*.
   d. The present delight in love will go on *forever*.

Conclusion
Having come into possession of eternal life:
   a. We receive the plan of God.
   b. We believe in the work of Christ.
   c. We are marked (sealed) by the Holy Spirit.
   d. We are given this token (earnest) of eternal glory.
      Let us go on demonstrating this excellence (glory) forever.

Word Meanings Essential to Interpretation

. 13   *You also.* This epistle is addressed to a church composed primarily of
Gentiles.

Included in Christ. This phrase lifts the reality of Christian faith to
being united to Christ.

The Word of truth. They heard a gospel of salvation. Its message
revealed man's condition and proclaimed the way of escape.
"Having heard" was an enlightening experience.

Having believed. Hearing is followed by believing. Hearing was
necessary but believing in Christ was the exercise of faith in surrender of self, actually trusting him.

Marked with a seal. The word used in legal documents was to mark
ownership, to protect against tampering. It was:
a stamp of approval,
an authorization to serve,
a mark of identification,
a stamp of validity, and
a sign of ownership.

Promised Holy Spirit, as predicted by the prophets. The Spirit is a
special gift to the church. The Spirit is the instrument of marking
the believers.

v. 14   *The deposit or earnest of inheritance* (assurance of it).
It is:
partial—a token of final consummation,
"a deposit made as assurance of delivery,"
an actual portion of the purchased possession, and
a pledge of what God has prepared.

The *full inheritance* is salvation viewed as God's gracious and abiding gift.

Redemption. The context determines the particular aspect of the
"gospel of salvation" that pertains to the consummation of saving
grace. It is the final step in the divine process of saving mankind.

Purchased possession is basically redemption finalized. The hope is
shared by Jews and Gentiles. It is enlarged, glorified, and confirmed.

The praise of his glory. God's purpose in redemption will be accomplished and he will receive praise for such "excellence." The
church will enter the final phase of benefits from redemption with

eternal praise. The church will partake of the heavenly glory and will praise God forever.

The Holy Spirit in Preaching

There is something awesomely unique in writing about the Holy Spirit's role in preaching. It defies objectivity and refuses to yield to the criteria for sermon evaluations. The Spirit works behind the scenes and within the orbits of divine purposes. Lloyd M. Perry has made a broad assertion to explain the Spirit's influence upon preaching:

> The Holy Spirit guides the preacher to the passages upon which he is to preach. Illumination, insight, and discernment are provided during preparation of the sermon. He guides the preacher to illustrative material and ideas. The preacher's memory is stimulated so that he can recall parallel passages of Scripture. The Holy Spirit provides boldness and confidence at the time of presentation. He unifies the audience and creates attentiveness. It is the work of the Spirit to convict of sin, righteousness, and judgment. He finally fixes the Word in the minds and memories of the hearers, follows it up, and causes it to be productive.[1]

In this brief discussion we are considering the key to preaching effectiveness. There is no substitute for the Spirit's engagement in the study or in the pulpit. Even the talents with which the Spirit has gifted persons for preaching are not enough. The Holy Spirit uses them and works through them, but they are inadequate without the direct influence upon speaker and hearer. John R. W. Stott has identified the Spirit's action in a sincere and humble servant in a preaching ministry:

> A humble mind [being submissive to the written Word of God], a humble ambition [desiring an encounter between Christ and his people], and a humble dependence [relying on the power of the Holy Spirit]—this is an analysis of a preacher's humility. It indicates that our message must be God's Word, not ours; our aim Christ's glory, not ours; and our confidence the Holy Spirit's power, not ours.[2]

The Holy Scriptures inspired by the Holy Spirit are the basic resource for preaching. Expository sermons, drawn as they are directly from biblical passages, are open channels for divine communication of the Word of God. Here is the setting in which the Spirit can work effectively in making an impact upon the mind and heart of the hearers. The following comments assume a vital faith in and unreserved commitment to the word of God.

There are five specific points in the process of preaching where the need for the Spirit's involvement is most obvious: in preparation, in delivery, in motivation, in the hearts of the hearers, and in the reflections following the sermon.

Once the Holy Spirit has led in choosing the right passage of Scripture, the preacher must rely on the Spirit's illumination of the meaning of the text. The Spirit is present in the exegetical process, bringing to mind understandings from past experience with the Word. J. Daniel Bauman makes a strong appeal for greater sensitivity to the role of the Spirit:

> When open to the Spirit, [one] will discover topics, content, illustrations, passages of Scripture.... The task is to study diligently, providing the Holy Spirit with material to use, and to study receptively in order that there may be a minimum of distortion between the Holy Spirit's purpose and our understanding of that purpose.[3]

The preacher is always in need of the Spirit's anointing in the pulpit. This is the time when help is needed to achieve clarity of expression and restraint from saying the wrong things or even saying the truth in the wrong way. This is less crucial if the Spirit was involved in the preparation of the outline. The Spirit is always available to direct the formation of sentences to identify the major points. Generally, the Spirit engages the insights discovered in the study.

Delivery requires more than structure and content. Paul refers to the communication of the gospel as going beyond the dynamics of human eloquence and artful skills, saying, "Our gospel came to you not simply with words, but also with power, with the Holy Spirit and with deep conviction."[4]

This concept of pulpit performance puts the emphasis upon the presence of the Spirit. The preacher, under the Spirit's anointing, has freedom to convey the Word of truth without seeking the favor of the audience. The spiritual power invested in the combination of the Word and the Spirit is the dynamic that makes sermon delivery effective.

The third factor in the Spirit's engagement in expository preaching pertains to the speaker's urge to communicate. The preacher's own experience of salvation and of biblical understandings are directly related to the Holy Spirit. The spiritual impulse to share the benefits of the gospel are of the Spirit. The inner sense of urgency to promote the kingdom of Christ emerges from a conscious relation to God. These factors of awareness are used of the Spirit to motivate action in pulpit proclamation.

The people in the pew are also subjects of the Spirit's indwelling. The convictions that develop from hearing a sermon are planted in the mind and heart of the hearer by the Spirit. Thus, the Spirit works at both ends of the evangelical process.

This is also true of what happens after the sermon has been preached. The immediate response of a few at the door is no measure of success among all the people present. Persons carrying impressions of truth will have additional reflections, responding in one way or another without verbal testimony or social expression. And so the work of the Spirit goes on in perpetual influence upon beliefs and behavior.

CHAPTER 9

Analysis of the Text

Guidelines
Outline: The Church in Prayer
Ephesians 1:15-19a (Sermon 5)
Word Meanings Essential to Interpretation
Introduction to Alternate Outlines
    Outline A: The Church with the Spirit's Presence
    Outline B: The Church as the Object of Divine Hope
    Outline C: Christian Privileges
The Writer's Intention

Guidelines to Analysis of the Text

After having selected a text, the next step is to analyze the passage. The purpose of analysis is to discover the parts of the text that lend themselves to investigation.

One approach to the analysis of a passage is to investigate the context. This includes reading the entire book from which it is taken. Even more important are the thoughts immediately before and after the chosen passage. By this effort the general trend of thought can be discovered. After orienting oneself in this way, one is ready to examine the text to extract its content.

One begins by reading and rereading the chosen passage to discover the subject it treats and the main thrust of thought, preparing a work sheet for jotting down the points in consecutive order from the text. The main points of emphasis should be underscored.

Next, the collected list of ideas can be transferred onto a (second) clean sheet of paper. On this second sheet one can begin to classify the major ideas and put them in order of thought sequence. Then one is ready to collect the secondary thoughts and place them in a position of modifiers to the main points (from three to five in most sermons). These subordinate points are formulated in complete sentences that show a direct relation to the primary sentences. While this study is in process, words and phrases are identified which need careful study. This becomes the initial step in exegesis, the benefits of which are used in shaping the outline from the material at hand.

The most common design in expository sermons is the analytical form in which the order of the main divisions follows the pattern of thought in the text. At times some rearrangement of primary thoughts is necessary to achieve the desired effect. This optional order is referred to as a synthetic outline. Although the synthetic outline has a different sequence, it also limits itself to the confines of the text in adopting the same thoughts as the analytic outline.

Whatever approach is made in analyzing the text and constructing an outline, it is well to remember a number of guidelines during the study:

1. Give attention to the progression of thought.

2. Note any accumulation within the text of ideas, principles, or teachings.

3. Discover any groupings of similar sentiments, pairing of words or phrases, or parallelisms on the basis of similarity.

4. Notice any contrasts of ideas including appositions.

5. Watch for statements of cause and effect.

6. Distinguish between primary and secondary ideas, especially modifiers.

7. Look for any repetition of phrases or words and try to discover their significance.

8. Note transitional words, clauses, or phrases that indicate direction of thought, especially connective words such as *because, therefore, whereas,* and *finally.*

Once the main points are identified, one should make sure that the subheads serve in a supporting or modifying role. These can make or break the coherence of thought in the outline.

Sermon 5
The Church in Prayer
Ephesians 1:15-19a

Introduction

In light of God's plan for the church, of Christ's purpose in the church, and of the Holy Spirit's promises to the church, there is concern that the church measure up to divine expectations. On this account the church is involved: (a) in fulfilling the eternal purpose of God, (b) in proclaiming the redeeming work of Christ, and (c) in engaging the power of the Spirit in its life and witness. The prayer expresses essential meanings of the church's relation to God, keeping steadily in view his glory and his interest in the affairs of the church as his "purchased possession."

Theme: The church receives *spiritual blessings.*
  A. *Spiritual blessings* originate in **divine relationship.** (1:15-16).
   1. The **divine relationship** is sustained by *faith.*
    a. *Faith* in Christ as Redeemer builds confidence.
    b. *Faith* in Christ as Lord yields obedience.
   2. The **divine relationship** is enhanced by *love.*
    a. *Love* for the saints is a mark of discipleship.
    b. *Love* for the saints is occasion for thanksgiving.
  B. *Spiritual blessings* rely on knowledge of **divine truth.** (1:17)
   1. We learn to know God better through the *Spirit's* **revelations.**
    a. The *Spirit* illuminates revealed truth.
    b. The *Spirit* conveys meanings of redemptive truth.
   2. We learn to know God better through the *Spirit* of **wisdom.**
    a. The *Spirit* gives wisdom to apply truth.
    b. The *Spirit* gives wisdom to communicate truth.
  C. *Spiritual blessings* accrue through **divine understanding.** (1:18)
   1. An enlightened mind can **understand** diving *calling.*
    a. The *calling* involves God's purpose to redeem.
    b. The *calling* involves God's hope in the church.
   2. An enlightened mind can **understand** divine *inheritance.*
    a. God's *inheritance* in the saints is full of riches.
    b. God's *inheritance* in the saints is full of glory.
  D. *Spiritual blessings* are provided in **divine power.** (1:19a)
   1. God's **power** in the church is *limitless.*

a. God's power is *unlimited* in transforming grace.
b. God's power is *unlimited* in sustaining grace.
2. God's **power** in the church is *eternal.*
    a. God's power produces the quality of *eternal* life.
    b. God's power is extended into *eternal* events.

Conclusion
The answer to our desire for a more intimate relationship with the Father is in the Spirit's indwelling. The human responsibility is to exercise faith and love.

The answer to our desire for adequate knowledge of divine truth is in the Spirit's illumination. The human responsibility is to search the Scriptures for the deeper insights into the things of God.

The answer to our desire to comprehend the purpose and hope of God in the church is in the Spirit's promptings (spiritual impulses). The human responsibility is to acknowledge our needs and privileges in Christ.

The answer to our desire to see the significance of the church to God's holy will and pleasure is in the Spirit's enabling power. The human responsibility is to obey the leading of the Spirit.

Word Meanings Essential to Interpretation

v. 15   *Your faith.* Addresses Gentile Christians, as the context so clearly indicates.

Lord Jesus Christ (cf. v. 3). Faithfulness to Jesus as Lord is respectfully and gratefully acknowledged.

Love for all the saints. Some manuscripts do not have the word *love.* In others, however, it is used in complete correspondence with its appearance in Colossians 1:4. It does appear here in the "Received Text" within verse 15.

v. 16   *The Church in Ephesus* was included in Paul's prayer list. This combination of intercessory prayer mixed with thanksgiving was characteristic of Paul's concern for the churches.

v. 17   *God of our Lord Jesus* refers to the relationship of Jesus with his Father from the viewpoint of his humanity. God is a glorious Father, the one to whom glory belongs.

The Spirit of wisdom and revelation. Wisdom and revelation are special forms of the Holy Spirit's activity. The Spirit possesses the wisdom of God. Here thanksgiving is extended to prayer for their spiritual enlightenment.

Know him better. The knowledge, not of mere facts *about* God, but the knowledge that comes from personal acquaintance with him and his ways. This is the way in which God's gifts are dispersed to those who really know him by experience.

Revelation. Whereas wisdom involves general illumination, revelations are insights to the mysteries of God.

v. 18 *Eyes of understanding* are spiritual eyes to see the essential elements of faith, particularly hope. This is generally thought to refer to the heart as the seat of motivation and spiritual perception, the seat of private thought and will.

Hope of your calling. The principle of hope in its broader sense of designated expectation, not a "hope so"! Specific petitions for the church: Eyes to recognize the hope of the call, eyes to appreciate the riches of glory, eyes to realize his exceeding power.

In hope the Christian church must be made ready for the ultimate call to heaven. In hope the Christian church finds joy in participation. In hope the Christian church relies upon divine promises.

Appreciating the *riches of glory.* Glory is an essential characteristic of salvation. Glory represents the excellence of saving grace.

Realizing the *exceeding power* of our Lord. It is a power that exceeds human effort, a power that effects spiritual resurrection.

Introduction to Alternate Outlines

This brief introduction provides explanations for three alternate outlines on this passage. The preferred outline in the series focuses on "spiritual blessings." Outline A focuses on the presence of the Holy Spirit. Outline B focuses on God's hope in the church. Outline C focuses on individual Christian privileges.

These differences in focus depend on the speaker's purpose. This primary decision is made early in the process of sermon preparation, then expressed in formulating the theme (proposition).

After the statement of the theme has been carefully formulated, one can begin to identify related ideas discovered in the process of textual analysis. Formulating headings or main divisions is not necessary at this point. One does not yet need to set ideas in any order of sequence. Obviously, the order of ideas in the text may provide some impression of sequence.

At this stage it is important to go through the text to identify the ideas that relate to the adopted focus or purpose, including the theme. As one jots down these ideas one can think of ways they are related to the purpose of the emerging sermon.

Outline A focuses on the function of the Holy Spirit in the church. It is an abbreviated edition as compared with the previous one on spiritual blessings. It follows the same model of structure but the adopted theme achieves a different purpose. The stated theme, "The church is sustained by the Holy Spirit," puts the emphasis upon the role of the Spirit. This is evident in the sentences that form the main divisions.

The first line of subdivisions further promotes the theme. These, however, are ideas drawn from a knowledge of other Scriptures in support of the content of the text. The second line of subdivisions have supporting ideas drawn from analogies of faith.

The use of this emphasis on the Holy Spirit is in the direct line of thought contained in the preceding context. It offers a good connection in the series of messages.

Outline B is another abbreviated outline in which a different focus is achieved by the selection of a word that holds prominent significance in the passage. The problem is complicated a bit further by the two possibilities of interpreting the word *hope*, which is used here as a point of emphasis. The title of the sermon already raises the question Whose hope? The believer's or God's? I have chosen the latter to illustrate a use different from that of the usual interpretation.

In "The Glory of God in the Christian Calling" by William O. Carver, the author selected the word *glory* to unify his treatment of the entire epistle of Ephesians. In the book God's *hope* in the church and his *inheritance* in the church are shown to have special meaning. The church is his possession:

> This is to be understood by God's hope in calling us, not what we may hope in that he has called us. . . . Each Christian needs to know what God's hope is for Christianity as a whole; and what each needs to find is the use God intends to make of him in fulfilling that hope.[1]

The argument for this interpretation becomes more convincing when seen in the light of its modifier, "the riches of his glorious inheritance in the saints." Thus "hope" is clearly regarded as the wealth which God sees in the church.

The next item in this knowledge has a bearing also on the interpretation of the word *hope*.

> It has to do with God's resources for possessing his inheritance and so realizing his hope in his redeemed people. The hope, the inheritance, and the power are all God's and the glory is all his. . . . In so great an enterprise, with so glorious an end, in which God's hope is fulfilled in his inheritance, the divine energy of God is the only power for producing the outcome and working in all stages of the process.[2]

This interpretation does not preclude interpreting hope as the believer's expectation of immortality and a share of divine glory. A typical explanation of this view by the renowned scholar B. F. Westcott is that the hope is "for all Christians." The "one hope when you were called" (cf. 4:4) is kindled and sustained in us by the fact that God has called us in to his presence. Such a divine call is a revelation of human destiny. Such hope enters within the veil where Christ has entered (Heb. 6:19).[3]

This interpretation has similar implications for faithful believers. The passage can also be used to define the position of the "called-out ones." A sermon with that emphasis may have equal validity with that of the following Outline C.

Outline C presents another alternative. As indicated in an earlier chapter, the main emphasis of this entire series of messages from Ephesians is on the church as a corporate body of believers. It was recognized at that point that one could design a series with a focus on individual Christian experience. Outline C is an illustration of this other use of the passage. Obviously, the church is composed of individual believers to whom these biblical principles apply with equal validity.

The structure is basically the same. However, a different approach is taken in application.

Outline C has another distinction from that of Outlines A and B. Full sentences are not used in every case in marking the divisions of ideas. Further comment on this method follows the outline.

Sermon 5-A
The Church with the Spirit's Presence
Ephesians 1:15-19a

Introduction
The church must find its place in God's plan.
It must keep steadily in view God's glory.
The church must find its role in Christ's program.
It must keep steadily in view Christ's return.
The church must find its character in the promise of the Holy Spirit.
It must keep steadily in view the Spirit's power.

Theme: The *church* is sustained by the **Holy Spirit.**
A. The **Spirit** gives *quality* to the *church.*
    1. The *quality* of faith is inspired by the Spirit.
    2. The *quality* of love is prompted by the Spirit.
B. The **Spirit** gives *meaning* to the *church.*
    1. The church finds *meaning* through the wisdom of the Spirit.
    2. The church finds *meaning* through the revelation of the Spirit.
C. The **Spirit** gives light to the *church.*
    1. The Spirit *affirms* God's hope in the church.
    2. The Spirit *affirms* God's inheritance in the church.

Conclusion
    a. The answer to our desire for adequate knowledge of divine truth is in the Spirit.
    b. The answer to our desire to comprehend God's purpose and hope in the church is from the Spirit.
    c. The answer to our desire to see the significance of the church in God's holy will and pleasure is in the Spirit.

Sermon 5-B
The Church as the Object of Divine Hope
Ephesians 1:15-19a

Introduction
    In light of God's plan for the church, Christ's program for it, and the Holy Spirit's promises to the church, the church has a responsibility to measure up to divine expectations. This prayer expresses the church's relation to God, keeping in view his glory and his hope in the church.

Theme: God has *hope* in the church.
  A. *Hope* is based on a personal **relationship.**
    1. The **relationship** is sustained by faith.
    2. The **relationship** is enhanced by love.
  B. *Hope* is based on **knowledge** of divine truth.
    1. We **know** God's intent better through the Spirit of wisdom.
    2. We **know** God's intent better through the Spirit of revelation.
  C. *Hope* is based on **understanding.**
    1. An enlightened mind can **understand** divine hope.
    2. An enlightened mind can **understand** divine inheritance.
  D. *Hope* is based on divine **power.**
    1. God's **power** in the church is limitless.
    2. God's **power** in the church is eternal.

Conclusion
  a. The exercise of faith and love opens the church to a walk with God.
  b. Repeated communications from the Spirit provide insights into the will of God.
  c. Prolonged searchings of the Spirit lead to greater awareness of the church's position in Christ.
  d. Persistent impulses from the Spirit create a keener sense of the church's role in God's kingdom.

The following sample outline is an example of using a passage of Scripture to focus on individual Christian experiences. The former outlines (A and B) kept a focus on the corporate body of believers, the church. Obviously what is a privilege to a single believer is also open to others and indeed to the church whose membership is composed of a variety of people. Basically, the letter (epistle) was written in an address to the church at Ephesus (and some scholars believe to other surrounding churches). It was no doubt read in other churches and is now applied to the universal church.

Sermon 5-C
Christian Privileges
Ephesians 1:15-19a

Introduction
Spiritual blessings are available "in Christ." The eternal purpose of God, the redeeming work of Christ, the indwelling presence of the Spirit—all work together to the praise of his glory.

Theme: Faith qualifies for spiritual *privileges.*
  A. The *privilege* of spiritual insight: "wisdom and revelation." (v. 17)
    1. To know more about God.
    2. Ability to perceive divine truth.
    3. Knowledge of personal fellowship and searching.
  B. The *privilege* of spiritual illumination (v. 18a) enlightened for learning and living a purified inner life.
    1. The mind opened to spiritual implications.
    2. Emotions purified to love.
    3. The will equipped to obey.
  C. The *privilege* of spiritual experiences. (v. 18b, 19a)
    1. Experience hope.
    2. Riches of inheritance.
    3. Greatness of his power.

Conclusion
    Prayer touches the core of Christian life and duty. Human response engages these divine resources.

Reflection

The formulation of ideas to be expressed in preaching the sermon with this outline depends upon a combination of memory from preparation and the inspiration of the moment while delivering the message. This is not to depreciate the action of the Holy Spirit during delivery of the sermon. But the preacher has less distraction in the study to interfere with hearing the voice of the Spirit. Standing before an audience, one encounters unpredicted competitive sounds and scenes.

Another disadvantage is the ease with which the train of thought can deviate from the theme, or even from the purpose of the message. When that occurs, the audience misses the impact of the truth that was intended.

The Writer's Intention

The writer's purpose in writing may not always appear "on the surface." There are numerous statements in New Testament books that indicate clearly to whom and to what intent the message was written. A good illustration is 1 John 5:13, "I have written to you . . . that you may know that you have eternal life."

It is not uncommon to discover a distinct pattern in writing. For instance, in Ephesians the first three chapters are devoted to statements of doctrine about the church. The second half is clearly given to expressions of the practical aspects of church behavior. One can also see the personal experience involved in the corporate expression of believers living in a pagan society.

Another illustration of purpose in writing is that stated near the close of the Gospel of John (see 20:30): "These are written that you may believe that Jesus is the Christ, the Son of God, and that believing you may have life in his name." This gives the interpreter a clue to the meanings of Jesus' miracles. They are signs of his deity and of his redemptive mission.

In that verse, two other elements of truth are announced: faith and life. The interpreter can find in the Gospel narratives and declarations an intention to have people experience these realities. It simply means that we are to interpret the Gospel with its various passages in light of this stated purpose.

Norton Sterrett has some suggestions for finding the purpose and plan of a specific book: (1) Note any specific statement that announces purpose. (2) Observe any personal references to the readers and the points of application. (3) Look for indications of structure. (4) When the purpose or plan is clear, interpret the various sections in harmony with it. He offers a good illustration of how these suggestions work out in Philippians. (See 2:1-8, especially.) "The phrases *the same mind, the same love, full accord,* and *one mind* show that Paul is bothered about the quality of fellowship of the Philippian Christians."[4] Here Christ's death is used as an example of humility. One must go to other Scriptures to find teachings on atonement.

In the Ephesian epistle, there is a simple statement in the first verse that identifies the writer as Paul who at the time was serving a prison sentence. The letter is addressed to the "saints in Ephesus." This setting clearly serves as a background for understanding the occasion for writing.

Of particular interest is what can be learned about the church at Ephesus. They are regarding as "saints" and "faithful" people who are the object of the writer's concern for the welfare of the church (and possibly other churches in the area). They were of Gentile extraction who had demonstrated "faith in our Lord Jesus" and "love for all the saints." Gentiles by birth, they grew up under a Jewish stigma for being uncircumcised (2:11). They were "separate from Christ, excluded from citizenship in Israel, foreigners to the covenants of promise, without hope and without God in the world" (2:12).

The redeeming feature in this picture of Gentile futility and darkened understanding is the benefits of God's grace among them. Therefore "now" since they have been delivered from darkness, they are called to live "as children of light" (5:8). As imitators of God they live a life of love and moral purity. Their possession of spiritual realities is what this series of messages is all about.

Note the autobiographical remarks which reflect the spirit of Paul, "the prisoner of Christ Jesus." The list of personal characteristics submitted as sermon 12-B (see chapter 16), gives a more complete picture of the apostle. It should be noted here, however, that he repeatedly identified with the spiritual experiences of Christians at Ephesus.

CHAPTER 10

Exegesis

Guidelines to Exegesis

Exegesis is an important part of interpretation. It refers to a detailed examination of the passage to be used. It is the process by which speakers can arrive at an assurance that they are representing the meaning of the text as accurately as possible. This can be a major task in preparing to preach, depending on the complications of the text.

Several helpful principles can help in the process:

1. Assume that the section under study has one and only one meaning.

2. Anticipate the likelihood that scholars may sharply disagree on the point.

3. As much as possible use other Scriptures dealing with the same issue.

4. Never adopt an interpretation that contradicts an assured doctrinal portion of any general or specific Bible teachings.

5. Attempt to learn what the text meant to the writer and to the persons addressed.

6. Try to ascertain what the words of the text most plainly mean in light of the historical situation that called for the writing.

In the process of tracking down the original sense, one finds new suggestions from the study of words and phrases. Sharp distinctions sometimes emerge from grammar study, (e.g., whether the verb conveys the idea of continuing action or completed action). For this and other reasons, the preparation of an expository (or textual) sermon must take into account the details of literary analysis.

This emphasis upon the basic original meanings of Scripture carries with it an important mandate to translate those meanings into contemporary concepts. We must remember that the inspired Word has both a universal and timeless application of principles. After having the original meaning at hand we must ascertain what that principle means to us today. After all, the application of truth is the ultimate goal of these studies. In addition to believing what we proclaim, we also want to preach with integrity. To do that we must build sermons on a solid foundation of accurate exegesis.

The particular exercise that the average minister can handle is the study of words and phrases. There are some grammatical niceties that have a bearing on final results of the overall investigation. Those who have some knowledge of Greek and Hebrew have an advantage in exploring such linguistic implications. Others will need to rely on commentaries, Bible dictionaries, Bible encyclopedias, and specialized helps such as word studies. Regardless of the amount of such resources immediately available, one should do all one can to satisfy the demands of faithfulness in handling the Word of God.

The goal of exegesis is to be completely objective. This is an ideal that is difficult to achieve. Personal presuppositions may need to be corrected by an exegetical study. In the process of learning God's message from the Bible, we have to take care to find the exact meaning of specific texts. James S. Stewart says, "The strongest and most helpful preaching is that which expounds a text or passage in dynamic relationship to its actual setting in Scripture. Loyalty to the Word of God demands scrupulous care in exegesis."[1]

Sermon 6
The Church in the Fullness of Christ
Ephesians 1:19b-23

Introduction

In the preceding verses of this first chapter of Ephesians we have seen how the wonderful plan of God is administered. It is accomplished through the redemption that is in Christ Jesus. It is made effective by establishing his presence in the church through the indwelling of the Holy Spirit. It has been brought to our attention, through the Spirit's illumination, that God has hope in the church. Here is a clear and definite proposal that the redeemed are God's inheritance (bought with the blood of his Son). We are now prepared to see further implications of the marvelous work of redemption.

In this section we are told about an expectation the church has in the final consummation of history. The body of believers (the body of Christ) is to become the fullness (or completion) of Christ.

Theme: Christ achieves his fullness in the **church.**
   A. The **church** is invested with **divine power.**
      God has hope in the church.
     1. **Divine power** was exerted in Christ's *resurrection.*
       a. *Resurrection* power is the norm of Christian experience.
         (1) Christian experience relies on divine action.
         (2) Christian experience reflects divine character.
       b. *Resurrection* power is the source of Christian strength.
         (1) Christian strength is derived through active faith.
         (2) Christian strength is derived through supernatural energy.
     2. **Divine power** was demonstrated in Christ's *ascension.*
       a. Christ's *ascension* introduced a new order.
         (1) The new order was designed in the heavenlies.
         (2) The new order took form in the church.
       b. Christ's *ascension* preceded a new presence.
         (1) The presence of the Spirit was predicted.
         (2) The presence of the Spirit was confirmed.
   B. The **church** is directed by **divine authority.**
      God has riches in the church.
     1. **Divine authority** accompanied Christ's *exaltation.*
       a. His *exaltation* established his mediatorial position.

(1) Christ's mediation pertains to church needs.

(2) Christ's mediation pertains to divine purpose.

b. His *exaltation* established prevailing grace.

(1) Grace is identified with being in Christ.

(2) Grace is identified with reigning with Christ.

2. **Divine authority** accompanied Christ's *victory.*

a. Christ's *victory* is potentially real in a disordered world.

(1) His victory gives a position above all rules and authority.

(2) His victory gives a position above powers and dominions.

(3) His victory gives a position above every title.

b. Christ's *victory* is real in the church.

(1) The church is the body of Christ.

(2) The church is the bride of Christ.

c. Christ's *victory* projects a future triumph.

(1) His triumph will give unopposed rule.

(2) His triumph will give unlimited glory.

C. The *church* is invested with **divine fullness.**

God has power in the church.

1. **Divine fullness** is attached to Christ's *mission.*

a. His *mission* is assigned to the church.

(1) The church proclaims Christ as Author of everything good.

(2) The church proclaims Christ as Giver of good everywhere.

b. His *mission* is to proclaim the gospel.

(1) The gospel conveys his secret of truth.

(2) The gospel conveys his glory of deity.

2. **Divine fullness** is attached to Christ's *headship.*

a. His *headship* assures the church of strength.

(1) Strength is utilized in spiritual administration.

(2) Strength is utilized in functional activities.

b. His *headship* assures fullness in the church.

(1) Fullness is conferred in the wealth of God's grace.

(2) Fullness is expressed in moral victories.

(3) Fullness is accepted through spiritual obedience.

Conclusion

The church has received its spiritual blessings on the merits of Christ's redemptive work. In light of the resources made available through the power of the resurrection, the church is being shaped according to a heavenly design. It is destined eventually to complete the projected fullness of Christ in the age that is yet to come. In the meantime she needs to make herself ready as the designated bride of the coming King. Even now, Christ is completing his fullness in the church.

Word Meanings Essential to Interpretation

. 19 *That power* has reference to the preceding sentence—point number 3 in Paul's prayer for the church. It identifies God's action. Christians should know the power of God.

The working of his mighty strength. Paul "piles synonym on synonym as he describes how God's power (dunamis) operates according to the inworking (energeia) or the strength (kratos) of his might (ischus)."[2] Note the emphasis on "working"; God's strength is inherent in his divine nature but this "working" is his activity in the church.

. 20 *Christ's resurrection.* The strength which God exerted in Christ's resurrection (past participle; completed action) is the measure of power now operating in the church.

Seated at his right hand. The early apostolic preaching associated Christ's resurrection with his exaltation (or enthronement). This indicates the Father's sharing of sovereignty with his Son. The authority vested in the exalted Christ is essential to our understanding of his lordship.

Heavenly realms is the location of the throne from which Christ exercises the authority given to him. This is a dominant thought in relation to the work of the ascended Christ.

. 21 *Principalities and powers.* It is difficult to determine the specific role of each agency listed. What is important is the superiority of Christ over all. His name is above every other name.

Present and future age indicates the scope in time of the authority and work of Christ.

. 22 *Under his feet.* God has given Christ supreme authority to be head over everything. This appointment was made in deference to the church.

. 23 *His body* identifies the close relationship of Christ and the church. The term *body* is equated with the term *fullness*. The fullness is ascribed to the One who "fills everything in every way." Christ is complemented by the body, the church.

Fullness of him. The interpretation of this hinges on the grammatical structure in which it occurs. The passive voice would mean the church receives elements of spiritual values. Some scholars take this view. But there is stronger evidence to interpret the church as filling up Christ's spiritual realities. In that sense the church is the fullness of Christ. So instead of the church reaching its fullness in Christ, "all things are contributory to him and he himself finds his fullness in the sum of all things that he brings into a living union with himself."[3]

Introduction to Alternate Outline

There is a delicate distinction of meaning in this passage. It illustrates the importance of exegetical studies. Does this passage emphasize the manner in which the church receives the "fullness" of God? Or does it identify the church as the means by which Christ receives "fullness"? There are arguments in favor of both views.

I have chosen the latter interpretation. God conditions the church as a complement to Christ as his body. Christ in his present and future role in eternal governance is made complete (fullness) in his union with the church. That conjunction obtains in Christ's sovereignty over political and spiritual powers.

In one sense this combination of Christ's superior authority with the union of the church with him constitutes the goal of God's political action. God's power operates according to the inner workings of the strength of his might to accomplish his purposes in redemption—both now and in the future.

The following outlines are drawn from the same passage of Scripture. They appear in this comparative study as illustrations of the effect of interpretation upon the focus of the sermon message. Although they appear to be in conflict, neither contradicts the other. The summation of doctrine is drawn from other New Testament teachings. Both represent valid elements of the biblical doctrine of the relation of Christ to the church and of the implications of redemption.

The issue to be identified in this exercise of interpretation pertains to the meaning this message conveys to the church. The first outline fulfills the purpose of exalting Christ. It inspires members of the church to live in the power of the resurrection and in respect for the honor and dignity of its Head. The second outline puts the focus on the effect God's working has upon the life of the community of faith. It applies the meaning of the power of the resurrection to the Christian life and Christian duty. In that position the church completes God's purpose in his Son.

Sermon 6-A
The Church in the Power of the Resurrection
Ephesians 1:19b-23

Introduction

There is victory for the church in the power of the resurrection. The Spirit of wisdom and revelation teaches the exceeding greatness of that power when applied to human need. When this power is released within the body of believers the appearance of spiritual realities will demonstrate the "working of his mighty strength."

This identifies Christ as the source of all spiritual blessings. Christian experience draws upon the same strength exerted in the resurrection of Christ.

Whereas the record of Jesus' crucifixion is provisionary truth, the proclamation of his resurrection identifies present spiritual realities. The believer's identification with Christ in resurrection experience indicates the nature of God's redemptive "working."

The church is made up of persons who are committed to the risen Lord.

Theme: Divine fullness is received through ***resurrection power.***
  A. ***Resurrection power*** is now available in the *risen* **Christ.** (v. 19)
    1. *Resurrection* power is released by faith.
    2. *Resurrection* power operates out of the supernatural.
    3. *Resurrection* power is a New Testament standard.
  B. ***Resurrection power*** is measured by *God's act* in **Christ.** (v. 20a)
    1. This *power* is a continuation of dynamics in Christ's resurrection.
    2. This *power* is a consequence of God's work in Christ's resurrection.
    3. This *power* is made accessible and actual in relation to Christ.
    4. This *power* is the stepping stone to moral victory.
  C. ***Resurrection power*** comes from the *exalted* **Christ.** (v. 20b)
    1. Christ's *exaltation* is the guarantee of mediation to the church.
    2. Christ's *exaltation* gives him official authority over the church.
    3. Christ's *exaltation* confirms his lordship to the church.
    4. Christ's *exaltation* verifies his headship to the church.
    5. Christ's *exaltation* established his dominion over all.
  D. ***Resurrection power*** is demonstrated in the *victorious* **Christ.** (v. 22a)
    1. This *power* is potentially real in a disordered world.
    2. This *power* is actually real in the church.
      a. This power sanctifies the church.
      b. This power energizes service in the church.

3. This *power* gives moral freedom to act responsibly.
  a. The church acts in separation from the world.
  b. The church acts in the power of a new affection.
E. *Resurrection power* is invested by the *replete* **Christ.** (vv. 22b-23)
  1. The *headship* of Christ offers controls to the church.
  2. The *headship* of Christ offers fullness to the church.
    a. Fullness is realized in the wealth of his grace.
    b. Fullness is expressed in purity of life.
    c. Fullness is expressed in the performance of his will.
  3. The *headship* of Christ is a current reality in the church.
    a. He provides spiritual administration.
    b. He provides functional energy.
    c. He provides ethical direction.

Conclusion
  The church achieves levels of spiritual realities in the risen
    Christ, the fullness of God.
  The church is in a position of access to resurrection power.
  The church has as its Head:
    —a living Person in whom we believe
    —an ever-present Lord in whom we confide
    —a conquering King on whom we depend

The Importance of Word Study

As mentioned in the discussion of exegesis above, it is important to ascertain the meaning of words as a part of any preparation of an expository sermon. Words are the means of putting thoughts into forms of expression. When words are put together into careful combinations, they convey certain meanings. Under divine inspiration we have such combinations which convey God's message.

In the process of interpretation we have the challenge of identifying God's thoughts and his intention for their use. The interpreter must therefore attempt to discover the exact meaning of the text. An effective clue is the meaning of important words in each sentence. This leads to an understanding of the distinct meaning the sentence was intended to convey.

The sermon outlines in this series are accompanied by "word meanings" to assist in this process of interpretation. In the case of sermon 6, the definitions included help the reader find meanings in the text. There is not always full agreement on these issues, but at least the study introduces reasons for the accompanying outline structure.

It must be acknowledged, however, that the same word can often have different meanings. An illustration of this is in verse 23, where the word *body* occurs. Here it is an analogy used to designate an intimate relationship of the church to Christ. The comparison is drawn from the human body. The body is useless without being related to its head.

Another case is the use of the word *house*. Ordinarily we use it to refer to an earthly dwelling place. Beyond that the Scripture refers to the physical body as "our earthly house" (2 Cor. 5:1, KJV) and Jesus spoke of heaven as his "Father's house" (John 14:1). Also in the Corinthian passage we have "an eternal house in heaven." In each case the other words in the sentence (the context) make the meaning clear.

A word's most common meaning should prevail unless there is some element of truth in the context that identifies a different usage. An illustration of this is the word *call* (called, calling) in Ephesians 4:1 as compared with its use in 1 Corinthians 7:20-21. The word in both places refers to being called to salvation. This is in contrast to its ordinary use in naming an object or person, like "thou shalt call his name Jesus." Again the context makes clear what meaning obtains.

There is a verse in 1 Corinthians which says, "Let every man abide in the same calling wherein he was called." This has been used to support the contention that a person who has been remarried after divorce (his first spouse still living) should remain in that same marital status. But this is not necessarily so. As Vincent says of this use of the word in the New Testament, "calling always signifies the call of God into his kingdom through conversion,"[4]

That it refers to the call to salvation and related elements of saving experience is seen clearly in the references from 1 Corinthians 7:

"As the Lord hath called every one, so let him walk" v. 17, (KJV). The alternate reading from NIV: "Each one should retain the place in life that the Lord assigned to him and to which God has called him."

"Was a man already circumcised when he was called?" (v. 18).

"Let every man abide in the same calling wherein he is called" (vv. 20-21, KJV). The alternate reading from NIV: "Each one should remain in the same situation which he was in when God called him. Were you a slave when you were called?"

"He that is called in the Lord, being a servant, is the Lord's freeman." The alternate reading from NIV is very similar.

"Brethren, let every man, wherein he is called, therein abide with God." The alternate reading from NIV is, "Brothers, each man, as responsible to God, should remain in the situation God called him to."

The word *situation* misses the point of emphasis in the original Greek. There is no justification to use that word in translation of the word *calling*. As Godet puts it, "The word *call* cannot denote the earthly state or profession; it is applied here as elsewhere [see references above] to the call to salvation."[5] The same Greek word *kaleō* is used throughout this entire passage as it appears in other passages in New Testament books, such as Romans 8:30, 1 Corinthians 1:9, 1 Thessalonians 2:12, and Hebrews 9:15. In each case, *kaleō* is translated *called* (see the NIV) and is used particularly of the divine call to partake of the blessings of redemption.

In our study of Ephesians we find the word *called* used (see 4:1, 4) in the same sense, pertaining to redemption. The detailed explanations here illustrate the importance of (1) careful study, (2) recognizing the general use of a word, and (3) taking the context into account.

Of course, some words go through a process of change, influenced by their cultural use. A good illustration of this is the word *prevent* as it appears in the King James Version of 1 Thessalonians 4:15. At the time the translation was made, the word was used to mean "go before," which was a proper translation from the Greek manuscript. Now a more common word conveying that thought is *precede*. See the NIV: "We who are still alive, who are left till the coming of the Lord, will certainly not precede those who have fallen asleep."

Some practical procedures in word study can help in accurate interpretation. Not all preachers will have a command of the Hebrew and Greek languages. But anyone can look up words in a good

Bible dictionary. By referring to a concordance one can see how the word is used in other passages of Scripture.

Relating a word to its context also gives a clue to its own meaning. For instance, Jesus used contrast effectively when he referred to the "narrow way" in contrast to the "broad way."

Ephesians 2

Interpretation

Guidelines to Interpretation

As indicated above, exegesis is essential to interpretation. After the selection of ideas under the control of the exegetical exercise, one goes on to test the validity of those ideas for the adopted purpose of the sermon. One should be convinced that the reading of the text gives the impression it was meant to convey.

This requires a careful examination of the words and sentence structures used in the text. It necessitates extensive study and honest application. One should be satisfied with nothing less than deep conviction that the prepared sermon is a fair representation of the Word of God.

When one undertakes to develop and apply the teachings of a selected passage of Scripture, one must be respectfully honest. The preacher has no authority in the pulpit (or anywhere else) to use the words of Scripture in any other way than to convey the meaning the Spirit of God intended them to have. A Scripture passage may have several applications, but it has only one essential meaning.

In order to study the text minutely, it is necessary to have good "tools." An exhaustive concordance (Strong's, Young's, or Smith's) is indispensable. It is a primary source of word study. For New Testament passages, *Vincent's Word Studies* and *Robertson's Word Pictures* are good additional help. With a concordance one can learn how the same word is employed elsewhere in the Bible. With a word study book one can ascertain the definition of words in their setting and in light of comparative study. The serious expositor will also want to examine the best accessible commentaries to see what meaning the commentator has found.

Another aspect of exegesis is the careful examination of grammatical structure. That often yields an interesting sidelight which enables the interpreter to see the specific meaning of a phrase or sentence. In the passage used in chapter 10 (Eph. 1:19b-23), the phrase "power for us who believe" occurs. This conveys the idea of present and continuous believing. This power is therefore available to the "now believing ones." Commentaries that include exegetical helps are particularly helpful in this regard. One should not rely on any one single commentator, however. Comparisons with several other commentaries provide a double check for the process.

In every case the student of the Bible will compare other Scripture passages with the particular meaning drawn from the text under consideration. Not only can one interpret Scripture with Scripture; one can also confirm or reject a conclusion arrived at in the study of the text alone. But one can never accept an interpretation of a single passage which contradicts the plain statement of truth found in another Scripture.

Another essential factor in interpretation is the immediate context of the given passage. The trends of thought which precede and follow the selected portion also give a clue to the meaning.

While searching for meaning one should raise serious questions. Who is the speaker? (In this case, Paul.) Who is the audience to whom the message is addressed? (In this case, the Ephesian church.) What is the general subject being treated? (In this case, the relation of Christ to the church.)

The "word meanings" that follow each primary outline provide some help for interpretation. They are intended to serve as suggestions for further study. They usually discuss the major elements of truth but are not intended to be comprehensive comments.

The following summary of principles of interpretation are not only reminders of what has been proposed, but suggest topics to be discussed in later chapters. More will be said about interpretation in this and following chapters.

Summary of Principles of Biblical Interpretation

1. *Contextual considerations* forbid lifting a passage out of the unit of thought in which it occurs.

2. *Word studies* are essential, but need to be subordinated to contextual and grammatical influences.

3. *Grammar* identifies the limits of interpretation but aids in conveying the true meaning.

4. The *writer's original purpose* in addressing the subject is a key to interpretation.

5. The *analogy of faith* is the final test to the meaning of a specific passage.

6. *Historical factors* throw light on the application of principles.

7. Guidelines for current practices are best found in *New Testament teachings*, rather than in the Old Testament economy.

8. The *Holy Spirit* can and does overcome human bias.

Other Principles of Interpretation

1. Avoid the use of arguments from silence.

2. Resolve alleged contradictions by examining the purpose and literary boundaries of the passage.

3. Understand figures of speech to convey literal truth through the use of concrete language.

4. Regard symbols and types as physical pictures of spiritual realities.

5. Read parables with a view to finding one central point for emphasis.

6. Interpret prophecy by recognizing that fulfilled prophecy is the key to the unfulfilled.

7. Poetry is understood as expressions of deep feelings in response to human circumstances.

Sermon 7
The Church: A Resurrected Body
Ephesians 2:1-3

Introduction
The hand that raised Christ from death has made the church alive by divine power. God is now acting again with that resurrection power that turns death into life, exposing the state of human nature. It is death to be alienated from God. It is life to know him.

Theme: **Believers** are raised from **death** to life.
  A. **Believers** are resurrected from a state of **sinfulness.**
    1. The state of **sinfulness** is derived from *human nature.*
      a. *Human nature* transgresses the will of God.
      b. *Human nature* without forgiveness remains dead.
    2. The principles of **sinfulness** are evident in *sins.*
      a. *Sins* alienate people from God.
      b. *Sins* constitute dead material that remains.
  B. **Believers** are resurrected from a state of **domination.**
    1. The **domination** of the world has a decaying *influence.*
      a. It *influences* habits of living.
      b. It *influences* standards of behavior.
    2. The **domination** of Satan constricts with *evil forces.*
      a. *Evil forces* develop evil intention.
      b. *Evil forces* develop a disposition of revolt.
    3. The **domination** of a spirit of disobedience exalts *self.*
      a. The *self-life* contradicts the will of God.
      b. The *self-life* ignores moral imperatives.
  C. **Believers** are resurrected from a state of **sensuality.**
    1. **Sensuality** is an expression of *carnal desires.*
      a. *Carnal desires* represent the cravings of sinful nature.
      b. *Carnal desires* follow natural impulses.
      c. *Carnal desires* follow the line of indulgences.
    2. **Sensuality** is an expression of *evil thoughts.*
      a. *Evil thoughts* emerge from corrupt affections.
      b. *Evil thoughts* follow the trend of a depraved mind.

c. *Evil thoughts* are related to selfish desires.

D. *Believers* are resurrected from a state of **condemnation.**

1. All sin is the object of God's fixed *displeasure.*
2. Disobedience can never be a matter of *indifference.*
3. The condition of depravity unresolved is under *condemnation*
4. Separation from God invokes his *wrath.*

Conclusion

The presence of death is a constant concern. Some Christians show symptoms of advancing death—a creeping paralysis of the spirit. To be alive to world influences is a sign of death in relation to God. The church must face the evidences of death and employ resurrection power for deliverance.

Word Meanings Essential to Interpretation (2:1-3)

. 1 *Sinfulness.* To be dead in trespasses is to have a society the object of need.

To be dead through trespasses is the result of persistent offenses.

To be dead is to be removed from divine power. It means being without moral power.

Sins refers to more than occasional acts. It usually refers to social action.

. 2 The *prince of the power of the air* is a spirit active in evil and an air tenanted by evil spirits.

The spirit . . . in the children of disobedience refers to a conscious resistance to the will of God. People are exposed to assaults of evil from without. Satan has agents of evil all over the world.

. 3 *Sensuality* is a condition among people of disobedience.

Lusts of the flesh refers to natural impulses that need only provocation of some kind. This corruption expresses itself in fulfilling desires of flesh and in following the promptings of the mind.

Conversation: behavior, manner of living.

Fulfilling: carrying out impulses.

Desires: pressures of the "willings."

Mind: thoughts which originate action.

Children of wrath emphasizes a connection by birth into a relationship with the natural order—an order essentially antagonistic to God's order. Therefore it is the object of divine displeasure when there is indulgence in its ways. "There is a birth principle of evil,

which, if suffered to develop, will bring upon itself the wrath of God" (Westcott).
Wrath refers to God's holy hatred of sin.

Introduction to Alternate Outline

In light of the emphasis on structure, the alternate outline that follows illustrates the disadvantage of forming main divisions and subdivisions in phrases. Observe the similarity of content. It is based closely on the Scripture passage. It represents a form of expository treatment. The question remains, however, whether the speaker will be able to communicate as clearly from this as from the other. Many of the thoughts to be expressed are in poor literary quality. The only person who can use this outline effectively is one whose extemporaneous skills have been well cultivated.

There is another difference in this outline. It is expressed in the terms of approach. The other outline has a positive mood; this one produces a negative effect. While the description of depravity in the text is realistic and needs exposure, the "good news" should not be suppressed or neglected.

The justification for the use of the positive approach is the expression in verses 4 and 5, "But . . . God made us alive." These verses could well be included in the text, putting an even greater emphasis upon the concept of the resurrected life. Later sermons will reflect that emphasis.

Another criticism of this alternate outline is that the prominent thought of the theme is "alienation from God." But the points and subpoints do not consistently reflect this emphasis. Here and there are assumptions that this is the case. It appears, however, that the theme was formulated independent of determining the succession of thought patterns.

Sermon 7-A
The Church Out of Death
Ephesians 2:1-3

Introduction

1. The hand that raised up Christ has made the church alive. The exceeding greatness of God's power was demonstrated in this "quickening."

2. This change can be compared with Christ's resurrection. God is act-

ing over again in us. This resurrection power turns death into life.

3. Previously we saw the divine encounter with humanity. Now we view human experience and the state of human nature.

4. It is life to know God; death to be alienated from him.

Theme: Spiritual death is a state of alienation from God.

A. *A state of sinfulness:* the dead material with which God works.

    1. Trespasses, transgressions, "falls."

    By the act and fact of transgression, people became dead and reflect their a depraved human nature and conduct.

    The doom of sin lies in a person's unforgiven spirit.

    Separation from the fountain of life eternal.

    2. Sins: the principle of sinfulness rather than sinful acts.

    Sin is an inherent principle in humanity.

    3. A dead person's outlook:

    His works are dead.

    His joys are a shadow.

    His hopes are a dream.

    His soul is in a coffin.

    His spirit is crushed under sense activity.

    He is cold and powerless as a tree cut off, a fire gone out, a heart stopped beating.

B. *A state of domination:* a sphere of activity or a habit of living.

    1. According to the standards of the world with its customs and traditions: rotting with corruption, molding in decay, people shaped after this world and under the control of the spirit of the age.

    The governing principle is evil.

    The conduct is controlled by an evil pattern.

    A soul in sympathy with God finds this world incompatible with his or her spirit.

    2. According to satanic domination,

    lives controlled by evil forces shape our behavior after evil intention.

    Satan possesses people and assumes direction of their lives, creating a moral atmosphere conducive to the accomplishments of his evil ends.

    To be in subjection to Satan is to be bound in moral temper and disposition with the leader of the revolt against God.

    3. According to domination of disobedience, associated with children of disobedience.

    Evil spirits in contrary action affect opinions, feeling, and conduct.

    The moral issues become clear.

C. A *state of sensuality:*
   1. Fulfilling the desires of the flesh: where appetites of natural man rule, following natural impulses and urges, rendering obedience to sensual desires.
   2. Fulfilling desires of the mind, including intellect and affections, following ideas of a depraved mind, governed by personal ideas, controlled by unleashed thoughts, biased by self-life.
D. A *state of condemnation:*
   1. All sin is the object of God's fixed displeasure.
      Disobedience is never a matter of indifference.
   2. Born in condition of depravity.
      God's smile or frown is the sunshine or gloom of the inner life.
   3. Carries judgment everywhere,
      Separating ourselves from God brings his wrath upon us.

Conclusion
   Some Christians show symptoms of advancing death, a creeping paralysis of the spirit.
   Some people are powerfully alive in relation to the world of sense, yet are utterly dead in relation to God.

Principles of Interpretation

Any use of the Bible in communicating divine truth involves the exercise of interpretation as indicated in the guidelines at the beginning of this chapter. After one selects ideas identified in the analysis of the text, one must subject them to the findings of the exegesis. After that screening, the ideas are then tested with the view of complying with the adopted purpose of the sermon. This concerns not only the particular meanings drawn from the text, but also their suitability to this particular sermon. They are also subject to the scrutiny of the total process of interpretation.

This requires a careful examination of the words and sentences in the text. It requires extensive study and honest application.

The results of the process of interpretation are strongly influenced by the interpreter's convictions about the Bible. For this reason it is well to have settled the question of the inspiration of Scripture. Related to that, however, are several other presuppositions. One is the recognition that the New Testament has greater authority in shaping the beliefs and lifestyle of the Christian, even though the Old Testament and the New Testament constitute a unity of truth in the revelation of God.

Interpretation also requires a living faith characterized by insight received through the new life in Christ. This includes a readiness to obey what is learned about God's will. Without obedience the process of interpretation is an empty endeavor. Obedience leads to understanding as surely as understanding leads to obedience.

A subtle influence that affects current patterns of interpretation is the pressure of secular social practices. Culture must constantly be judged by the Bible.

Compromise with world standards is sometimes justified by a spurious use of the Scriptures. Interpreters who do this seem to be able to extract from Scripture whatever upholds their preconceived positions. Such exercises precipitate an erosion of the true meaning of God's Word.

> It is not a peculiarity of conservative evangelical theologians that they are guided in their view of the Bible by what they think of it. Presuppositions there must be, but the difference between presuppositions of conservative theology and the presuppositions of other groups is that those of the former are provided by the Scripture itself, whereas those of the other groups are of human origin. The presupposition of conservative theology is that the Bible demands an approach in reverence and faith. It claims to be the Word of God and must be examined and interpreted in that light. . . . The basic principle of biblical interpretation which emerges from this point of view is that the sense of Scripture is to be found in the grammatical meaning of the words. . . . Every word is therefore to be accepted in its normal meaning and in the context of the style of writing in which it appears.[1]

We will discuss this matter further in the next chapter under the heading "Theological Guidelines to Interpretation."

Theological Interpretation

Theological Guidelines to Interpretation

We develop understandings by theological guidelines. It is inevitable that we bring faith concepts into our approach to biblical studies. It is therefore essential that we hold respect for the Bible as the Word of God. This position is held in contradiction to the view held by some that one must be totally unbiased in any attempt to find the meaning of a passage of Scripture. While this may serve as a caution against the tendency to read into Scripture what we want it to say, we insist that the Bible must be approached in a different way than classical literature or any other form of human communication. After all, this is God's Word written.

Another principle that serves as a guideline is the authority of Scripture. The doctrine of inspiration affirms the validity of biblical truth. Sermons must be prepared with that in view. In order to speak for God, one must have confidence in the record of his revelation. When we preach the Word we attempt to declare what God wants expressed in human language.

We are committed to a Christological view of the Scriptures. By this we mean that we look for references and allusions to Christ as the divinely appointed Redeemer and Lord. Any interpretation of Scripture that denies the deity of Christ may well be held in doubt. Our Christian faith holds him in a supreme position in all matters of redemption. Any interpretation of a biblical passage that casts an unfavorable reflection on his incarnation is inconsistent with the whole tenor of the New Testament. The analogy of faith comes to the rescue of any such attempt to misrepresent our Lord.

The message of the Bible is addressed to all people. It is a book for the people. It is intended to reach into every class, race, or nation. Its teachings are for the rich and poor. It is intended to meet the heart needs of intellectuals and the uneducated. It has universal applications for a people in all walks of life, regardless of vocational engagements or political commitments.

There is also a basic unity in the Bible. Even though its writers were drawn from a variety of ethnic backgrounds and it covers a broad and diverse history, there is a consistent thread of truth that follows the development of the community of faith. When we come to the Bible with a settled conviction that God means to convey divine truth through it, we have a firm foundation upon which to build an attitude of acceptance toward individual passages. This sets the tone for research studies and for preparation to preach the gospel.

In interpretation one should recognize the distinction between the Old Testament and the New Testament. Each represents a different "dispensation." Basically the New Testament is a fulfillment of the Old. We give our primary loyalty to the teachings of the New Testament. It represents God's intention to establish a new economy with new characteristics. Christ is recognized as the central point of redemption. Furthermore, his work has opened the way for the unique role of the Holy Spirit in the life of the church.

The meaning of discipleship also emerges from this truth as a distinction that gives to the Christian faith a unique quality of belief and behavior. It puts the focus on the lordship of Christ and on the servanthood of believers. New Testament Scriptures are heavily weighted with this truth. Obviously, then, one should be on the alert to see how the meanings of Scripture can be applied to contemporary relationships.

Sermon 8
The Church: A Redeemed Community
Ephesians 2:4-10

Introduction
Paul now looks at the whole Christian community. Here we see the results of life-giving experiences of God's grace: It is provided for all that accept Jesus Christ. He is the Redeemer of lost humanity. Faith in him yields a blessedness known only to true believers. The utter helplessness of the natural person calls for a divine initiative. God offers deliverance from that sinful state described in the previous verses.

Theme: The church is redeemed by **divine grace.**
  A. **Divine grace** reflects the **nature** of God. (vv. 4-5)
    1. God's **love** motivates redemption.
      a. **Love** gave the life of his Son.
      b. **Love** gives life and peace to his own.
    2. God's **mercy** extends opportunity for salvation.
      a. **Mercy** extends opportunity for repentance.
      b. **Mercy** extends opportunity for forgiveness.
    3. God's **grace** provides eternal life.
      a. **Grace** offers life to transgressors.
      b. **Grace** offers strength to the helpless.
  B. **Divine grace** reflects the **purpose** of God. (vv. 5-6)
    1. God **purposed** to make the church *alive* with Christ.
      a. *Living* with Christ engages saving grace.
      b. *Living* with Christ engages righteousness.
    2. God **purposed** to have the church *resurrected* with Christ.
      a. *Resurrection* power is extended to penitent sinners.
      b. *Resurrection* power is extended to faithful saints.
    3. God **purposed** to have the church *seated* with Christ.
      a. This *position* with Christ establishes heavenly citizenship.
      b. This *position* with Christ assures heavenly privileges.

C. **Divine grace** reflects the **intention** of God. (vv. 7-10)
  1. God **intends** to put his grace on *display*.
    a. The *display* shows incomparable riches.
    b. The *display* shows divine kindnesses.
  2. God **intends** to put his gifts on *display*.
    a. It will *display* the results of faith.
    b. It will *display* the results of obedience.
  3. God **intends** to put his *workmanship* on display.
    a. God's *workmanship* is a creation in Christ.
    b. God's *workmanship* is designed for good works.

Conclusion
  Let us worship God for what he is.
  Let us thank God for what he has purposed.
  Let us serve God for what he intends us to do.

Word Meanings Essential to Interpretation

4   *God.* In this context the emphasis on God's action in redemption shows his desire to satisfy his great love. It emphasizes the motivation back of God's redeeming act.
  Mercy. The motivation of love is further supported by the element of mercy.
5-6 The communal effect of redemption is explained in verses 5-6.
  The community of faith is characterized by:
    1. Being *quickened* together with Christ.
    2. Being *raised up* together with Christ.
    3. Being *seated* together with Christ.
  In Christ. Resurrection, enthronement, and heaven are all made available in Christ.
7   *Ages to come* refers to those periods of time now coming.
  The purpose of God is kept in focus.
  The demonstration (showing) is for his glory.
  It is a display of grace.
  Grace is the unmerited favor of God, the key to our salvation.
  This grace is offered in kindness.
  This makes the church a glorious witness to the amazing wealth of God's grace.
  It is intended to attract others to faith and hope.
8   The *Gift of God* is received by grace through faith.

The actual benefits of redemption are on display.

vv. 9-10   *God's workmanship.* Our salvation cannot be of ourselves. The emphasis is on God.

"Self-assertion is fatal to spiritual life" (Westcott).

God's intentions are for the redeemed

to enter into good works,

to accomplish his purposes, and

to demonstrate the benefits of his grace.

Guidelines on Structure

Pulpit power finds major support in an adequate structure for the sermon. There are other contributing factors, such as oratorical talent, breadth of learning, experience, and the intensity of feeling and observation. But these alone do not make an expository sermon effective. Structural excellence enhances any or all of these for effective communication. Good homiletical habits in this regard are vital to pulpit success.

Generally, an exposition of a passage of Scripture follows the progression of thought inherent in the selected text. But if the goal adopted for the delivery of the message can be achieved more effectively with a rearrangement of the order of points, there is no law against it. This is particularly true when the point of persuasion can be sharpened thereby.

The basic pattern consists of topic (subject, title), theme (proposition), introduction, body (discussion), climax, and conclusion. Within this skeleton arrangement, bringing together these units must achieve unity, progression, coherence, and impact.

Other factors that influence the arrangement during the process of construction are the purpose of preaching from this passage, the intended focus on its influence, and the composition of the anticipated audience. Some secondary effects to be kept in mind are elements of information it can convey, experience of commitment it can produce, forms of action it may induce, and expressions of devotion it may stimulate.

Structure involves the arrangement of ideas drawn from the text so as to express the relation of the parts to the whole in keeping with the theme.

The theme (or proposition) forms the basis of the selection of material. It states the concept around which ideas are organized. That will become evident in the phrasing of the main divisions. It serves as a guide to help one speak to the point. The preacher must never lose sight of the central idea. It is a safeguard against wandering out into irrelevant thoughts.

Structural Components

Title. The title is a label on the sermon. It does not control the shape of the structure nor does it specify the content of the message. Its main purpose is for public advertisement. It should be brief, attractive, suitable, and suggestive. It should be protected from abuse such as promising too much, misrepresenting the content of the message, or overplaying the dramatic.

Theme (proposition). The formulation of a sentence that expresses the central idea of the message requires a thorough knowledge of the content of the text. It must have strength of imaginative force to influence the statements of the main divisions.

This is probably the most delicate sentence of the entire structure. It carries the weight of control over the entire outline. It determines the direction of thought movement through the progressive stages of development. It must express a major idea contained in the text. Time spent on this component is worth it. Developing a cohesive structure can save a person a lot of mental energy.

Main Divisions. The sentences that are formulated must speak to the main thrust of the message. They are comprised of sentiments that relate material in the text to the adopted theme. Usually they contain generalizations which are open for further elucidation. They need specific ideas that support the main thought.

These main divisions are mutually exclusive as to thought and mutually adaptive as to proportion in comparison with each other. As much as possible they should have equal force in terms of importance to the thought development. A concerted effort is required to achieve uniformity in patterns of expression.

Main divisions are coextensive in thought with the theme. Moving from point to point, they represent a progression of thought to a strong finish, preferably to a climax that reinforces the importance of the central idea of the message.

Subpoints. The subheads are the modifiers of the main divisions.

Usually they are the particular elements that describe further the meanings expressed above them. Again, these are complete statements that are obviously related to the main points.

These sentences are best understood in their relation to the main thrust of the sermon when they pick up a main thought in the sentence it modifies. These, too, are mutually exlusive to avoid duplication of thought. They are mutually adapted to similar forms of expression. That means they are parallel in thought patterns.

An outline so constructed stands out clear and sharp for the memory to retain its progression. If I have a preaching engagement I like to reflect on the outline the evening before. Just before turning over to sleep, I like to review my outline—particularly the main divisions—as a final refresher for the upcoming occasion.

Only such ideas may be used as subpoints as can be supportive to the main sentence. This may mean discarding some of the ideas accumulated in the study because they do not contribute to this purpose.

Introduction to an Alternate Outline

This outline is submitted as an example of several deviations from the regular pattern represented in the main stream of sermon construction.

Observe that the title and theme both indicate a different approach. Whereas the former outline gives more attention to elements of community, this focuses more directly on the effect of divine grace on the individual believer.

The difference in structure is most sharply observable here in the formation of the main divisions. Here we have phrases to mark the trend of thought. In the other we have complete sentences. In this alternate outline, however, the subpoints become more clear with full sentences. This combination of phrases and sentences makes the outline more useful and more acceptable, especially under point C, where the assumption of the phrase completes the sentences of the subpoints.

In this alternate outline less concentration of thought is achieved by repetition of expression. Observe the italicized words in order to follow the progression of thought. This kind of concentration enhances the effect of communication.

Sermon 8-A
The Church: Saved for a Purpose
Ephesians 2:4-10

Introduction

This resumes the former theme: the life-giving experience of God's grace is obtained through faith.

The utter hopelessness of "natural man" calls for divine initiative in grace, calls for a deliverance from sinful state.

We see God's (1) nature, (2) salvation, and (3) purpose.

Theme: God was moved to exercise his grace in the redemption of man.

A. *The divine motivation.*

1. God is rich in *mercy.*
   He delights in mercy.
   He is eternally disposed to save.
   He has a deep desire to help the miserable.
2. God is great in *love.*
   It was on account of his love that he moved.
   He was constrained to intervene.
   God so loved that he gave.
   There is power in his unlimited love.
3. God is marvelous in *grace.*
   See the gratuitous nature of salvation.
   Humanity was helpless and ill-deserving.
   No way to redeem ourselves.
   No way to induce salvation.
   By grace you are in a saved state.

B. *The divine experience.*

By virtue of our union with Christ we have been quickened, raised, and seated together.

In our experience with Christ we have been made alive, raised up, and seated in the heavenlies.

Parallel in pattern to 1:20: raised and exalted.

1. God made us *alive.*
   a. He made us to live along with Christ.
      (1) Having made him alive, thinking at the same time of giving us life.
      (2) By anticipation he extended life to us.
   b. He communicated life to counter death.
      This is the initial step in the process of restoration. It brought us into new and actual state of life.

2. God *raised* us up.

With the resurrection of Christ he intended to raise us up. He anticipated our experience.

In our union with Christ we have this experience. This is an expansion of the meaning of *quickened* and is not to be taken as a succeeding step in the experience.

Quickened: disappearance of the condition of death.

Raised: appearance of permanent participation in the heavenlies.

3. God *seated* us in the heavenlies.

a. These are heavenly realms and relations.

State into which believers are introduced by regeneration.

State of purity, exaltation, and favor with God.

b. We are citizens of heaven.

We belong to heaven.

We are under laws of heaven.

We have the privileges of heaven.

c. In our union with Christ we are exalted in position and power.

C. A *divine purpose*.

1. To put his grace on display.

a. In the ages to come (periods of time)

Spaces of time in which *showing* takes place (''rolling cycles of eternity'').

b. Exceeding riches of his grace.

Display of his omnipotent power.

c. Kindness toward us through Christ.

2. To bring glory to God.

a. Grace through faith and not merit through effort.

Not the outcome of moral fitness.

Not the result of moral effort.

Not human strength or insight.

b. Gift, not reward.

c. Divine workmanship, not human works.

The fact accomplished.

3. To produce good works in saints.

a. Creation in Christ.

b. Planned to be so.

Conclusion

Let us worship him for what he is.

Let us praise him for what he provided.

Let us serve him for what he did in us.

Inspiration

"All Scripture is God-breathed and is useful for teaching, rebuking, correcting and training in righteousness, so that the man of God may be thoroughly equipped for every good work. . . . Preach the Word; be prepared in season and out of season; correct, rebuke and encourage—with great patience and careful instruction" (2 Timothy 3:16-17; 4:2).

This is a major claim of the Scriptures. The Bible claims to be the product of God's action in human writers. This claim rests primarily on the fact that God has spoken. Revelation gives substance to the Bible. What is contained in the Bible indicates that God did not leave the world without an adequate self-disclosure of his nature and an accurate record of his purpose and will.

This latter point especially applies to our use of the book of Ephesians as the basis of a series of sermon messages. The process of interpretation engages the principle of divine inspiration which establishes authority for the proclamation of any message drawn from a Scripture passage.

The following outline supports the assumption expressed in above section on theological interpretation.

Introduction: Our starting point is divine inspiration.
Inspiration makes the Bible a unique book.
    Preaching is the proclamation of a unique message.
The New Testament is an infallible record of the redemptive purpose.
    Portions from the Ephesian letter may be used with divine authority.
        It bears the marks of authentic truth.
        It can be used with full confidence.
1. The basis of inspiration is revelation.
    God has acted.
    God has spoken.
2. The meaning of inspiration is "God-breathed."
    Divine in-breathing infused human gifts with truth.
    Divine control insured accuracy in recordings.
    Divine supervision assured conveyance of divine purpose.
3. The nature of inspiration is dualistic.
    It produced a blending of human and divine elements.
    It combined a fusion of human and divine functions.
    It engaged a combination of human and divine insights.

4. The method of inspiration engaged the Holy Spirit.
   The Spirit worked in a supervisory capacity.
   The Spirit illuminated spiritual insights.
   The Spirit gave substance to redemptive purpose.
   The Spirit chose qualified writers.
   The Spirit assured infallibility.
5. The extent of inspiration followed lines of veracity.
   It safeguarded words to convey divine meanings.
   It supervised the recording of facts (inerrancy).
   It validated every part (plenary).
6. The purpose of inspiration achieved validity of purpose.
   It preserved the integrity of the message.
   It retained the authority of the message.
   It guaranteed the power of the message.
7. The evidences of inspiration go beyond human reason.
   The Scriptures have internal claims.
   The Scriptures have sanctifying power.
   The Scriptures have a unique unity.

CHAPTER 13

Biblical Interpretation

Guidelines
Outline: The Church: A Ransomed People
Ephesians 2:11-13 (Sermon 9)
Word Meanings Essential to Interpretation
Introduction to Alternate Outline
Alternate Outline 9-A: The Church Brought Near to God
The Context

Biblical Guidelines for Interpretation

A major issue arises in the difference between the Old Testament and the New. It is our task to resolve whatever problems emerge from this distinction. That is done by observing the context of a passage and examining the overall unity of the Bible. It is also helpful here to recognize the principle of progress in revelation.

One begins by affirming that the plan of redemption was in effect in Old Testament times. However, it is also quite evident that the new covenant bears the marks of a long-expected fulfillment: the Redeemer has come! The church operates under the full redemptive privileges and final standards of behavior identified in the New Testament.

Our studies in Ephesians are based on the principle of apostolic authority expressing the will of God. These sermons concentrate on what the inspired Scriptures have to say to the church. This is a conscious attempt to highlight meanings in the texts that relate to the position and nature of the church. Having accepted the teachings of the New Testament, we have a pattern for the practice of Christian faith. We look for that again in this sermon outline (sermon 9).

The New Testament view of the Old recognizes God as the same person as that of the New Testament references (notwithstanding the different Hebrew words for his name). It simply recognizes God's acts in redemptive purposes as he deals with the universal problem of sin. It sees the person of Christ in occasional appearances on earth (theophanies). He is represented in types and figures and in specific prophetic announcements.

There is much emphasis in the Old Testament upon God's choice of Israel to represent the divine mission. The New clearly includes Gentiles and Jews alike to be the church. (See sermon 9 below). Note the tearing down of the wall of partition between them.

We could also make a point of God's dealing with individual believers. While that holds an interesting challenge for study and pulpit exercises, I have chosen to follow God's dealing with the church as a corporate body of believers. That is clearly identifiable in the passage we have under consideration as well as in sermon 10, and more or less prominently throughout the book.

A careful comparison of the two dispensations paves the way to understand the distinctions for purposes of interpretation. Norton Sterritt presents a helpful list of contrasts:[1]

1. The Old was a preparation for the final revelation in Christ.

2. The Old contains predictions of Christ's incarnation whereas the New records the fulfillment of the plan of redemption.

3. In the Old, God was primarily concerned with developing one nation (Israel) while the New incorporates people of all nations.

4. In the Old we see that which is partial; it finds its perfection in the New arrangement.

5. Therefore the new covenant becomes the standard for the church and its mission.

Jesus' Sermon on the Mount repeatedly asserts the priority of his teachings over the Old Testament practices. Among these upgraded standards is the Christian's relation to war. "Thou shalt not kill" has broad implications that call for the practice of peace and goodwill. When Jesus said, "Do not resist evil," he established the base for the practice of nonresistance. These point directly toward the new covenant. What we have in Ephesians is a detailed expression of New Testament standards of behavior, especially in the second half of the book.

Sermon 9
The Church: A Ransomed People
Ephesians 2:11-13

Introduction

In light of the miracle of mercy (vv. 4-10) we come now to view the status of a ransomed people. The church is made up of people who having been dead in trespasses and sins are now raised to life. It is a people who were dominated by evil but now are the workmanship of God. This passage speaks particularly to the point of Gentiles who were far off from God but now are brought near to him by the blood of Christ. This was the ransom price for God's saving purpose to be achieved in Christ.

Theme: Union with Christ *overcomes* human **barriers.**
  A. Union with Christ *overcomes* natural **barriers.**
    1. The blood of Christ overcomes the **barrier** of *exclusion.*
      a. Those *excluded* because of human descent are now included.
      b. Those *excluded* because of being outsiders are now brought in.
    2. The blood of Christ overcomes the **barrier** of *alienation.*
      a. *Aliens* from the people of God can now be accepted.
      b. *Aliens* from Christ can now be brought into divine favor.
  B. Union with Christ *overcomes* religious **barriers.**
    1. The blood of Christ overcomes the **barrier** of *estrangement.*
      a. *Estrangement* is healed by promise of forgiveness.
      b. *Estrangement* is healed by promise of grace.
    2. The blood of Christ overcomes the **barrier** of *hopelessness.*
      a. *Hope* is established by the reality of atonement.
      b. *Hope* is established by the reality of resurrection.
  C. Union with Christ *overcomes* spiritual **barriers.**
    1. The blood of Christ overcomes the **barrier** of *separation.*
      a. *Separation* from God is closed by the atonement.
      b. *Separation* from God is closed by mediation.

   2. The blood of Christ overcomes the **barrier** of *rejection.*
      a. Those *far away* are brought near to God.
      b. Those *far away* are brought into the fold of God.
   D. Union with Christ *overcomes* emotional **barriers.**
      1. The blood of Christ overcomes spiritual *doubts.*
         a. Being in Christ *assures* favorable relation to God.
         b. Being in Christ *assures* membership in family of God.
      2. The blood of Christ overcomes fear of *future.*
         a. Being in Christ supports hope for *future* blessings.
         b. Being in Christ supports hope for *life after death.*

Conclusion
   In Christ we have access to the kingdom of God.
   In Christ we are brought near to God.
   In Christ we are accorded fellowship with God.
   In Christ we have hope for a glorious future.

Word Meanings Essential to Interpretation

v. 11   *Therefore.* Wherever this word appears, it serves as a signal to the importance of the immediately preceding thoughts, relating what follows to the previous paragraph.

Gentiles in the flesh refers to people in their outward, natural, ethnic designation. We refer to them in terms of human descent. This passage deals with the racial hostility toward them as "outsiders."

Circumcision is a ceremonial practice among the Jews. They ascribed to external rites objective powers conveying grace and securing divine favor. Their reference to the Gentiles as the uncircumcized was a degrading remark.

Done on the body by hands of men refers to the external rites.

v. 12   *Separate from Christ* means they were living without the effects of the atonement, without the power of the resurrection, without the influence of his mediation, and without the hope of his second coming.

Citizenship in Israel is belonging to God's chosen people and enjoying the privileges of divine administration.

Aliens represent being opposed to God's society. They were not only "outsiders" but antagonists.

Foreigners to covenants of promise. The Greek text sharpens the word promise to "the promise," pointing to the Messiah. To be a foreigner meant they did not qualify for commonwealth privileges.

Without hope. They had nothing to hope for. Their hopelessness left them in darkness about their future.

Without God. The objects Gentiles worshiped were not real gods. They were living in sickness without healing, in hunger without bread.

. 13   *In Christ.* This phrase is the key to the administration of God's saving grace. The answer to human need is found "in Christ."

Blood of Christ refers to the atoning effect of Christ's death on the cross. It symbolizes the saving act in redemption. It is the ransom price God paid to redeem lost humanity to himself.

Brought near is to have access to God in personal fellowship, to be conscious of sonship with the Father, and to be in a position of constant communion with him. It also refers to the reconciliation of whole peoples—foreigners and citizens.

Introduction to Alternate Outline

The alternate outline submitted here clarifies the difference between an outline that has unity throughout its structure and one that is only partially unified. Several observations for your consideration:

1. This outline uses phrases as subpoints which are merely suggestive for use in the pulpit. The preacher will have to formulate appropriate expressions while speaking.

2. This outline vacillates between historical elements (Jew-Gentile relationship) and contemporary application of principles. Consult the section on application for further study. This point is illustrated in the contrast between the main divisions A and B. Division A is basically historical, whereas Division B relates to contemporary Christian experience.

3. This outline allows the speaker leeway to follow unrelated thoughts in the sermon. This is illustrated in the main division C, especially subpoints 2 and 3. These digressions are not necessarily inappropriate, but such excursions would not advance the theme very well.

There are some advantages in this less restrictive structure, especially for speakers who feel at home with extemporaneous delivery. However, such sermons tend to leave the impression that the preacher was not ready. While the audience may have been exposed to a wide variety of ideas, they may lack the focus of a prevailing thought.

This outline carries some commendable features:

1. This outline uses the material in the text to shape one's overall treatment of the Scripture. Observe the quotes from the text in divisions A, B, and C. Division D has a byline that is more of a summary expression of the last sentence in the text.

2. Various explanatory points clarify background assumptions. An illustration of this is in main division A. (See the subpoints under point 2.)

Sermon 9-A
The Church Brought Near to God
Ephesians 2:11-13

Introduction
   Wherefore refers to a previous condition:
   —Buried in sins but are now raised in life.
   —Restless in guilt but are now restored to freedom.
   —Dominated by evil but are now workmanship to God.
Remember. It is good to recall the former condition.
   Think of what you were "then."
   Think of what you are "now."
   How we were brought to conversion—not so much "how" as the fact.

Theme: Union with Christ overcomes barriers to God.
   A. Union with Christ overcomes exclusion. Gentiles in the flesh are far away from God.
      1. The uncircumcised were indifferent and sensual, symbols of corruption, debasement, and ignorance.
      2. The circumcised were critical and censorious. Theirs was a superficial faith—flesh only. Theirs was an artificial means—by hands only.
   B. Union with Christ overcomes alienation.
      Aliens from the commonwealth of Israel are estranged from God.
      1. Being without Christ.
      Living apart from saving blessings.
      Living without privileges of divine grace.

2. Being alienated from divine favor.
   Alienated from divine society.
   Having no personal fellowship with God.

C. Union with Christ overcomes estrangement. Strangers from the covenants of promise.

   1. The covenants were the only light of hope.
      The promise of redemption connected with them.
      Only guarantee of messianic blessings.

   2. An estrangement that leaves no hope.
      The state of those rejecting Christ.
      Those refusing him will perish.

   3. An estrangement that leaves no God.
      They will not hear him.
      They blot out thoughts of him.
      They defy his advances.

D. Union with Christ overcomes rejection: The answer to human need is found in Christ.

   1. Made right by blood. The blood:
      Makes atonement for sin.
      Forms the basis for forgiveness.
      Becomes the ground for reconciliation.

   2. Brought near to God:
      In conscious sonship.
      In personal fellowship.
      In constant communion.

Conclusion
   We are brought near to God.
   We are restored to fellowship with God.
   We are given hope in God.

The Context

To be able to understand fully the meaning of a passage of Scripture, one must see a passage in its proper relation to the whole. This may involve only what precedes and/or what follows immediately. Or it may pertain to the chapter from which it is taken.

"Anyone, no matter how soundly his views of biblical inspiration and authority may be, is in danger of ignoring the context, particularly if he unwittingly labors to sustain some biblically unsound system of interpretation, some mere sectarian dogma, or some

ecclesiastical heresy over which time and tradition have cast a halo."[2]
This quotation applies also to the practice of proof-texting to support
a preconceived doctrine. In expository sermons this is less likely to
happen, but even so, the principle obtains that we must consider
what goes before and after. When we are under pressure for time it is
too easy to concentrate on the passage itself without considering the
full implications of the context.

Norton Sterrett lists six guidelines in determining the significance of the context of any given passage (with a few exceptions, like
Proverbs).

> 1. Think of all the possible meanings you can from the verse
> (passage) in light of the context.
> 2. Read the verse (passage) in the context. Read enough to get the
> progress of thoughts or events. Note connections between words and
> thoughts.
> 3. Study the verse more closely. Note the connecting words again,
> especially those found at the beginning of sentences.
> 4. Note any main words that are repeated both in the passage and
> the context. It may indicate a major theme.
> 5. Write the section (passage and its context) in your own words.
> 6. Ascertain what the text means in the given context.[3]

"The superficial purpose of interpretation is that the hearers
may enter into the thought of the text fully and grasp its entire
contents mentally. But the deeper purpose is that the truth with all
its saving power may be brought to the apprehension of the hearer so
that it may reach his heart."[4] This is the paramount purpose in
preaching.

There is another aspect of contextual influence which is often
overlooked. It is sometimes referred to as prepositional guidelines.
The New Testament is full of significant prepositions. If one refers to
the text above (Ephesians 2:11-13) and to the other passages that
engage the influence of a preposition, one can find the following
uses: "Like the rest" (2:3, the fallen nature), "in order that" (2:6-7,
referring to God's resurrection power), "for" (2:10, indicates basis of
appeal), "therefore" (2:11, indicates a reminder), "for" (2:14), "but
now" (2:13, reflects a contrast), "for" (2:18), and "consequently"
(2:19, in applying previous thought). There are numerous others in

this epistle that accent various shades of meaning, either from the previous statement or from what is to follow, usually in sequence of action.

It should be clear at this point that by *context* we mean the passage itself along with those surrounding sections which bear on the interpretation of that passage. It is the interpretive frame of reference.

A word has its context in the sentence of which it is a part. Or it may be found more remotely in the paragraph. Meanings are understood in the light of what else is expressed in the paragraph. An illustration of this is the outline of sermon 9. The meanings of this passage are clarified by careful study of the preceding paragraph.

Each statement of Scripture is in agreement with the plain sense and tenor of the passage of which it forms a part. By divorcing a verse or paragraph from its setting, one may "prove" by the very words of Scripture not only absurdities, but completely false meanings.

CHAPTER 14

Literary Style

Guidelines
Outline: The Church: A Reconciled Brotherhood
Ephesians 2:14-18 (Sermon 10)
Word Meanings Essential to Interpretation
The Analogy of Faith

Guidelines for Literary Style

The emphasis on unity in the sermon calls for careful literary disciplines. The outline should convey clearly what the preacher plans to communicate. For that reason it is an advantage to state the theme (proposition), main divisions, and subpoints in complete sentences. This is an advance over the usual form of identifying divisions of thought by phrases.

Stating ideas in the form of sentences forces the speaker to think through (not just think about) the expression of a thought as it should be stated before an audience. When the entire outline is made up with sentences, thoughts can be communicated with greater accuracy and clarity.

Some insist that the speaker depend on the inspiration of the moment. But is it not reasonable to insist that it is better to do it in the quiet atmosphere of the study without human distraction? It is not unusual for a sermon to be interrupted by human distraction!

Some argue that a preacher should rely upon the guidance of the Holy Spirit while he is in the pulpit. But again, the divine guidance the preacher wants usually can best be received in the study environment. The Spirit who brings enlightenment to understand the Scripture can at the same time inspire the use of proper language to communicate truth. This is also most likely to happen when and where there is the least interference—in the study.

The whole process of sermon preparation is subject to divine guidance. It involves the combination of spiritual illumination and dedicated human skill. For that reason it is important to exercise care in using the Scriptures. We are called to preach the Word.

Having selected a passage of Scripture as a basis of sermon material, one should use every available means to arrive at the real meaning of the passage in its context of other truth. From the exegetical study and the process of exposition, one should be able to clarify purpose and formulate a theme to achieve that purpose. Selection of material from the notes taken during the study should be related to the theme.

It is important to eliminate elements in the notes (and even those within the text itself) that do not relate directly to the adopted purpose. This requires a clear concept of the desired focus. In the process of exegesis, one often makes interesting discoveries of truth unrelated to the theme. In the interests of making a persuasive impact, the preacher must eliminate ideas—however exciting they may be—that do not enhance the purpose of the sermon.

Sermon 10
The Church: A Reconciled Brotherhood
Ephesians 2:14-18

Introduction

Whereas this appeal is directed primarily to the prevailing tensions between Jews and Gentiles, the text has direct applications to our contemporary scene. The tension between adherence to the law and the freedom of the gospel has its contemporary religious duplication. So also does the social status of Jews as compared with that of the Gentiles. The basic principles of reconciliation among the ancient peoples have their current applications to the health of the church. The world of today is full of human barriers.

Christ is the source of Christian peace. He is the great mediator.

Theme: Reconciliation removes divisive elements from the church.
  A. **Reconciliation** resolves irritating **differences.**
     Walls of separation are removed in Christ.
    1. Christ removes the **dividing wall** of *race.*
      a. *Racial* barriers are removed by experience in Christ.
      b. *Cultural* barriers are removed by experience in Christ.
    2. Christ removes the **dividing wall** of *class.*
      a. *Psychological* barriers are removed in Christian fellowship.
      b. *Emotional* barriers are removed in Christian fellowship.
    3. Christ removes the **dividing wall** of *creed.*
      a. Barriers of *traditional interpretation* are resolved in him.
      b. Barriers of *ethnic priorities* are resolved in him.
  B. **Reconciliation** resolves **antagonistic** feelings.
    1. Feelings of **superiority** are overcome by common *need.*
      a. All persons *need* the Savior.
      b. All persons *need* the church.
    2. Feelings of **superiority** are overcome by common *love.*
      a. Love for Christ issues in *love* for others.
      b. Love for Christ issues in *caring* for others.
  C. *Reconciliation* relaxes prevailing **hostilities.**
     Enmity is slain to make one body.
    1. **Conflicting** opinions are *relaxed* by negotiation.
      a. Petty differences are *forgotten* in Christ.
      b. The spirit of independence is *merged* in Christ.
    2. **Conflicting** interests are relaxed in *commitment* to Christ.
      a. Self-interests give way to *kingdom interests.*
      b. Self-promotions give way to *the glory of God.*
  D. *Reconciliation* removes spiritual **competition.**
     Both those far away and those near have access to God.
    1. **Peace** is announced for *all.*
      a. Peace with God has been effected for *all.*
      b. Peace with others is achievable by *all*
      "All persons were made capable of a living unity" (Wescott).
    2. **Access to God** is open to all by one *Spirit.*
      a. The *Spirit* opens the way to God for salvation.
      b. The *Spirit* intercedes with God for victorious living.

Conclusion
    The removal of divisive elements in the church sustains brotherhood rela-

tionships. The reconciliation of prevailing hostilities enhances peace with God and with others.

Word Meanings Essential to Interpretation

v. 14   *Christ is our peace.* He is not merely a peacemaker; he is the essence of peace.

Jew and Gentile. Both are mentioned to emphasize reconciliation. The passage shows how hatred is resolved and unity is achieved. Christ operated in the arena of strife and discord—elements the church must handle.

Destroyed the barrier, the middle wall of partition. The separation was a strong tradition. The barrier represented a misguided position. The dividing wall of hostility in this case involved the whole Mosaic economy and the hundreds of legalistic accessions.

v. 15   *Abolished enmity* means "made to be without effect."

The law of commandments contained in the many ordinances became burdensome and divisive. The wall of partition and the enmity were dissolved. It was accomplished in his flesh.

Created one new man, making peace out of two hostile elements.

v. 16   *Reconciled both to God.* That is, the Jews and Gentiles became one people in Christ.

It was a restoration to original intention.

"Thereby," through the death on the cross, hostility was put to death, resolved.

v. 17   *The far off* refers to Gentiles, so designated because they were outside of Israel. The near (Jews) were also brought into peace. This removed the irritations of ritual pollutions, civil ordinances, and confinements of temple worship.

v. 18   *Access to God.* Note indirect reference to the Trinity here: Christ on the cross, God on the throne, and the Holy Spirit, the Agent. Human nature may yet reach the goal of its creation. Christ preached peace and brought in a new type of personhood.

The Analogy of Faith

This term refers to comparing Scripture with Scripture. Each passage is to be interpreted in the light of biblical teachings as a whole. A conclusion resulting from the biblical study of a passage may not contradict explicit teachings in other parts of the New

Testament. If it does, the findings need to be reassessed. They should be revised to fit into the pattern of truth established elsewhere. The Bible does not contradict itself if rightly understood.

In one sense the whole Bible is the context of any single passage. Biblical doctrines are formulated out of all passages relating to the particular subject under review. It is always good to compare an interpretation with some other passages as a check on one's conclusion.

The heresies and false doctrines promoted by cults and left-wing teachers are an example of the failure to use the analogy of faith to test interpretations. They claim to base their beliefs on the Bible but they use only certain passages (often out of context) to support their views.

Some people misuse the words of Jesus who said, "Inasmuch as ye have done it unto one of the least of these my brethren, ye have done it unto me" (KJV). This has been used to support the "social gospel," as though all one needs to do to obtain eternal life is to be generous to others. To rest a practice on this one verse without recognizing other teachings of Jesus which stress repentance and the new birth is to arrive at an unbalanced view.

This same principle is important also in establishing the practices of the church. Those who build their doctrine of the Holy Spirit on the book of Acts alone are left with a partial view of the Spirit's role in the church. Extreme positions can arise regarding the baptism of the Holy Spirit. One can understand this kind of experience only by taking into consideration the teachings of the whole New Testament.

While consulting parallel passages of Scripture is important, there is also a subtle danger of ignoring a scriptural truth because it appears only once. All Scripture is inspired. Each passage deserves recognition in the total body of truth, even if it occurs infrequently.

CHAPTER 15

Grammatical Interpretation

Guidelines
Outline: The Church: A Restored Habitation
Ephesians 2:19-22 (Sermon 11)
Word Meanings Essential to Interpretation
Principles of Exposition

Grammatical Guidelines to Interpretation

Grammar consists of not only the meaning of words but also the form in which they are used. Of particular significance is the tense of the verbs. Past tense is used of something that has already happened. Present tense indicates what is happening now. In the Greek language the present tense can refer to something that continues to happen. The imperfect tense refers to a past action that continued over a period of time. Of course, the future tense normally tells what is expected to happen. There is yet another major form of past tense called the aorist. When that is used it means the happening has occurred with finality. There is nothing more to be expected from it.

The text for sermon 11 has in it a good illustration of the simple present tense in relation to the word *all* (verse 21). It also illustrates present action with an indication that the process continues (verse 22). The words *built together* are one word in the Greek text. A loose translation could read "built together with harmonious fitting together of the parts now and in time to come."

In 3:17 the prayer for Christ's indwelling is that it may be a decisive action (aorist) in the present and a permanent ongoing experience.

The application of grammatical structures is seen in the relationship of words used together. Words used in combination convey thoughts more explicitly than one word can express. Therefore, a knowledge of grammatical principles can aid interpretation, making a specific point clear. "Grammar may not always show us the actual meaning, but it will show us possible meanings. We cannot accept any meaning that does violence to [the total statement and context]. Thus grammar is important in understanding the Bible. This is not strange. Essentially it means that we understand the Bible according to the laws of human language."[1]

Figures of speech make reading more delightful and suggestive. In the case of our common speech we say, "That argument doesn't hold water." The figure is true but in a technical sense it is not "literally" true. It is a different way of saying what we mean. It makes the truth more vivid and interesting. Our minds translate it automatically. It assumes, however, that both the speaker and the listener make that translation on the basis of knowledge from previous exposure to the idea.

In our text a figure of speech is used to identify Gentiles called "uncircumcised." (See 2:11, sermon 9.) In the last four verses of Ephesians 2 one finds such words as household, foundation, cornerstone, building, and temple, each one representing a specific spiritual concept.

In a general sense figurative language is used to convey deeper meanings (or meaning on a different level). Sometimes a suggestive word is used like *light* (Eph. 5:8), or *belt* of truth (Eph. 6:14), or *shield* of faith (Eph. 6:16). Most of these uses are quite evident in meaning. Some, however, require sound literary judgment to discern their meaning. For instance, in 4:16 Paul uses the analogy of the whole body to say that we are joined and held together by every supporting *ligament*. We need some perceptive ideas of what *ligament* here represents.

Some metaphors reflect a larger reality. The expression (referring to Jew-Gentile tension) "the *dividing wall* of hostility" says a great deal about racial conflict in the secular world (Eph. 2:14).

These and other principles are taken into consideration in the sections following each primary outline called "Word Meanings." They are all intended to provide helps in interpretation.

Sermon 11
The Church: A Restored Habitation
Ephesians 2:19-22

Introduction

This passage expresses in a rather complex thought pattern the outcome of reconciliation. "Strangers" who had been excluded from the rights of the heavenly kingdom are now given citizenship. "Foreigners" who have not shared in kingdom privileges and blessings are now accorded full participation in heavenly benefits.

Theme: The church brings people together under God.
    A. People are brought *together* in a Christian **commonwealth.**
      We are "fellow citizens with the saints."
      This is an ever-expanding kingdom.
      1. This **commonwealth** of saints indicates the *status of the saved.*
      a. *Saved* people are separated from the world.
      b. *Saved* people live under the laws of heaven.
      2. This **commonwealth** is a sharing together in kingdom *privileges.*
      a. People share together in *privileges* in Christian liberty.
      b. People share together in *privileges* of divine care.
      3. This **commonwealth** is in heavenly *citizenship.*
      a. Our *citizenship* assures us of divine security.
      b. Our *citizenship* assures us of equal rights.
    B. People are born *together* in a single **household.**
      We are of "the household of God"—a growing family.
      1. The **household** is made up of God's *children.*
      a. God's *children* are born of the Spirit.
      b. God's *children* are under the Father's care.
      c. God's *children* are in the Father's will.
      2. The **household** is a family of *believers.*
      a. *Believers* become fellow members of one family.
      b. *Believers* enjoy a tender and sacred relationship.
      c. *Believers* find intimate fellowship with one another.

C. People are built *together* on the same **foundation.**
This is "foundation of apostles and prophets" and Jesus.
 1. The **basis** of union is divine *revelation.*
   a. The *apostles* were the initial agents of conveyance.
   b. The *prophets* proclaimed the providence of God.
 2. The **point** of *union* is Jesus Christ, the cornerstone.
   a. People are built together in *union* with him.
   b. People are joined together in *common faith* in him.
D. People are fit *together* in a growing **temple.**
The church is a "building fitly framed together."
 1. The **structure** of the **temple** has *many parts.*
   a. It is composed of *many holy people.*
   b. It is bonded together by *faith in Christ.*
 2. The parts of the **structure** must *fit together.*
   a. It depends on *harmonious relationships.*
   b. It relies on *function of each part.*
 3. The **structure** grows as a *sanctuary.*
   a. Being *holy*, it is set apart for worship.
   b. Being *holy*, it is consecrated for service.
E. People are put *together* for a divine **habitation.**
The church is "builded together for an habitation of God" (KJV).
The church is the one dwelling place for a fixed abode or residence.
 1. The church is **built** for *occupancy.*
   a. It is built to *suit the owner.*
   b. It is a *residence* in the collective life of redeemed.
 2. The church is **built** for the *Holy Spirit.*
   a. He regards the collective body *his headquarters.*
   b. He makes the *presence of God* real.

Conclusion
In union with Christ and in fellowship with the saints, the church is constructed of spiritual material for a temporary but continuing residence of God.

Word Meanings Essential to Interpretation

v. 19   *Foreigners* are sojourners without rights of citizenship.
Fellow citizens refers to the fellowship of all believers in which we have equal privileges in the commonwealth of God's kingdom.
Members of God's household indicates that Christians can enjoy the intimacy of family relationships.

20   *Foundation.* This was laid by the apostles and prophets of the New Testament age.

    Cornerstone. Christ is the point of unity where the "stones" are put together.

21   A *building* has all its parts put together in a special way. *This* building becomes a holy temple in the Lord in a continuous growing process.

22   *Builded together.* We are constantly being built together to make a permanent dwelling for the Lord. This dynamic constant reflected in the present tense and the static image of a stone structure is an interesting contrast of metaphors.

    Through the Spirit. The "habitation" is indwelt by the Holy Spirit.

Principles of Exposition

Exposition is an exercise that follows closely that of exegesis. In fact, exegetical results are essential factors in arriving at valid statements of biblical meanings. In this process the interpreter formulates an understanding of the meaning of the text.

Another distinction emerges in comparing exposition with application. Exposition is concerned with the meaning of Scripture at the time it was written and with the relevance of that meaning in today's culture. The application takes those meanings into consideration and makes that relevance more explicit in contemporary life.

"To expound Scripture is to bring out of the text what is there and expose it to view. The expositor pries open what appears to be closed, makes plain what is obscure, unravels what is knotted, and unfolds what is tightly packed."[2] The task of the preacher is to use the findings of exegesis in such a way as to make the message plain for the average person in the pew.

Two major areas of exegesis include the historical origin of the Scripture and its grammatical structure. These same principles apply to the process of exposition. Exposition demands the exercise of a rigorous discipline. It aims to determine what the original author meant and what meaning that holds for today. It is concerned with using the results of such preliminary studies to determine the content of the sermon. Exposition acts as a controller of what may be said. It prescribes what is pertinent to the purpose of the message.

The testimony of Paul in his letter to Timothy speaks to the point of faithfulness to the Scriptures. "What you heard from me, keep as the pattern of sound teaching, with faith and love in Christ Jesus. Guard the good deposit that was entrusted to you—guard it with the help of the Holy Spirit who lives in us."[3] When he wrote to the Corinthians he said, "Men ought to regard us as servants of Christ and as those entrusted with the secret things [mysteries] of God. Now it is required that those who have been given a trust must prove faithful."[4] Thus preachers must take great care in making sure they represent the mind and will of God. The exposition is the key to faithfulness in acknowledgment of that trust. It serves in the context within which the "reflective function of preaching" takes place.

There have been various attempts at defining the act of preaching. One succinct and comprehensive definition calls true preaching "the story of God's redemptive activity in Jesus Christ, of God's personal approach and holy action regarding salvation, demanding surrender and faith."[5] A sermon that is based on careful exposition can be delivered with full confidence that it has divine authority.

> The church needs to listen attentively to his Word, since its health and maturity depend on it. So pastors must expound it; it is to this they have been called. Whenever they do so with integrity, the voice of God is heard, and the church is convicted and humbled, restored and invigorated, and transformed into an instrument for his use and glory.[6]

PART IV

Ephesians 3

CHAPTER 16

Historical Interpretation

Guidelines
Introduction to the Outline
Outline: The Church: The Mystery of God
    Ephesians 3:1-6 (Sermon 12)
Word Meanings Essential to Interpretation
Introduction to Alternate Outline
Alternate Outline 12-A: The Secret of the Ages
One Other Approach
Alternate Outline 12-B: The Dispensation of Grace

Historical Guidelines for Interpretation

Events in the Bible took place at certain times and places in history. They occurred within the culture of a people in ancient times. The New Testament relates specifically to the culture of Palestine of the first century. This poses a challenge to students of the Bible to acquaint themselves with the cultural patterns of that time.

Jesus' use of commonly understood expressions is a part of the biblical account. These do not always convey the same meaning in our current language. When he invited a person to "take up his cross daily," he clearly meant it to symbolize the experience of spiritual death. Instead of referring to possible human difficulties that might

149

stand in the way of progress, it actually calls for a dying to self. We have our modern way of expressing the same idea in terms of spiritual conversion and moral renewal.

There is a prominent element of historical truth present in the book of Ephesians. It has a singular influence upon the interpretation of the book's message. The fact that Ephesians refers to feelings of hostility between Jews and Gentiles indicates a special concern about their being united "in Christ." This epistle was written to the Gentile "section" of the church in order to build a bridge of understanding. Knowing this helps us to understand the implications of the universality of the gospel. (See 2:11-22). The first 13 verses of the third chapter speak clearly to this issue.

The term *mystery* was well understood by the Gentile readers as it is used (and explained) in sermon 12. For us in our time, it needs explanation. In the New International Version the word *mystery* is used three times in this passage. But in *The Living Bible* it is omitted entirely and is replaced with expressions such as "special work of showing God's favor to you Gentiles," "the secret plan of his that Gentiles, too, are included in his kindness," and "in olden times God did not share this plan with his people."

To use this principle in determining the meaning of a Scripture passage, one must consider carefully those points in it that appear hidden and try to understand the background as a help to discover its meaning for today. A knowledge of what it meant to the first readers of the passage will help to determine its meaning for today. We have an obligation to put into modern practice the meaning it had when it was written.

This is illustrated in Jesus' institution of the ceremonial practice of footwashing. It was customary in that day for the host to wash the feet of a guest upon entrance into the house. The reason for that custom is clear from a knowledge of the climate and lifestyle of the times. But this was an occasion in the "upper room" with Jesus and his disciples in relation to mealtime. When Jesus washed the disciples' feet, it was not for the purpose of cleansing upon entrance. That, according to custom, was already done. What Jesus initiated had a deeper significance than complying with an ordinary custom. He established the practice as a symbolic reminder of the servanthood to which the followers of Jesus are called.

However, sometimes appeal is made to ancient cultural practices in order to nullify the force of religious teachings. This is a common way of dealing with portions of Scripture that interfere with self-designed freedoms. For instance, the Scriptures that condemn the wearing of jewelry are often too easily dismissed on the basis that they reflect a culture that no longer exists.

The social pressures that motivate deviations from biblical standards are upon us. They influence interpreters to engage in arguments that minimize the force of specific prohibitions for Christian behavior. Interpreters so influenced say such passages do not apply to modern culture. But it must be said that the principle does have an application.

When we accept the doctrine of the inspiration of Scripture we commit ourselves to making application of biblical principles in our time. Cultural patterns change from generation to generation. However, that does not automatically imply that any truth which was expressed in an outmoded cultural pattern does not apply in our modern culture. The revealed truth must still remain in effect in the changed culture even if that principle is expressed in a modern application. The ethical principles in the sermons that follow are taken from chapters four, five, and six.

Introduction to the Outline

Paul's reference to himself as "prisoner of Christ" indicates an actual incarceration. It represents a double life and address. His life was in Christ while being held by the Roman government under Nero's administration. He was suffering for the sake of Gentiles. In another sense he was suffering for Christ's sake. He was undergoing hardship for the sake of Christian principles. It gave him an opportunity to demonstrate his loyalty to Christ.

Paul possessed the revelation of the great secret "hidden in God." It was not that he made a discovery of divine truth but that he received a revelation about the extension of redemptive purposes. It taught him that the love, mercy, and grace of God are meant for all humanity.

In his testimony before King Agrippa Paul said he heard a voice from heaven say, "I am sending you to open their [Gentiles] eyes and turn them from darkness to light and from the power of Satan to

God, so that they may receive forgiveness of sins and a place among those who are sanctified by faith" (Acts 26:18).

In this mandate he became a transmitter of grace. His mission was to serve as a messenger of Christ and to extend the range of redemption to all people. The gospel he preached elevated Gentiles to the same height of dignity as that of the Jews. This special truth committed to Paul became a stewardship of grace. The passage under consideration is a primary step toward an affirmation of acceptance of the Gentiles.

Sermon 12
The Church: The Mystery of God
Ephesians 3:1-6

Introduction
A mystery is a truth not previously made known but now is understood. The application of this truth extended the range of divine grace to include all people. It represents God's intention to share the full benefits of redemption with Jew and Gentile alike.

Theme: The *mystery* of God is an extension of his **grace.**
   A. The revelation of the *mystery* came with the dispensation of **divine grace.** (vv. 2-4)
      1. The truth of the *mystery* is seen in the universality of God's **grace.**
         a. **Grace** is extended beyond the bounds of Israel.
         b. **Grace** is understood to be extended to all.
      2. The knowledge of the *mystery* is made known in **Christ.**
         a. The **grace of Christ** declares a ransom for all.
         b. The **grace of Christ** declares a mansion for all.
      3. The stewardship of the *mystery* is an application of **grace.**
         a. Applied **grace** assures forgiveness of sin.
         b. Applied **grace** assures the hope of glory.
   B. The meaning of the *mystery* is expressed in the **gospel of grace.** (vv. 5-6)
      1. The **gospel of grace** declares all believers *fellow heirs.*
         a. Being *fellow heirs* with Christ engages the new covenant.
         b. Being *fellow heirs* with Christ involves the new dispensation.
      2. The **gospel of grace** declares all believers are in *one body.*
         a. Being *fellow members* gives to all the same dignity.
         b. Being *fellow members* gives to all the same identity.
      3. The **gospel of grace** declares all have equal share in the *promise.*

a. The *promises* in Christ offer redemption to all.
b. The *promises* in Christ offer hope for all.

Conclusion
We rejoice in the administration of God's grace.
We worship with the gospel of God's grace.

Word Meanings Essential to Interpretation

1   *For this reason* refers to that which immediately precedes. The Gentiles to whom Paul was sent are also subjects of divine grace. A prisoner of Christ speaks. Christ's cause kept him in prison.

2   *The administration of grace* was assigned to Paul. This represents a divine arrangement. Paul was chosen for this particular enterprise. He was an accredited mouthpiece of divine grace.

3   *The mystery* refers to the central truth of the universality of the gospel. It represents truth only now made known. Previously it was a secret—"hidden in God." "Truths which are the characteristic possession of Christians are 'mysterious' " (Westcott).

4   Paul's *knowledge* of the mystery of Christ pertains to the revelation of truth in the gospel. It refers to the revelation of Christ's significance.

5   *The gospel* refers to the "good news" of saving grace. Gentiles no longer needed to become Jews to be included in redemption.

6   The mystery indicates that through the gospel believing *Gentiles* are incorporated in the body of Christ. Union with Christ constitutes union with one another.

Introduction to Alternate Outline

The alternate outline that follows looks at the same passage from a different perspective. It draws ideas from the text for immediate contemporary application. It focuses on church status and functions. Although it reflects conditions of the apostolic church, it bypasses the historical analysis involved in preparation and moves immediately to designations of current life in the church. It simply takes the principles discovered in the study of the passage and applies them in today's church activity.

Sermon 12-A
The Secret of the Ages
Ephesians 3:1-6

Introduction: The historical setting presents the apostle Paul as an interpreter of the mystery that is now revealed.

Theme: The church makes a universal appeal with the **mystery** of the gospel.
    A. The church functions in a **stewardship** of the **mystery**. (vv. 2-3)
        1. This **stewardship** is a special blessing of *divine grace*.
            a. *Divine grace* opens a universal opportunity of salvation.
            b. *Divine grace* applies the universal purpose of redemption.
        2. This **stewardship** is an application of God's *intention*.
            a. God *intends* salvation for all who believe the gospel.
            b. God *intends* kingdom membership for all believers.
            c. God *intends* all believers to have equal privileges in Christ.
    B. The church promotes an **understanding** of the **mystery**. (vv. 4-5)
        1. This **understanding** involves God's purpose in *Christ*.
            a. *Christ* announced the universality of the gospel.
            b. *Christ* provided redemption for all humanity.
        2. This **understanding** involves the illumination of the *Spirit*.
            a. The *Spirit* acts as Revealer of the truth.
            b. The *Spirit* acts as Agent of the truth.
    C. The church applies the **meaning** of the **mystery**. (v. 6)
        1. Believers **become** fellow *heirs*.
            a. The spiritual *inheritance* includes a common fellowship.
            b. The spiritual *inheritance* includes a common hope.
        2. Believers **become** fellow *members*.
            a. Believers *become members* of the same body.
            b. Believers *become members* of the same family.
        3. Believers **become** fellow *partakers* of the promise in Christ.
            a. Believers *share together* in the promises of forgiveness.
            b. Believers *share together* in the promise of victory.

Conclusion
    The Church is God's investment of grace.
    The Church is God's display of grace.
    The Church is God's instrument of grace.

One Other Approach

The following proposal relies more upon the progression of thought in the passage. It allows for greater expansion of ideas and for a more particular application of its meaning. In this case more use is made of the historical background of facts. What is needed for homiletical development is the translation of principles into current application.

To get a start in forming the structure one selects major ideas from each of the verses as they appear in the text. A greater awareness of the nature of the church can thus be achieved. The phrases used below will then be expanded into sentences and the subpoints determined by the meaning of those sentences.

Sermon 12-B
The Dispensation of Grace
Ephesians 3:2-6

Verse 2: The Administration of God's Grace
Verse 3: The Mystery Made Known by Revelation
Verse 4: Insight into the Mystery of Christ
Verse 5: What Is Now Revealed by the Spirit
Verse 6: This Mystery Is That:
   a. Gentiles are heirs together with Israel.
   b. Gentiles are members together of one body.
   c. Gentiles share together in the promise.

CHAPTER 17

Achieving Variety

Guidelines to Achieving Variety

Sermons are generally classified as topical, textual, or expository. It is not my intention to discuss each of these. Our focus is on expository preaching. However, Merrill Unger spends considerable time and space to show how both topical and textual sermons can be developed with expositions of Scripture.[1] Although this distinction has merit, it tends to be a bit confusing when referring to expository preaching.

There is a sense in which textual sermons are basically constructed over the expository pattern. One verse or even two verses can be developed in a fashion similar to that of an expository sermon. The divisions for the outline are discovered in the chosen text. The difference comes in using Scripture from other parts of the Bible for supportive elements to enlarge on the ideas identified in the text. Sermon 1 could be called "textual expository message" to use Unger's designation.

> If the speaker expounds what the text or passage actually means, he is perforce compelled not only to break it up into leading words or clauses and use these as the headings of his discourse, but he must relate the passage to its context in order to arrive at its accurate meaning. If the preacher does this, in a very definite sense he will be preaching an expository sermon, though of the textual variety.[2]

Taking a topical approach to the sermon preparation of an expository message is less obvious. Unger says, "In this type of Bible exposition the topic determines the context of the sermon and the Scriptures themselves determine the manner in which it is developed."[3] He lists such sermons as doctrinal, biographical, and ethical.

It is important in both of these forms to apply the expositional process to all the Scriptures that are employed in the development of the sermon. This exercise gives it the flavor of expository effects, but it also demands considerable time to do that. Few preachers are willing to put that much effort into the preparation of a sermon.

This leaves the matter of achieving variety in expository preaching for further explanation. It is important to avoid any monotony in the pulpit service. This can be done with different approaches influenced by content of the text. Perfecting the skill of developing an effective pattern tends to lead to some similarity of structure. But even that can be modified to accommodate differences in the design. However, certain standard practices are used to achieve unity in diversity. Having a clear notion of a familiar procedure to be followed step-by-step can give one confidence. This does not necessarily produce monotony, for there are other factors that put variety into sermon delivery.

A look at the variety of preaching functions indicates a wide range of possibilities to meet human need. The sermon can be used to heal social hurts. That calls for a specific approach and application to a particular problem. The sermon can be used also to exhort people about deviant behavior. It can edify believers in their reach for deeper devotional experience. (And there are usually some persons in the audience with guilt feelings.) These and other purposes have a strong bearing upon the selection of Scripture to be used as a text. Or, if one follows a series of passages, any particular passage may dictate a possible use or purpose that may be achieved.

This emphasizes again the preacher's purpose. The choice of purpose determines the development of the sermon material. The variations of thought in a series of passages open the way to adapt various purposes from one sermon to the next.

However, "each passage will call for a sermon structure all its own. If the preacher allows the passage to be his guide, he will soon find that his sermons have a great and colorful variety."[4]

Variety is achieved in how one treats the text in light of changing needs, community moods, and current circumstances. In addition, the constant change of materials and emphases is certain to create freshness and variety.

Charles W. Koller finds variety in the appeals from the pulpit for instructing, encouraging, approving; or correcting, warning, and rebuking.[5] He says, "The presentation of theological truth must be comprehensive enough to illuminate the mind, to stir the emotions, to move the will, and to win the whole man. To every man and to every mood there is an effective and an ineffective approach. And to every approach there are degrees of attractiveness and persuasiveness." In view of these assertions he submits seven basic appeals:

1. The appeal to altruism, a benevolent regard for the interest of others.

2. The appeal to aspiration, the universal hunger for spiritual happiness.

3. The appeal to curiosity, susceptibility to that which appears novel, unfamiliar, or mysterious.

4. The appeal to duty, the divine urge to do a thing because it is right, or refrain from a thing because it is wrong.

5. The appeal to fear, the fear of consequences. God uses this approach when lesser appeals have failed.

6. The appeal to love, love of self, love of others, or love of God.

7. The appeal to reason which is merely an appeal to intelligent self-interest.[6]

Kohler concludes his discussion of appeals in biblical preaching: "Whatever the inclinations or special aptitudes of the preacher may be, he will strengthen his ministry, enlarge his faithfulness, and advance his own mental and spiritual development by maintaining a variety of appeals with the many diversities of his people constantly in view."[7]

Introduction to the Outline

This passage continues the explanation of the mystery. It focuses more directly on grace. It expands the meaning of the mystery in terms of the unmerited favor of God in declaring the universality of the gospel. In the course of magnifying this extended privilege to the Gentiles, the nature of the gift is explained in terms of experience.

Sermon 13
The Church: A Demonstration of God's Grace
Ephesians 3:7-13

Introduction

Paul, a servant of the gospel, received from God the gift of grace to be shared with the church. He counted himself totally unworthy to be given an assignment to deliver such unsearchable spiritual riches. For him to explain now what God had in mind all through the ages was beyond human resources. He depended on the revelation of God's eternal design to open the door of salvation to the Gentiles. Through all the changes of time, the divine intention was secretly incorporated in the developing providence of his redemptive purpose.

Theme: God conveys his **mystery** through the church.
    A. The proclamation of the **mystery** promotes the gift of divine **grace.** (vv. 7-8)
        1. The gift of **grace** extends the range of *redemption.*
          a. *Redemption* is determined by the purpose of God.
          b. *Redemption* is provided by the power of God.
        2. The gift of **grace** proclaims the *riches* of Christ.
          a. The *riches* of Christ are a provision for all believers.
          b. The *riches* of Christ become the possession of all believers.
    B. The fellowship of the **mystery** engages the **grace of wisdom.** (vv. 9-11)

    1. The **grace of wisdom** is a benefit of the new *dispensation*.
       a. Divine wisdom brings to light the *purpose* of creation.
       b. Divine wisdom brings to light the *nature* of election.
    2. The **grace of wisdom** is put on display in the *church*.
       a. The *church* exhibits the goodness of divine mercy.
       b. The *church* exhibits the nature of divine judgment.
    3. The **grace of wisdom** makes the mystery known to *heavenly beings*.
       a. *Angels* desire to know the meaning of redemption.
       b. *Angels* were involved in the message of redemption.
  C. The purpose of the ***mystery*** is realized through **faith**. (vv. 12-13)
    1. All people may approach God by **faith.**
       a. *Faith* gives freedom from apprehension of rejection.
       b. *Faith* gives freedom to engage in Christian privileges.
    2. All people have **access** to God in the name of *Christ*.
       a. Being in *Christ* gives confidence in divine provision.
       b. Being in *Christ* gives confidence in divine providence.

Conclusion

We rejoice in the dispensation of grace.

We worship in the provision of grace.

We serve to enhance the display of grace (in the church).

Word Meanings Essential to Interpretation

v. 7   *The gift of God's grace* came through the working of God's power. This operation refers to moral and spiritual effects.

v. 8   *Unsearchable riches of Christ.* These were given for distribution among Gentiles. The scope of Paul's ministry was twofold:
       a. To proclaim the gospel to Gentiles.
       b. To show to all people the fullness of the gospel to solve human problems.

v. 9   *Administration* of this mystery (or dispensation of) to show the purpose of evangelizing Gentiles. Hidden in God previously, it now includes admission of Gentiles into covenant privileges.

v. 10   The *intent* of preaching Christ was to enlighten people. The church was to make known the hidden truth of admitting Gentiles to put God's wisdom on display.

    Principalities and powers in heavenly places. This refers to beings or powers beyond earthly realms. It expands our present knowledge of the immensity of the universe. These heavenly beings were told about the mystery.

v. 11 His *eternal purpose* was accomplished in Christ. It was only lately disclosed as the eternal plan.

v. 12 *Access with confidence.* Now all can approach God with freedom and confidence, with the right to address him, and with the right to access—these are all coupled together through faith.

The Biographical Use of a Passage (3:1-13)

Paul shared his personal experience as an encouragement to his Gentile audience. These elements of truth are not directly related to our focus on the church. However, they can be used to build confidence in the providence of God. They relate more particularly to individual and community experience in appropriating the grace of God. The main divisions could be formulated as follows:

Sermon 13-A
The Prisoner of Christ

A. Paul regarded his imprisonment a service to Christ.
B. Paul discovered the universal privileges in Christ.
C. Paul served as a transmitter of the grace of Christ.
D. Paul served with dignity for the riches of Christ.
E. Paul suffered hardships and persecution for the sake of Christ.

Another biographical sermon can be constructed from the direct statements of Paul as they appear in these verses (3:1-13). Contemporary applications can be drawn by "translating" them into modern personal characteristics. A nine-point discourse could be developed as follows:

Sermon 13-B
Characteristics for a Christian Leader

1. I (am) a prisoner of Christ. (v. 1)
   Translation: He is one who identifies with Christ.
2. I (received) the stewardship (administration) of God's grace. (v. 3a)
   Translation: He is one who gives priority to divine anointing.
3. I (received) the mystery by revelation. (v. 3b)
   Translation: He is one who holds divine revelation in high regard.
4. I (have) insight into the mystery of Christ. (v. 4)
   Translation: He is one who possesses spiritual insights.

5. I became a servant of this gospel. (v. 7)
   Translation: He is one who is committed to the gospel.
6. I am less than the least of all God's people. (v. 8a)
   Translation: He is one who possesses the spirit of humility.
7. I was given grace to preach the riches of Christ. (v. 8b)
   Translation: He is one who has adopted a clear purpose in serving.
8. I was given grace to enlighten others of this mystery. (v. 9)
   Translation: He is one who shares freely of universal privileges.
9. I ask you not to be discouraged because of my sufferings; they are for your glory. (v. 13)
   Translation: He is one who remains loyal to the cause.

CHAPTER 18

Making Application

Guidelines for Making Application

One of the most important elements in preaching is the use of application. The audience needs help to understand how to put the appeals of Scripture into practice.

Application means to relate, to involve, to move to action. When the preacher uses application in a sermon, he speaks to the audience in such a way that they see how the sermon is appropriate, fitting, and suitable for them. Application means to show to the audience that they can use and put to a practical personal use the truth of the message.[1]

Preaching carries the opportunity and responsibility to show the audience how to put truth to work. The preacher's role is to help people solve their spiritual problems and to provide guidelines for living and serving in the will of God. That makes applications right on target. People want to know how to respond to biblical teachings.

Having selected a purpose, a preacher must plan a strategy to reach the identified goal. That calls for a thorough study of the Scripture passage, clear thinking about its meaning, and a careful survey of its possible bearing on Christian life and duty.

> Application is the rhetorical process by which truth is brought to bear directly upon individuals in order to persuade them. . . . It helps the audience see the relevance of the truth and what the truth has to do with them. . . . It answers the question, "So what?"[2]

In that same discussion Perry points to an important sequence in sermon preparation. First, one must analyze the text. From that one produces an exposition. (See chapter 22.) This is all essential to the sermon, but it is not enough. Application is needed to complete the process. The full-blown sermon can then emerge and be delivered with confidence.

> The chief part of what we commonly call application is persuasion. It is not enough to convince people of truth; nor enough to see how it applies to themselves, and how it might be practicable for them to act out—but we must "persuade men."[3]

At this point the reader might do well to review the discussion on expository preaching and the Holy Spirit (see pages 78ff). This does not mean that we ask the Spirit to confirm our plans without having invited the Spirit's influence at each step along the way. We do not want to neglect the importance of guidance and illumination throughout the process of preparation. But this is especially true in designing the application.

In effect the application conveys the purpose of the sermon. For that reason it must be based on the content of the text, and indeed on the general direction of the sermon itself. It deserves very careful preparation in forming the statement. "The language of application should be direct but tactful, straightforward, but courteous and all inclusive, yet personal."[4]

This raises the question of different types of application. The quote above refers to direct application as distinguished from those that are merely suggestive. Some preachers prefer making no formal statement at all. They are satisfied to present an exposition and leave it to the audience to make their own applications. This may be appropriate for handling debatable ideas, but generally, the purpose of the sermon can best be achieved with some form of application.

> A sermon rises or falls in its application. In fact it is questionable whether a sermon is really a sermon unless it contains some form of application. The gospel of Jesus Christ must bring the hearer under its claims, search his heart and mediate a divine encounter.[5]

At times a "continuous application" may be appropriate in which an application follows each main division. When an application is made at the close of the message ("compact application"), it generally requires reiteration of expositions made during the course of the message. Continuous applications follow immediately the various points of discussion. With the method of "continuous application," however, it is difficult to achieve a strong focal impact on a selected theme.

Another approach, particularly useful with a text that has historical background, involves extracting the universal principles and stating them in contemporary thoughts. An illustration of this is found in the sermon outline of Ephesians 2:11-13. While the text treats relationship between Jews and Gentiles in biblical times, the sermon concentrates on elements of unity and Christian experience in our time.

Sermon 13-A includes other examples of translating biblical statements into contemporary thoughts. In sermon 13-B the bylines under each statement of biographical fact form the divisions of the message.

In these examples the process of analysis led to the adoption of biblical principles expressed by church leaders at the time of writing. They applied truth in their historic situations. The textual analysis is followed by a normal process of exposition. Then the elements of truth drawn from the exposition were translated into meanings that are essentially contemporary applications. In that sense the entire sermon is an application.

The more common practice is to reserve application for the end of the message. Often it becomes a part of the conclusion. It may be expressed as a guideline to put to practice what has been emphasized in the body of the message. This can be used effectively if the progression of thought has led naturally and logically to the point of suggesting "how to...."

A word of caution is in order here. One must avoid any chance to "tack on" a moral appeal that is not supported by the discussion that precedes it.

Introduction to the Outline

This is the last passage from the "doctrinal" part of the epistle. It is marked off from the second part by a gracious doxology.

The outline of this passage is drawn from the analysis of the text. As in other Scripture passages there are major concepts to be identified. That is reflected in the main divisions with the words *power, faith,* and *love.* These words emerge as important ideas around which supporting truths are clustered.

It is not my intention to suggest that this is the only way to treat such a text: alternate outlines are also included in this chapter. And there are yet other designs. However, in the process of developing one's own structure, one should employ the general principles of development expressed in the previous and following chapters.

Sermon 14
The Church: The Fullness of God
Ephesians 3:14-21

Introduction

Who dares to pray for the church to be endowed with the wealth of God's glory? That glory means everything that renders him worthy of human adoration. The prayer conveys an expectation of inward strength for the believer according to divine grace and power. It is directed to the Father of our Lord Jesus Christ on behalf of the entire family of believers.

Theme: The church is endowed with the *fullness* of God.
    A. The church finds *fullness* in spiritual **power.** (v. 16)
        1. Spiritual **power** develops dynamic *personalities*
          a. Such *persons* have enlightened minds.
          b. Such *persons* have refined emotions.
          c. Such *persons* have resolute wills.

    2. Spiritual **power** involves the *Holy Spirit.*
       a. The *Spirit* enlightens the believer.
       b. The *Spirit* energizes the believer.
       c. The *Spirit* operates from within the believer.
  B. The church finds *fullness* through the exercise of **faith.** (v. 17)
    1. **Faith** appropriates *Christ's presence.*
       a. *Christ* becomes the way of our behavior.
       b. *Christ* becomes the truth of our believing.
       c. *Christ* becomes the life of our being.
    2. **Faith** appropriates Christ's *provisions.*
       a. Christ's indwelling brings *light* to our understanding.
       b. Christ's indwelling establishes *mastery* of our desires.
       c. Christ's indwelling gives *hope* to our expectations.
  C. The church finds *fullness* in experience of **love.** (vv. 18-19)
    1. Being rooted in **love** motivates *service.*
       a. *Service* is prompted by the grace of God.
       b. *Service* is prompted by obedience to God.
    2. Being established in **love** gives power to *witness.*
       a. The *witness* involves fellowship with the saints.
       b. The *witness* involves fellowship with God.
    3. Being commended to the **love** of Christ sets the *standard* for Christian experience.
       a. The *standard* surpasses human knowledge.
       b. The *standard* represents knowing Christ by experience.

Conclusion: the doxology (vv. 20-21)
  Divine power exceeds our imagination.
  Divine power is at work within us.
  Divine glory is on display in the church.

Word Meanings Essential to Interpretation

v. 14 *For this reason* refers to the preceding thoughts but may also include the closing verses of chapter 2, especially "being built together to become a dwelling in which God lives by his Spirit." The posture in prayer to the Father indicates an urgent appeal.

v. 15 The Father's *whole family*—deceased saints and living believers—all bear the marks of divine characteristics.

v. 16 *His glorious riches* are the resources of divine grace, the virtues at work in believers.

        Power through his Spirit indicates the channel through which God energizes the believer's will.

Inner being carries the notion of innermost personality, "the essence of the man which is conscious of itself as a moral personality."[6]

v. 17   *Christ may dwell in you* indicates an abiding presence, "a dwelling in which God lives" (2:22). This adds an element of permanence to the strengthening mentioned in verse 16.

Faith is the medium of appropriating these divine favors. Faith opens the door to receive his grace.

v. 18   *Rooted and grounded* is a comprehensive term that indicates the foundation for the indwelling. They represent the consequences of Spirit and Christ action.

Grasp *the love of Christ,* Christ's love for us in four-dimensional quality—the vastness of divine action.

v. 19   *Love that surpasses knowledge.* We must know that love goes beyond a mere concept to the point of experience.

The fullness of God is what God imparts through Christ. All the fullness of God dwells in him (Col. 1:19).

vv. 20,   *Immeasurably* goes beyond what we ask or think. *Glory* refers to
21   God's many-sided excellences. These are to be found in the church, where God's fullness is on display.

Introduction to Outline 14-A

This abbreviated outline (without letter subpoints) illustrates several other factors not featured in the previous outline.

The first element that catches the eye is the title. This is a different approach to using the same passage. The focus here is on the pastoral concern for the church and the sermon highlights the expectations of the intercession. It uses the same basic concepts of the other outline but puts them into another mold. Another difference pertains to the use of quotes from the passage. It should not be difficult to fill in the subpoints similar to those of the first outline.

This is another illustration of achieving variety in expository sermons. Although the same basic structure is in use, the approach and adopted purpose make the difference.

In this outline both the introduction and conclusion are drawn directly from the text. This is another factor that contributes to variety in sermon construction.

Sermon 14-A
A Pastoral Prayer for the Church
Ephesians 3:14-21

Introduction, vv. 14-15

In the previous section, the believer's position in Christ is explained to show that "we may approach God with freedom and confidence." In light of that marvelous privilege this passage reflects a kneeling pastor who addresses God as the Father of all saints both in heaven and on earth. E. K. Simpson refers to this scene and to this intercession as being "comparable to some heavenly breeze, set in motion by the Spirit of the Lord, (as) it sweeps across the aeolian harp strings of the apostle's soul, waking chords of celestial music of unearthly beauty and superlative grandeur. . . . It is in such passages as these that inspiration rises to its full stature."[7]

Theme: Pastoral concerns anticipate divine favors.
  A. The church needs strengthening by *divine power.* (vv. 16-17a)
   1. *Divine power* comes out of "glorious riches."
   2. *Divine power* is conveyed by the "Spirit."
   3. *Divine power* indwells the "inner being."
   4. *Divine power* is available through "faith."
  B. The church needs the motivation of *divine love.* (vv. 17b-18a)
   1. *Divine love* is the "root" of Christian virtue.
   2. *Divine love* is the "foundation" of spiritual "power."
   3. *Divine love* is the emblem of "togetherness."
  C. The church needs the endowment of *divine fullness.* vv. 18b-19)
   1. *Divine fullness* expresses the "love of Christ."
   2. *Divine fullness* "surpasses (human) knowledge."
   3. *Divine fullness* represents the "measure" of grace.

Conclusion (vv. 20-21)
  God's ability surpasses all human endeavor.
  God's involvement goes beyond what we ask or think.
  God invests his glory in the church.

Another alternative follows the concept of resources to be used for the health of the church. It picks up the phrase *out of his glorious riches* (v. 16). The following outline developed under the influence of that thought is presented here in reduced form.

Sermon 14-B
From the Wealth of His Glory

Theme: The **church** realizes the *full scope* of salvation.

Introduction: The Father of all the redeemed is requested to apply his own attributes to the spiritual progress of the church.
A. The **church** grows by an inner *strengthening* of the Spirit.
   The church is made a powerful instrument.
B. The **church** grows with a permanent *indwelling* of Christ.
   The church is made a suitable habitation for deity.
C. The **church** grows with a clear *understanding* of God's purpose.
   The church is made aware of God's plan.
D. The **church** grows under a deep *conviction* of love.
   The church is taught the meaning of love.
E. The **church** grows toward a full *expression* of divine fullness.
   The church is directed to express the full intent of God.

Conclusion
   To give glory to God is to cause his excellence to be seen and acknowledged "throughout all generations."

Ephesians 4

CHAPTER 19

Making Explanation

Guidelines
Introduction to Part V
Outline: The Church with Christian Graces
Ephesians 4:1-3 (Sermon 15)
Word Meanings Essential to Interpretation
Collecting Ideas

Guidelines to Making Explanation

Preach to be understood. This is a major consideration in communication. Since Scripture corresponds to human need, we have urged the use of the expository method in preaching. The presentation of biblical content is made effective through explanations. It is a matter of making communication effective.

The previous emphasis was on the importance of careful exegesis and analysis of the text in preparing a sermon. We must now consider what follows. Those results of that exegesis and analysis must be translated into the language of the average layperson. A typical congregation has a cross-section of various age-groups. It has people who think on different educational levels. Few are acquainted with technical terms. Ideas need to be expressed in words that are commonly understood.

The preacher must also keep the children in mind and use simple language, simple enough for a child to understand. Explanations help to clarify meanings and to sharpen the verbal imagery for the listener.

I have previously urged the discipline of word study. That is one source of understanding to assist the audience in grasping the truth. There is no need to give long details about the origins of words and the history of their usage. In a brief sentence, the point can be made without explaining to the audience the process by which the meaning was discovered. Often the idea can be conveyed in simple contemporary speech. In each case the speaker moves on without calling undue attention to the process.

Some expressions seem foreign to us and some members of the congregation will not have them in their vocabulary. So lest we be misunderstood, explanation needs to be made. As Lenski puts it, the preacher explains "for the practical purpose to enable the hearer to grasp what the text says on the point and may not misunderstand or draw false conclusions."[1] Again, we are here dealing with results and not processes. One should take the results of private study and select from them what is appropriate for public consumption, using only what is necessary to communicate the meaning, and moving on with further thoughts on the theme.

> Many matters of truth and duty are obscure and, without help, practically unintelligible to the popular mind; many questions are sadly perplexing. To answer such inquiries, to clear up difficulties, and make as plain as possible the way of truth and the path of duty, is, as well as the explanation of Scripture, an important part of ths preacher's work.[2]

In fact, it is a part of the functional element of preaching.

Other simple literary forms that help to make meanings clear include definition, exemplification, comparisons, and parallel passages. Doctrinal meanings need clarification and application. Occasionally questions arise as to what is true and right in practical conduct. A word of explanation is needed. Often after making an application of a biblical principle, the communication becomes more effective by suggesting "what to do and how to do it."

The section labeled "Word Meanings" after each regular outline is intended to provide some of the material with which explanations are made. The explanation of the word *mystery* after sermon 12 is an example of this. *Father's whole family* is explained following sermon 13. The word *fullness* is incorporated in the theme and main divisions as an example of incorporating a word as a dominant concept of the entire message.

Introduction to Part V

With Part V we notice a change in the line of Paul's thought. Here we pass from statements of doctrine to the development of guidelines for Christian practice. In the previous chapters practice was only implied. In the following chapters the focus is on behavior. Doctrine is announced and enforced in practical living. Truth and life are interwoven. Doctrine runs itself into life. Practice feels its footing in doctrine. We are now turned in the direction of learning to live as members of the church.

A preview of the titles in this section will help to understand the progression of thought in the series. The focus is on the church and the functional elements of truth about it. It carries forward specific observations on the believer's participation in the life of the church.

In these studies of Ephesians the corporate experience of the believers is emphasized with a secondary note on individual experience. The following list of titles provides an overview of this division:

The Church with Christian Graces
The Church with Christian Commitment
The Church with Christian Gifts
The Church with Christian Unity
The Church with Christian Morality
The Church with Christian Integrity

Although the focus of these sermons is on the church, they do not ignore the implications for the individual believer. Obviously Christian idealism in the body of Christ finds its realism in the experience of the individual members of that body. For that reason it is appropriate to incorporate meanings of individual faith in the comments about the church. This should not weaken the impact of truth concerning corporate behavior.

Sermon 15
The Church with Christian Graces
Ephesians 4:1-3

Introduction

Christian graces represent the quality of life designed for the community of faith. The church hears an urgent appeal "to live a life worthy" of the divine calling. Members of the body of Christ are summoned to give themselves in full response to the meaning of the gospel and its call to service. This involves a worthy walk which qualifies persons to be engaged in divine action. The Christian calling is given top priority in the practical aspects of living. To walk worthily of our calling requires a clear commitment to the meaning and purpose of the grace of God.

Theme: The church certifies itself with **Christian graces.**
A. The *Christian walk* is characterized by **humility.**
   1. **Humility** is a disposition of *dependence.*
      a. *Dependence* springs from a sense of human limitations.
      b. *Dependence* springs from a sense of unworthiness.
   2. **Humility** is a disposition of *lowliness.*
      a. *Lowliness* is an honest recognition of personal inadequacies.
      b. *Lowliness* is an honest appraisal of personal assets.
B. The *Christian walk* is characterized by **gentleness.**
   1. **Gentleness** (meekness) exercises tolerance toward *injustice.*
      a. *Injustice* is tolerated without irritation.
      b. *Injustice* is tolerated without resentment.
   2. **Gentleness** *submits* to providential circumstances.
      a. The spirit of *submission* accepts losses without bitterness.
      b. The spirit of *submission* accepts reverses without complaint.
C. The *Christian walk* is characterized by **long-suffering.**
   1. **Long-suffering** exercises *restraint* under provocation.
      a. *Restraint* keeps a cool temper when one is unjustly accused.
      b. *Restraint* forgives under clouds of misrepresentation.
   2. **Long-suffering** *preseveres* under discouragements.
      a. *Perseverance* is essential to progress.
      b. *Perseverance* is essential to integrity.
D. The *Christian walk* is characterized by **forbearance.**
   1. **Forbearance** is *reluctant* to condemn.
      a. It *overlooks* the mistakes of others.
      b. It *tolerates* the frailties of others.
   2. **Forbearance** *bears* with the failures of others.

    a. It *refrains* from imputing evil intentions.

    b. It *absorbs* embarrassments created by others.

  E. The **Christian walk** is characterized by **peace.**

    1. The bond of **peace** is initiated by the *Spirit.*

      a. The *Spirit* operates from within to produce peace.

      b. The *Spirit* operates from within to preserve peace.

    2. The bond of **peace** engages human *effort.*

      a. Keeping peace involves *cultivating* Christian graces.

      b. Keeping peace involves *achieving* Christian maturity.

Conclusion

  The achievement of peace relies upon the disposition to receive it.

  The cultivation of peace depends on eagerness to achieve it.

  The preservation of peace depends on a willingness to guard it.

Word Meanings Essential to Interpretation

1 *Urge* or *beseech* carries the idea of giving diligence to the appeal.

In the Lord may have either of two thrusts: "to entreat you in the Lord" or "I, the prisoner in the Lord." Either is grammatically correct (Westcott).

Worthy of the calling. To walk worthy of the benefits of conversion. The Christian life is to correspond with the expectations of Christian faith. It calls for a demonstration of the reality of being identified with Christ.

2 *Humility* or *lowliness* is a dependence on God.

Gentleness or *meekness* is an open consideration of others, especially when one is under provocation.

To be *long-suffering* is to be patient under trials that come about through adverse circumstances or the unreasonableness of people.

Forbearance. In the case of real grievances or occasions of offense, to avoid being upset. To let love find expression in relating to others.

3 *Endeavoring* is to make every effort (in one's attempt to achieve unity in the brotherhood).

Unity of the spirit. "Oneness in the faith and knowledge of Christ must issue in oneness of spirit" among believers. This unity demonstrates the work of the Holy Spirit.

Bond of peace: the element that cements all of these graces into a lifestyle that expresses the "worthy walk." Christ is our peace.

Collecting Ideas

Closely associated with the task of making explanation is the task of collecting ideas. This is in less general demand in expository sermons than in many topical messages. In the process of preparing an expository message on a specific passage of Scripture, the lines of thought are somewhat predetermined. However, even within such proximity there is occasion to collect ideas and put them together to support the adopted theme.

In the development of an adopted thought from the text, there are occasions to put ideas into an order that will accomplish the adopted purpose. In the preparation of a sermon it is important to give careful attention to the matter of order in presenting a chosen line of thought. The development of that thought requires the selection of ideas related to the theme. It must promote the chosen objective. Whatever is chosen from the text needs to be set in an orderly fashion so as to make a contribution to consistent progress of thought.

Thus, one must develop a structure that is logical in its projection and clear in its expression of ideas. It needs to be an accurate representation of the selected biblical passage. The truth of the chosen text will need to be restated in the language of contemporary usage.

The Scripture passage on which the above outline is based is full of ideas with very little descriptive material. The words *humility, gentleness, long-suffering, forbearance,* and *peace* are not defined within the text. The collection of ideas that support their meanings must be drawn from other parts of the Bible. In conveying the meanings of these words, one needs to rely upon concepts gleaned from biblical sources outside of the text.

It should be observed that the nature of the structure or outline has a bearing on how one discovers ideas suitable for the development of a full-blown sermon. Within that regular structure we find numerous ideas that fit into the overall purpose of the sermon.

The ideas for the development of the outline are derived from the immediate and remote elements of truth in the context. They constitute the supporting elements that expand the outline. The ideas are discovered through reading, through reflection, and from research. There are times when the text itself provides a large share of the ideas for the sermon development.

In the outline above it is evident that the sentences used to form the structure call for descriptive elements, illustrative material, explanations, and expansion of meanings. These must be implicit in the suggestive elements. Definitions and the "Word Meanings" section above contribute significant ideas and shades of truth to enrich the total impact of the message.

CHAPTER 20

Formulating a Conclusion

Guidelines
Introduction to the Outline
Outline: The Church with Christian Commitment
Ephesians 4:4-6 (Sermon 16)
Word Meanings Essential to Interpretation
Progression of Thought

Guidelines to Formulating a Conclusion

We have previously considered the importance of having a distinct purpose for every sermon. As W. E. Sangster says, "That dreadful vagueness which hangs over so much preaching derives in the main from the fact that it is not clearly aiming to *do* something."[1] When the preacher has a clear objective in mind, the message will be focused on that purpose. A carefully designed conclusion indicates what is expected from the influence of truth expressed in the text.

The conclusion can accomplish this purpose in a variety of ways. It can make a swift restatement of the main idea and show what can be done about it. Or it can present some vivid material to "bring home" the point of the message. It also offers an opportunity to persuade acceptance of the truth. In some cases it may even identify a form of procedure that puts the truth into action.

The major purpose of the sermon usually determines the form of the conclusion.[2] It may be a plea, a warning, a challenge, a thanksgiving or praise, an exhortation, a projection with direction, or it may conclude with an encouragement. A suitable illustration may achieve a combination of these elements. Depending on the nature and purpose of the message, the conclusion can be accomplished with a call for decision (in public or private). There are times when it would be effective to use the conclusion as a winding up of the last point. (See the conclusion in sermon 15.) This is particularly applicable when the points of the sermon are designed to be accumulative in logic.

> The conclusion is the moment in which listeners can come nearest to seeing the idea whole and all at one time. It is the moment in which the issue can be seen in its clearest and felt at its sharpest focus. It can be carried into life service where, if anywhere, it must be resolved. The conclusion is the last chance to accomplish the sermon's purpose.[3]

The preparation of the conclusion stands at a high priority in designing a sermon. It is important to finish the sermon on a positive note. Whether it is a clarification, a recapitulation, or a winding up of the last point, it should embrace the truth with an affirmation of divine purpose.

There are times when it is entirely appropriate to close the sermon with prayer. Instead of making an appeal for acceptance, the prayer can become the equivalent of application.[4] However, the prayer should be directly related to the substance of the message and particularly to the last point. Such closing words are more likely to be remembered than any single item in the general discussion. Last impressions are usually the most lasting.

In any case the conclusion should be swift, strong, and full of interactive interest. This allows for no introduction of new ideas. It must concentrate on a major aspect of the theme and translate the Scripture into the language of common life. It calls for a concise statement that applies the theme to contemporary life.

Introduction to the Outline

The analysis of this text led to the adoption of a particular structure—one that pursues the matter of unity in the church. This message focuses on how to unify the church in doctrine. It uses the concept of commitment as a means to achieve doctrinal unity.

This outline illustrates how to use supportive truth expressed in other portions of Scripture as subpoints. They flesh out the key words that appear in the text. The unifying element of "belief" is engaged to identify the nature of human response.

In the discussion of application in chapter 18, several alternatives are mentioned. One of them is to formulate the headings of the main divisions in terms of personal living. In this outline we move from the historical setting to current reality. The corporate body is being addressed here. The commonality of commitment is a point of emphasis in this entire series.

The introduction in the outline refers to a list of words as having been included in the universal creed. However, the context does not suggest it be used as a creedal formula. Rather, it represents a point or points to which the church pledges loyalty.

Sermon 16

The Church with Christian Commitment
Ephesians 4:4-6

Introduction
The "bond of peace" is extended to the expression of Christian beliefs. This passage is composed of simple declarations of truth commonly accepted among true believers. It looks at biblical positions that represent a universal Christian creed. Although these declarations do not take the form of exhortations they represent the essential elements of Christian doctrine affecting practice.

Theme: The church unifies itself through **commitment** to Christian **beliefs.**
   A. The church is **committed** to **belief** in one **body.**
      1. The **body** is composed of all true *believers* in Christ.
         a. *Believers* in Christ have a common salvation.
         b. *Believers* in Christ have a common subsequent Christian experience.
      2. The **body** is composed of believers who accept *each other.*
         a. Believers accept *each other* in faith.
         b. Believers accept *each other* in love.
   B. The church is **committed** to **belief** in one **Spirit.**
      1. The Holy **Spirit** indwells each *believer.*

  a. The *believer* is born of the Spirit.
  b. The *believer* is indwelt by the Spirit.
 2. The Holy **Spirit** dwells in the *church.*
  a. The *church* is the habitation of the Spirit.
  b. The *church* is an agent of the Spirit.
C. The church is *committed* to *belief* in one **hope.**
 1. **Hope** is an anchor for present *encounters.*
  a. *Encounter* with evil relies upon hope for security.
  b. *Encounter* with hostility relies upon hope for courage.
 2. **Hope** is centered in a common *destiny.*
  a. The *destiny* is set by Christ's return.
  b. The *destiny* is fixed by God's judgment.
D. The church is *committed* to *belief* in one **Lord.**
 1. The believer's life is subject to **divine** *control.*
  a. Divine *control* includes the believer's possessions.
  b. Divine *control* includes the believer's relationships.
 2. The believer's vocation is subject to **divine** *guidance.*
  a. Divine *guidance* is directed to the use of talents.
  b. Divine *guidance* is directed to the use of time.
E. The church is *committed* to *belief* in one **faith.**
 1. The common **faith** puts *confidence* in God.
  a. *Confidence* in God means relying upon his promises.
  b. *Confidence* in God means relying upon his providence.
 2. The common **faith** is centered in *Christ.*
  a. Believers in *Christ* embrace the same plan of redemption.
  b. Believers in *Christ* embrace the same truth of discipleship.
F. The church is *committed* to *belief* in one **baptism.**
 1. This involves the **baptism** of the *Spirit.*
  a. The *Spirit* binds all believers to the same covenant.
  b. The *Spirit* binds all believers to the same imperatives.
 2. This involves the **baptism** of *suffering.*
  a. The baptism of *suffering* identifies the believer with Christ.
  b. The baptism of *suffering* involves the believer in servanthood.
G. The church is *committed* to *belief* in one **God.**
 1. **God** is Father of *all* true believers.
  a. His will is addressed to *all* his children.
  b. His care is extended to *all* his children.
 2. **God** is a refuge to *all* true believers.
  a. His sovereign power is available to *all.*
  b. His persuasive pleas are directed to *all.*
  c. His imminent presence is available to *all.*

Conclusion

The unity of the church has its basis in a common commitment to biblical beliefs. Our challenge today is to make evident in life and service the reality of that unity. It calls for each member to express these elements of truth in a corporate Christian witness.

Word Meanings Essential to Interpretation

v. 4　*One body* refers to the invisible church, the so-called mystical body of Christ of which he is the Head.

One Spirit. There is only one Holy Spirit. The Greek word for spirit *(pneuma)* is never used in the New Testament of temper or disposition (Vincent). However, some scholars regard this as referring to a quality within the human organism. (See Westcott).

One hope. All true believers experience hope as a present element of fellowship with God in Christ. It is a spiritual reality associated with the heavenly calling. It also has a future aspect.

v. 5　*One Lord.* There is one Lord who is sovereign over all of life. This implies a confession of faith proclaiming that Jesus is Lord. His lordship includes his possession of and authority over all.

One faith. The principle of faith is applied to the people who embrace the same saving truth. It is the believing experience that puts confidence in divine revelation.

One baptism. This is the external sign of faith, the visible act that validates membership in the church. It is a symbol of membership in the body of Christ. It also has a mystical meaning in relation to identification with Christ.

v. 6　*One God.* As Creator, he is Father of all humanity. As Redeemer, he is Father of all who believe in his son Jesus Christ. The phrase *one God* represents the Trinity—Father, Son, and Holy Spirit—in the position of ruling, pervading, and sustaining all things everywhere.

Progression of Thought

We have previously considered the importance of identifying purpose and of setting a goal during sermon preparation. With these elements in focus the form of the outline needs to demonstrate a progression of thought. The sermon needs to move forward. The order in which thoughts are presented has a direct bearing upon effectiveness in communication.

Some general principles need to be observed in the development of the sermon outline. A sound structure can make the difference between failure and success in the pulpit. A proper design provides for the stream of thought to move from a specific starting point to a desired ending. It moves from one thought to another, and yet another, in progressive development of the formulated theme.

In the structure of a topical message the selection of appropriate passages of Scripture determines the material with which to arrange the progression of thought. In this procedure there is considerable liberty in shaping the content of the message. It is important, however, to have the elements of truth so arranged as to have the trend of thought arrive at the goal.

It expository preaching some limitations apply. It is expected that the sermon will emerge from the chosen text as one develops an outline from that material. In a series of messages covering an entire epistle, such as Ephesians, the borders of selection are somewhat predetermined. But even so there is plenty of variation in the subject matter to achieve variety. The basic structure may be quite uniform but the range of thought allows for differences of approach.

In the development of an expository sermon the perimeters of truth are determined by the selected portion of Scripture. Within that selection the preacher will identify the main divisions (and often the subdivisions) for the outline. If the arrangement of material in the text does not lead step-by-step in a progressive order, the points may be rearranged so that the development of thought leads directly to the goal, the intended purpose of the sermon.

Pulpit power relies much on structure. Without a proper arrangement of thoughts, the message may prove to be obscure. An outline that stands out clear and sharp is the first long step to freedom in the pulpit.[5] An effective outline serves to make the message a dynamic influence. It directs the line of thought in the direction of the sermon purpose. The continuity of thought may not be interrupted by unrelated ideas (however good they may be). Preachers must take their listeners along step-by-step until they reach their goal.

Preaching is communicating with people. Hearing the sermon

depends upon maintaining a flow in the development of the message. The design must be useful to the hearer; it should have an audible movement of thought. The audience must feel that the preacher is making progress in the pulpit. The thought structure must keep the listener in contact with the theme. A good audible design accommodates the audience.

For that reason it is important to arrange the parts so that the effect of hearing the message will result in continuity with the listeners' experience. Only a few structural divisions in clear and simple sentences are required to achieve that purpose. The developmental details must all be related to advancing the principal thought of the theme.

In a pulpit ministry the preacher needs to know how to reach the identified goal. That is why a well-planned outline to follow is necessary. It serves as a guide to achieve the stated purpose. For that reason thoughts need to be arranged in a proper sequence.

Generally, expository sermons reflect a deductive continuity. They begin with a general statement (usually the formulated theme), followed by particulars in support of the proposition. It moves from the general to the particular.

Within the discussion of particulars the inductive method of reasoning may be used with good effect. In this secondary function the speaker moves from particular points to a conclusion that represents a general principle. This is particularly useful in presenting an argument in which an analysis of a problem is followed by a solution.

In brief, the following steps may be helpful in building a progression: (1) fix the goal of the sermon, (2) formulate the theme for a beginning, (3) arrange a progressive order of thought between the beginning and the end, and (4) balance the strength of the points (work at development) with a proper continuity.

CHAPTER 21

Formulating a Theme

Guidelines
Introduction to the Outline
Outline: The Church with Christian Gifts
Ephesians 4:7-12 (Sermon 17)
Word Meanings Essential to Interpretation
Gifts in the Church

Guidelines to Formulating a Theme

I prefer using the word *theme* rather than *proposition*. These terms are used interchangeably in setting forth the gist of the sermon. It consists of a complete sentence that becomes the basis of the message.

The sermon theme is "a formulated sentence in which the unity of the sermon receives its adequate expression."[1] According to Andrew Blackwood, it ideally "consists of a complete sentence—simple, not complex; declarative, not interrogative; straightforward, not figurative; positive, not negative."[2]

Another term used is *thesis*. A sermon idea may take the form of a proposition to be proved or a thesis to be supported. "In either case an assertion is made that needs to be proved, or at least to be supported, by evidence, or reasoning, or both."[3]

I prefer the designation *theme* because its assumed function is to mark out a definite course of thought contained in the text without a call for proof. A *proposition* usually places a challenge to be proved.

In any case, it calls for the discovery of the "dominant thought" of the text. "Every text has a main theme . . . an overriding thrust."[4] Having found that dominant thought, the next step is to express it in a brief sentence that will serve as a guide in the further preparation of the sermon, giving direction to its structure.

A carefully formulated theme will state in a clear and telling way what the text means and how it is being used in a particular sermon. A text can thus be used to support more than one particular message. Its various elements of truth can allow for different emphases. A particular purpose may call for the use of specific singular thoughts that lie in the passage. And it will conform to that purpose of the message. This calls for a high level of intellectual and spiritual discipline.

The theme points in a chosen direction pertinent to the adopted purpose of the message. It forms the basis for building a thought structure that advances the selected truth in a progressive fashion.

The directive line can be indicated in various ways. One effective means of unifying the line of thought is with words that modify or identify the idea intended to be expressed. It may be a noun, an adjective, a verb, an adverb, or even a phrase. Repeated occurrence of such a word supports the unity of thought as it becomes more evident.

Another approach to sermon construction begins by determining a *subject.* Normally that could be expressed in a single word. It may appear in the text or it may be an impression left in the preacher's mind from reading the text.

The next step in this procedure would be to select the theme reflecting a particular aspect of the subject. It would most likely be expressed in the form of a phrase representing the main thought of the sermon. This, too, is drawn from the preaching portion of Scripture.

The formulation of a proposition would follow. This becomes the focal point of the sermon outline. (I have been calling this the theme.) The outlines in this book combine steps two and three into one procedure. In this case "the proposition announces the theme in sentence form."[5]

A statement of J. H. Jowett, often quoted by authors in the field of homiletics, reflects the foregoing emphasis.

> No sermon is ready for preaching . . . until we can express its theme in a short pregnant sentence as clear as a crystal. I find the getting of that sentence the hardest, the most exacting, and the most fruitful labor in my study. To compel oneself to fashion that sentence, to dismiss every word that is vague, ragged, ambiguous, to think oneself through to a form of words which defines the theme with scrupulous exactness— this is surely one of the most vital and essential factors in making a sermon; and I do not think that any sermon ought to be preached, or even written, until that sentence has emerged clear and lucid as a cloudless moon.[6]

Normally one should formulate the theme before arranging the structure of the sermon. Occasionally, however, during the process of further analysis and research, one may find it necessary to revise the theme to express a newly discovered truth. This is no excuse for a careless approach but rather is an accommodation to the text.

Introduction to the Outline

This is one of the more difficult passages of Scripture to translate into a popular sermon outline. But when planning a series of messages from a single book, the preacher should not bypass a text just because it raises problems of interpretation.

This passage has in it a diversion of thought that requires careful study to discover its relevance to the main stream of thought. The quotation from Psalm 68:18 is a Pauline illustration of adapting Old Testament Scriptures to New Testament thought.

The guidelines for formulating a theme can be tested in the outline below. The prominent word that ties the divisions together is *edify*. This concept carries the symbol of building which appears in the text and is used through the entire sermon. The word *church* is primary in the series of topics; in this sermon it is in a secondary position. It is the noun which prevails throughout, whereas *edifies* is the verb of action. A word of equal importance that appears throughout the message is *gift*. In some respect it deserves primary emphasis.

Observe that these three words and their meanings form a trio of elements that serve in concert to make the desired impact.

Sermon 17
The Church with Christian Gifts
Ephesians 4:7-12

Introduction
There is diversity in unity and unity has diversity. Different talents and abilities in the church are intended for service in a united effort. The manifestations of God's grace are as diverse as human personalities. "The intense demand for unity of all within one body for one great end of glorifying God in Christ, carries with it an equally powerful insistence on the personal responsibility of each member of the body" (W. O. Carver).

Theme: The church *edifies* itself with Christian gifts.
   A. The gift of **grace** *edifies* the church **in Christ.**
      1. **In Christ grace** gives *strength* for living.
         a. *Strength* is needed to cope with temptation.
         b. *Strength* is needed to cope with human limitations.
      2. **In Christ grace** provides *resources* for service.
         a. *Resources* are available for guidance.
         b. *Resources* are available for witnessing.
   B. The gift of **deliverance** *edifies* the church in **completeness.**
      1. The measure of **completeness** reaches *captive saints.*
         a. *Captive saints* needed atonement.
         b. *Captive saints* were delivered with perfection.
      2. The measure of **completeness** reaches *current saints.*
         a. *Current saints* trust in the crucified Christ.
         b. *Current saints* rely on the ascended Christ.
   C. The gift of **persons** *edifies leadership* in the church.
      1. **Apostles** edify the church in *mission.*
         a. Its *mission* meets spiritual needs.
         b. Its *mission* meets material needs.
      2. **Prophets** edify the church in *proclamation.*
         a. Its *proclamation* conveys exhortation.
         b. Its *proclamation* conveys comfort.
      3. **Evangelists** edify the church in *evangelism.*
         a. They engage in making *personal contacts.*
         b. They engage in making *mass appeals.*

4. **Pastors/teachers** edify the church in *doctrine*.
   a. They give *instructions* for belief.
   b. They give *instructions* for practice.
D. The gift of **leadership** *edifies* the church in *action*.
   1. It **brings** saints into the *body*.
      a. It *grows* by receiving new members.
      b. It *grows* by sharing spiritual experience.
   2. It **qualifies** saints for *service*.
      a. Their *work* includes the ministry of caring.
      b. Their *work* includes the ministry of sharing.
E. The gift of **administration** *edifies* the church with *diversity*.
   1. It provides **diversity** in *works* of service.
      a. *Works* of service are motivated by positive attitudes.
      b. *Works* of service are expressed in helping behavior.
   2. It provides **diversity** in distribution of *abilities*.
      a. Different *abilities* are used in cooperative engagements.
      b. Different *abilities* are used in community projects.

Conclusion

Christ is the Dispenser of gifts, distributing them according to the divine will. The church is responsible for the cultivation of gifts for the glory of God.

Word Meanings Essential to Interpretation

7   *Grace* refers to the favors of God as a characteristic of his being.

A *gift* is a particular endowment. (For a more detailed explanation refer to 1 Corinthians 12:4-6.)

Apportioned by Christ. The gifts are distributed according to the will of the Lord Christ, in varied measure to individuals.

. 8-
10   Quote from Psalm 68:19. This has been a "bone of contention" for centuries. The main problem centers in the meaning of Christ's descension "to the lower earthly regions." After repeated studies of this passage I have come to agree with the view that he descended to the Paradise section of Hades. Old Testament saints went down into that place where they were captive until "the spirits of just men were made perfect." At Christ's resurrection these redeemed souls with the benefits of atonement were transferred to their heavenly habitation. Christ's ascension put him in the position of divine authority to distribute "endowments" to be used for the glory of God.

v. 11   *Apostles*. The word was used originally to designate persons commissioned by Christ in his time on earth. Its use was extended in the early church. Persons who were engaged to preach and establish churches were called apostles.

v. 12   *Perfecting*. This is the only occurrence of the Greek word from which it is translated in the New Testament. It can be translated literally to mean "coordinate." It is expressed in NIV "to prepare God's people for works of service."

Work of ministry. The coordination of the saints is designed to facilitate their service to each other, a person-to-person influence and "ministry" within the body of believers.

Edifying identifies the purpose of ministering; namely, adding what is required to complete the body of Christ. This then refers to the final goal of preparing (coordinating) the saints.

Gifts in the Church

The church is expected to edify itself in love:

> Now you are the body of Christ, and each one of you is a part of it. And in the church God has appointed first of all apostles, second prophets, third teachers, then workers of miracles, also those having gifts of healing, those able to help others, those with gifts of administration, and those speaking in different kinds of tongues. (1 Cor. 12:27-28).

This indicates that all members do not have the same office. But all are related to Christ as Head of the body.

The body is not one member but has many parts. All operate under one head. We are members one of another because we are related to each other in Christ. Although each member communicates the meaning of the gospel, the entire church exhibits the teachings of Christ as his body.

The church demonstrates restored relationships. Because of human frailty this is an old problem. Relationships may be marred but the connection is nevertheless real. We do not look for that reality in human organization. It is achieved as each member acknowledges the control of his or her head. It can happen in the local congregation insofar as each member respects the headship of Christ and the leadership of the Holy Spirit. However, the entire congregation should think and live in accordance with this understanding. We can all live with the privileges and limitations of a restored relationship.

> There are different kinds of gifts, but the same Spirit. There are different kinds of service but the same Lord. There are different kinds of working, but the same God works all of them in all men. Now to each one the manifestation of the Spirit is given for the common good. (1 Cor. 12:4-7).

The church needs to be aware of its potential. It has a diversity of endowments to perform different functions in order to build up the body of Christ. For that reason it needs to cultivate individual gifts as they appear within the group. The Spirit works in all members to profit everyone. The gift of the Spirit is for everyone, but the gifts of the Spirit are bestowed individually according to divine purpose. These are not designed for personal display of capability but are for the benefit of the entire body. The particular purpose is for the upbuilding of the entire church.

> Frequently, though not always, the gifts bestowed accord with natural talents and endowments, but they always transcend them. They are supernatural, but make use of and increase the natural abilities.[7]

CHAPTER 22

Exposition

Guidelines to Exposition

In the previous chapters we have alluded to the process of exposition without naming it as such. The task in implementing the principle of exposition is to discover what in the text stands for all time. After having completed one's exegesis, the logical next step is to move from what it meant at the time it was written to what it has meant since then in general principles.

Although the exegesis of a text enables the student of Scripture to learn about a past event represented in the passage, the exposition translates that information into universal principles. Having at hand an understanding of the grammatical and historical accuracy of the text, one is prepared to form an opinion of its meaning for today. The challenge is to express that truth in current language so it can shed light on life for today. In one sense it is a form of making application of the text to current human issues.

The sentences in the outline below are all in the present tense. They reflect Paul's time and circumstances. However, when one uses the process stated above the universal meanings of that time are translated into our time. The result in these assertions are applicable today.

The discipline of exposition brings into sermon preparation a valid respect for the text. This has less to do with structure than with content. "To expound Scripture is to bring out of the text what is there and expose it to view."[1] Exposition makes plain what is obscure, unravels what is knotted, and unfolds what is tightly packed. The goal of this process is to open the Scripture in such a way that the hearers understand plainly its current application.

The principle of exposition is a functional element in biblical preaching and is vital for an understanding of expository sermons. This is evident in this entire series of sermon outlines developed from the book of Ephesians. Once a theme has been chosen, the development of the sermon is basically an exposition of that central idea.

Introduction to the Outline

The Sermon outlines from the fourth chapter of Ephesians follows a progression of thought. Each emphasizes a specific aspect of truth. Expressed in each of the themes, they are as follows:

The church certifies itself with Christian graces.

The church sanctifies itself through Christian beliefs.

The church edifies itself with Christian gifts.

The church unifies itself through Christian experience.

This passage is devoted to a specific objective in the life of the church.

The object of this manifold ministry is the perfecting [maturing] of every member after the pattern of Christ, that all, realizing the truth in life, may grow up to complete fellowship with him, who provides [resources] through the ministry of every part for the growth of the whole body in love.[2]

Sermon 18
The Church and Christian Unity
Ephesians 4:13-16

Introduction

The function of the ascended Lord is to achieve the perfecting (maturing) of the saints (the church). This involves bringing about a related unity that qualifies for spiritual service. The end in view is the building up of the body of Christ. "The standard and measure of this work on the part of consecrated members of Christ's body cannot be completed and perfected until we all together achieve the goal of unity" (W. O. Carver).

Theme: The church *unifies* itself through Christian experience.
  A. *Unity* is achieved through common experience of **growth.**
    1. **Growth** in *faith* depends on experience with God.
      a. *Faith* accepts the person of God.
      b. *Faith* acts on the promises of God.
    2. **Growth** in *knowledge of Christ* depends on experience with him.
      a. *Knowing Christ* means growing in identity with him.
      b. *Knowing Christ* means growing in union with him.
    3. **Growth** in the *fullness* of Christ depends on experience in heavenly relationships.
      a. *Fullness* is achieved through faith in him.
      b. *Fullness* is achieved through submission to him.
    4. *Growth* into *maturity* depends on experience in corporate relationships.
      a. *Maturity* is expressed in congenial relationships with neighbors.
      b. *Maturity* is expressed in positive relationships with saints.
  B. *Unity* is achieved through common experience of **maturing.**
    1. *Loyalty* to Christ is a mark of **maturity.**
      a. *Loyalty* to Christ acknowledges his headship.
      b. *Loyalty* to Christ accepts his lordship.
    2. *Purposeful* living is a mark of **maturity.**
      a. The *purpose* of exalting Christ is to establish Christian values.
      b. The *purpose* of exalting Christ is to counteract craftiness.
    3. Exercising *responsibility* is a mark of **maturity.**
      a. *Responsibility* stabilizes doctrinal position.
      b. *Responsibility* regulates social practices.
    4. Expressing redemptive *love* is a mark of **maturity.**
      a. *Love* is aggressively speaking the truth.
      b. *Love* is aggressively exercising goodwill.

C. **Unity** is achieved through the common experience of being in **Christ.**
    1. **Christ** is the source of *unity.*
       a. **In Christ** saints are harmoniously *joined together.*
       b. **In Christ** saints are firmly *held together.*
    2. **Christ** is the *Sustainer* of unity.
       a. Being **in Christ** *sustains* functioning together.
       b. Being **in Christ** *sustains* living together.
    3. **Christ** is the *manager* of unity.
       a. He *inspires* each person to do his or her work.
       b. He *inspires* each person to support others.
    4. **Christ** is the *occasion* of unity.
       a. He *produces* growth of the body.
       b. He *inspires* building up in love.

Conclusion
    Each member of the church in his or her own special way helps all other parts of the body so that the entire community of faith is healthy and growing, full of love.

Word Meanings Essential to Interpretation

13b *Knowledge* here represents full comprehension, completeness, and harmony of ideas and work.
    Mature indicates being full-grown, "perfect."
    Measure defines the "perfect" mature position, the point at which the fullness of Christ is received.
    Fullness is that quality of life which belongs to Christ and which is imparted to believers in the process of development.

14 *Infants* (children). This term is used to contrast with the goal of maturity. This figure of speech indicates a status of incompletion.
    Tossed to and fro represents the actions of influence on a person—like a boat among the waves of opposition.
    Winds of teaching refers to erroneous doctrines in contrast to teachings that build up in Christ. They tend to blow unstable people in every direction.
    Cunning, craftiness, and *deceitful scheming* are terms that describe the methods of those tending the system of error. They imply deliberate planning.

15 *Speaking the truth* includes living truthful lives. It means going beyond the state of speaking to that of walking in it. (This term is

found only here and in Galatians 4:16.)

In love refers to the brotherly relationship reiterated in verse 16. This moral element characterizes the church.

Grow up in him emphasizes the relation of the believers as a body with its origin and being in Christ. It indicates the sphere and direction of the maturing process.

v. 16 *Joined and held together* represents the present relationships within the whole body in the sense of a progressive experience. These two words represent the ideas of "harmony" and "compactness."

Grows and builds refers to the result of Christ's activity in motivating human action. Its purpose is to supply the means for achieving the goal. The two figures of speech are used to identify the dual response of the church: to stimulate "growth" and to "build" up the whole structure of people.

Each part. Each person has his or her own contribution to the whole body, making increase of itself in the atmosphere and spirit of love.

Transitions

The outlines submitted in this series from Ephesians do not include statements for use in making transitions—those points at which the speaker moves from one major thought to another. The assumption is that the circumstances and the composition of the audience have a direct influence upon the way in which the speaker makes transitions.

The settled ideas to be pursued become evident in the sermon structure. The most common and natural points at which the speaker informs the audience of the next step are following the introduction and in the movements from one main division to the next. "The transitions are guideposts, pointing from one idea to the next, so that both speaker and audience may be minded of precisely where we are."[3]

The nature of oral communication is such that careful transitions are essential to keep the audience involved in the chosen subject. The preacher has a perpetual concern not to lose the audience. "The speaker who cares anything at all about holding his audience may need to spend an entire paragraph of his address in orienting them before he moves on to a new idea."[4]

At some parts of the sermon the transition is crucial. If the audience should miss the introduction of a new idea, the preacher's message may be frustrated in that particular part of the message. Unless there are effective attention-getters from time to time throughout the sermon, one will begin to lose one's audience. To keep the level of interest from fluctuating, the audience must be kept at a high level of interest. Carefully worded transitions are essential to keeping their minds engaged.

A transition may at times summarize the points already made with an additional comment that emphasizes the relevance of the next idea. There is a distinct advantage in having the total structure of the message studded with carefully chosen words that provide unity in progression. Reference to the unity so achieved may be made briefly with only a suggestion that indicates another aspect of the prevailing idea. In the outline above the words *unity, growth, maturity,* and *in Christ* represent prominent aspects of the theme.

The phrase "the church unifies itself through Christian experience" is an illustration of repeating a phrase taken from the theme to introduce the main divisions of the sermon. In each case it is a part of the transition.

It is not necessary to identify these divisions with "second," "third," etc., when moving from one point to the next. Any appropriate remark that links the foregoing to the next can serve this function. Another way is to restate the previous division heads and simply indicate that the next consideration is open for discussion by announcing the division statement. "Clean, smooth transitions are a mark of excellence in a sermon."[5]

CHAPTER 23

Biblical Authority

Guidelines
Introduction to the Outline
Outline: The Church with Christian Morality
Ephesians 4:17-24 (Sermon 19)
Word Meanings Essential to Interpretation
Alternate Outline 19-A: Lessons in Morality

Guidelines to Biblical Authority

One evening I was reading a booklet about a specific social problem. The author made a simple but striking statement: "For final authority, we must turn to the Word of God." With what finality could this writer appeal to the Bible? Jesus referred to a trustworthy message when he said, "Blessed are those who hear the Word of God and obey it." (Luke 11:28). This was his ultimate resource for authentic communication about human behavior. God has spoken.

By authority we mean the right to command and enforce obedience. It involves speaking the decisive word on debatable questions. The exercise of judicial authority assumes the right to make laws and to enforce them. And the exercise of moral authority involves the application of standards of ethics in human behavior. Of course, there is only one absolute authority—that which rests in God.

The Bible is authoritative because it is a revelation from God. It has come to us through divine impartation of truth. Its message was recorded by inspiration. Thus the Bible is an instrument of communication of divine truth without any mixture of error in the original language by the original writers. It was "God-breathed by the Holy Spirit."

The Spirit is also involved in Christian discernment. Biblical authority is further supported by spiritual illumination. When the believing mind is exposed to the Word of God, the Holy Spirit becomes engaged in providing an understanding of what God has spoken. The Bible's authority is in this way substantiated by the witness of the Spirit. The substance of Scripture bears testimony to its finality. The Spirit works in our thinking and in the response of our hearts during the process of biblical studies.

The authority of the Scriptures is made available to the church through the application of valid principles of interpretation. These have been outlined in previous chapters. By this means we can discover the true meaning of a text and can use it with confidence. The writers of Scripture—especially of the New Testament—were in close proximity to the actual events they were recording and to the teachings they expressed.

This proximity to Christ gives authenticity to their witness. And this authenticity establishes the Bible's authority. They were able to report accurately and to reflect decisively the implications of their messages.

The New Testament is entirely credible; it is worthy to be believed and to be preached. It stands as the base upon which we rest our faith. Jesus by his own testimony not only found truth in Old Testament; he also declared truth in the new era.

The New Testament completes the revelation of God to us. The Bible as a whole has an internal unity which forms a strong base for the authority of preaching. We proclaim it as the very Word of God.

Introduction to the Outline

The Scripture passage under consideration lends itself to a twofold division. For that reason this outline is four levels deep instead of the usual three. The first three levels (capital letters, numerals, and lower-case letters) follow the basic outline of the text itself. The fourth level division employs concepts suggested by the divisions they modify. The supporting truths are drawn from the scriptural truth expressed outside of the text, but not in contradiction to it.

The text itself expresses the negative concepts reflected in the first main division. In order to comply with the principle of preaching with a positive outlook, those negatives are handled as objects to be overcome via positive statements.

It would not necessarily be wrong to use the derogatory elements as declarations against sin, since the second division is distinctly positive. However, as it is, it presents a real problem for the church and suggests a solution.

Sermon 19
The Church with Christian Morality
Ephesians 4:17b-24

Introduction
At first Paul expressed great confidence in the Ephesian church. Now he writes with concern for their moral behavior. Obtaining eternal life does not at once and in a moment change a person's moral temper. Habits are subject to the process of sanctification. However, ethical standards are reinforced by a new motivation. In every Christian's life, ethical progress must follow regeneration. The new life is no longer to be patterned after worldly practices. Grace requires moral reformation. To be "in the Lord" means maintaining a living relationship with him.

Theme: The church renews itself with moral disciplines.
  A. Moral discipline involves *renunciation* of **carnality.** (vv. 17b-19)
    1. *Renunciation* of carnality repudiates **sensuality.**
      a. The **sensual** way of thinking leads to moral *insanity.*
        (1) Moral *insanity* develops blindness to truth.
        (2) Moral *insanity* develops futility in judgment.
      b. The **sensual** state of mind is darkened in moral *discernment.*
        (1) Moral *discernment* is darkened with confusion.
        (2) Moral *discernment* is darkened with uncertainty.
    2. *Renunciation* of carnality restores **good behavior.**
      a. **Good behavior** is restored by *regeneration.*
        (1) *Regeneration* establishes new life in Christ.

(2) *Regeneration* motivates obedience to Christ.
  b. **Good behavior** is motivated by *fellowship*.
    (1) *Fellowship* with God stabilizes moral judgments.
    (2) *Fellowship* with saints reinforces moral behavior.
3. **Renunciation** of carnality copes with moral **insensitivity.**
  a. Moral **sensitivity** combats *sensuality*.
    (1) *Sensuality* is overcome by newness of mind.
    (2) *Sensuality* is overcome by discipline.
  b. Moral **sensitivity** counteracts *sensual indulgence.*
    (1) *Sensual indulgence* is overcome by spiritual commitment.
    (2) *Sensual desires* are overcome by spiritual activities.
B. Moral discipline involves **cultivation** of spirituality. (vv. 20-24)
  Discipline applies the ethics of Jesus.
  1. The **cultivation** of spirituality employs **faith in Christ.**
    a. **Christ** set standards of Christian *behavior.*
      (1) Christian *behavior* is regulated by the truth of Christ.
      (2) Christian *behavior* is motivated by the love of Christ.
    b. **Christ** set the pattern for Christian *conduct.*
      (1) Christian *conduct* is modeled after the example of Christ.
      (2) Christian *conduct* is patterned after the teachings of Christ.
  2. The **cultivation** of spirituality applies the **teachings of Christ.**
    a. The **teachings of Christ** identify the *new way* of life.
      (1) The *new way* of life adopts new ideals.
      (2) The *new way* of life expresses new desires.
    b. The **teachings of Christ** define *spiritual attitudes.*
      (1) *Spiritual attitudes* open the mind to moral guidance.
      (2) *Spiritual attitudes* open the mind to moral corrections.
  3. The **cultivation** of spirituality adopts **godly behavior.**
    a. **Godly behavior** expresses elements of *righteousness.*
      (1) *Righteousness* represents the will of God.
      (2) *Righteousness* represents the action of God.
    b. **Godly behavior** expresses *elements of holiness.*
      (1) *Holiness* reflects a separated life.
      (2) *Holiness* reflects a committed life.

Conclusion

We should continually be growing in moral improvement. Our current lifestyle should reflect Christian behavior as a valid representation of the new nature in Christ. We are called to live as children of light. Let our conduct be consistent with our membership in the new humanity.

Word Meanings Essential to Interpretation

v. 17   *So I tell you this* (NIV) or *therefore* (KJV) refers to the preceding appeal for consistent living in the church. It also pinpoints an urgency about what follows.

In the Lord highlights the writer's personal qualification to speak and speaks to the nature of his appeal.

Live as the Gentiles. The church is made up of called-out people. This negative appeal is intended to sensitize Christians to their relation to the unsaved world, the population of pagans.

Futility of their thinking (NIV) or *vanity of their mind* (KJV). This is a descriptive expression of mental delusion. It implies moral worthlessness, illusion of reality, and lost mental powers of distinction.

v. 18   *Darkened understanding:* a state of intellectual darkness in which the natural mind does not understand divine truth. A person's most trusted guide is turned to darkness. Mental and moral faculties are perverted. They are broken with futility.

Separated from the life of God. This "life of God" refers to the life God gives. This state of spiritual alienation results from a lack of commitment to the will of God and from no longer participating in God's kind of life.

Hardening of their hearts refers to the deadening power of sin at work resulting in the loss of one's sense of guilt.

v. 19   *Having lost all sensitivity.* The morally degenerate no longer feel guilt due to their willful defiance of moral restraint. Having gone contrary to the will of God so long, they cease to feel guilt's pain.

Given over to sensuality: complete surrender to evil. The continual lust for more indicates a total abandonment of right behavior.

v. 20   *To know Christ* is to have faith in him and to live under his lordship. One cannot continue worldly ways after learning to know Christ.

vv. 21-24   The phrase *truth that is in Jesus* introduces three basic elements of experience in the verses that follow:

1. Renunciation of one's previous immoral life. *Put off your old self* (aorist tense). Have done with it once and for all.

2. Constant renewal of spiritual life (present tense). *Be made new in attitude* (continuous action). This requires cultivation.

3. Appropriation of new privilege (aorist tense). *Put on the new*

self. This imperative calls for a decisive act, one that will help a person step into a position of personal power and victory.

v. 21　*Jesus.* This name is used instead of Christ to designate his historical name. It indicates a "believing fellowship with the historical Jesus, who is the Christ of prophecy" (Vincent).

v. 22　*Which is being corrupted* indicates the progressive condition of corruption. It emphasizes the need for continuous moral discipline.

v. 23　*Attitude of your minds.* This phrase does mean a change in the essence of the mind; it is that which gives the mind both its bent and its materials of thought.

v. 24　*Righteousness and holiness* are designated here as attributes of truth. "The new self finds its expression in these elements, the fulfilment of duties to others and to self, inspired and supported by the influence of the truth" (Westcott).

Alternate Outline

With the title *Lessons in Morality* we are introduced to another approach in preaching from this same passage. The introduction varies slightly from the other, but the basic material is the same. It differs most in its details and its structure. Both outlines make valid use of the biblical content.

Sermon 19-A
Lessons in Morality
Ephesians 4:17-24

Introduction

This passage follows Paul's expression of confidence in the church, his deep concern for the Ephesians' morality clearly continues here. The process of sanctification begins with conversion and continues with unabated zeal. Moral progress is supported by the application of ethical standards and is reinforced by new motivations. The new life is no longer patterned after worldly practices. This calls for a clear break with the way of the world and the adoption of principles of moral purity and inner chastity.

Theme: Faith applies moral *disciplines.*
   A. *Discipline* produces **moral improvement.**
      1. **Moral improvement** engages spiritual *discernment.*
         a. It discerns the evil in pagan practices adopted in "futility."

       b. It *discovers* the moral delusions of a worldly thought pattern.
   2. **Moral improvement** engages resources from spiritual *enlightenment.*
       a. Spiritual *enlightenment* uncovers darkened understanding.
       b. Spiritual *enlightenment* exposes perverted moral judgment.
       c. Spiritual *enlightenment* counteracts a blurred intelligence.
       d. Spiritual *enlightenment* corrects blindness to truth.
   3. **Moral improvement** engages the *life of God.*
       a. The *life of God* resolves spiritual alienation.
       b. The *life of God* counteracts spiritual ignorance.
       c. The *life of God* restores one from spiritual darkness.
   4. **Moral improvement** engages the cultivation of *emotional stability.*
       a. *Emotional stability* dissipates hardness of heart.
       b. *Emotional stability* supports patterns of good behavior.
   5. **Moral improvement** engages the *conscience* to monitor behavior.
       a. The *conscience* builds resistance to dissipation.
       b. The *conscience* disarms willful defiance of moral restraints.
       c. The *conscience* forbids indulgence in acts of impurity.
       d. The *conscience* reduces tendencies toward sensual vices.
 B. *Discipline* applies the ethics of **Jesus.**
   1. **Jesus** taught the regulation of human behavior by *truth.*
       a. *Truth* liberates people to obey God.
       b. *Truth* offers guidelines for moral behavior.
   2. **Jesus** taught against *indulgence* of deceitful lusts.
       a. Forbidden sensual *indulgence* is subject to self-denial.
       b. Forbidden sensual *indulgence* is subject to the Spirit's restraint.
   3. **Jesus** taught renewal of mind to identify the *regenerated.*
       a. The *regenerated* operate under motivation of divine grace.
       b. The *regenerated* operate under control of a renewed mind.
   4. **Jesus** taught godlikeness for *Christian behavior.*
       a. *Christian behavior* is characterized by righteousness.
       b. *Christian behavior* is characterized by holiness.

Conclusion

    We should be growing in moral improvements, raising the practices of current lifestyles to a higher level of living. Our lives should reflect our new nature in Christ. We must cope with the powerful influences in the pagan culture that surrounds us. Let us walk as children of light.

CHAPTER 24

Persuasion

Guidelines to Persuasion

Application brings truth to bear on the thought and conduct of persons. It is the natural sequence to the declaration of truth, showing how to make use of it in practical living. Persuasion is necessary to comply with the standards of biblical truth.

One way to persuade acceptance of the message is through appropriate illustrations. This awakens interest and attracts attention to the application. It also helps to achieve clarity, particularly in understanding the relation of Scripture to contemporary living.

Illustration can make an indirect application effective. It carries with it elements of persuasion. Occasionally it is appropriate to give one's own testimony. A story illustrating the successful results of a passage can be convincing.

A balance is needed between making certain that the gospel and its implications are known and giving recognition to the role that the individual and the Holy Spirit play in making application. Subtle, indirect applications have significant value and should therefore be developed along with the more common direct applications.[1]

Often this kind of approach is more persuasive. Reliance upon the Holy Spirit at that point is essential to making a permanent impact.

Much of our preaching is intended to be persuasive. Any given purpose that anticipates modifying attitudes or reinforcing convictions calls for a persuasive presentation of truth. It involves a conscious effort to influence thought and behavior.

Persuasion confronts people with realistic options. As a form of appeal to change, it calls for decision. Biblical history has many illustrations of divine efforts to influence the behavior of God's people. "Choose you this day whom you will serve" is the kind of communication that has in it an element of persuasion without coercion. This represents a valid approach with an obvious recommendation drawn from its context.

Three major goals are achieved by persuasive communication: (1) development of positive attitudes, (2) commitment to evangelical beliefs, and (3) adoption of Christian values. To reach these goals, persons in the audience should be led to recognize their own needs and to become involved in the communication process. The speaker will need to give attention to factors that will contribute to this motivation to change.

The application of truth to practice is a major function in preaching. W. W. Sangster says, "Application in homiletics means the pointed relation of the truth newly expressed in the lives of the people present."[2] The effectiveness of persuasion is enhanced when it is obvious that the speaker understands the immediate setting, the persons addressed, the times, the pressures of culture, and the needs of the current environment. The dynamic nature of its function in preaching makes persuasion a prominent feature in communication.

People are more inclined to accept an application if they think it is realistic. However, Christian truth is best expressed through a direct application to a specific issue, which may be controversial.

"Very few things are as persuasive as participation. If I hope to change behavior, I need to engage the other person in the process of change, and he shares in the task of persuading himself."[3] This principle applies also to addressing a congregation of worshipers. Persons can be given "ownership" by suggesting alternate proposals to resolve a given issue. Peruasion is achieved by giving the message in such a way as to allow people to respond in freedom.

Introduction to the Outline

The foregoing discussion of biblical authority forms the basis for confidence in the chosen text. This sermon contains a series of ethical standards for Christian behavior. As an expression of God's will in this matter, it represents what may be expected of the church.

The form in which these principles are presented calls for a series of points with less explanatory subdivisions. The speaker must carefully prepare each item on the list with a view to presenting concise explanations and illustrations in each case.

The outline represents an attempt to present clusters of truth, to enhance the discourse with "handles" to impress the audience in areas of ethical considerations. It will also assist the listener's memory.

When dealing with negative material, positive elements of experience point the way to satisfactory Christian experience. The outline provides a formulation of positive statements that together represent how to cope with evil.

Sermon 20
The Church with Christian Integrity
Ephesians 4:25—5:2

Introduction
This message focuses on the details of community conduct. There is a radical difference between the standards of an unregenerate society and those of the community of the redeemed. The ethics of the New Testament are unique in quality and motivation. They make a direct appeal to the enlightened conscience. They make vigorous demands upon the will. Much depends upon the group attitude to establish a corporate witness of faith. The predominant lifestyle of the group determines the strength of its witness.

Theme: The church purifies itself with Christian **integrity.**
A. **Integrity** marks the style of the **regenerated person.** (vv. 25-28)
   1. The **regenerated person** displaces falsehood with *truthfulness.*
      a. *Truthfulness* builds confidence.
      b. *Truthfulness* preserves unity.
   2. The **regenerated person** displaces resentment with *restraint.*
      a. *Restraint* averts potential evil.
      b. *Restraint* curtails satanic aggression.
   3. The **regenerated person** displaces stealing with *labor.*
      a. *Labor* involves stewardship of talent.
      b. *Labor* involves stewardship of possessions.
B. **Integrity** prevails in expressions of **new life.**
   1. The **new life** expresses itself with *wholesome speech.*
      a. *Wholesome speech* builds mutual confidence.
      b. *Wholesome speech* yields mutual benefits.
   2. The **new life** expresses itself with *Spirit sensitivity.*
      a. *Spirit sensitivity* promotes Christian assurance.
      b. *Spirit sensitivity* promotes divine guidance.
C. **Integrity** employs elements of a **new disposition.**
   1. A **new disposition** overcomes *negative feelings.*
      a. *Bitterness* is overcome by deliberate resolution.
      b. *Wrath* is overcome by foreclosing satanic dissension.
   2. A **new disposition** overcomes *persistent agitation.*
      a. *Brawling* is overcome by self-control over agitated impulses.
      b. *Anger* is overcome by self-discipline against selfish intent.
   3. A **new disposition** overcomes *compromise with evil.*
      a. *Slander* is overcome by the recognition of the rights of others.
      b. *Malice* is overcome by the cultivation of brotherhood.
D. **Integrity** motivates Christian practice in **new behavior.**
   1. The **new behavior** exercises social *graces.*
      a. It offers *kindness* to answer hostility.
      b. It offers *compassion* to answer futility.
   2. The **new behavior** exercises spiritual *privileges.*
      a. It extends *forgiveness* for offenses.
      b. It extends *love* for misdemeanor.
   3. The **new behavior** exercises loyal *devotion.*
      a. It offers the *life* for Christian discipleship.
      b. It offers the *service* for Christian witness.

Conclusion
   Our motivation to maintain moral integrity is found in:

1. A desire to hold faithfully our union with Christ in relation to the body of believers.
2. Determination to give no room to the devil in one's moral behavior.
3. Maintaining speech that does good to others.
4. Keeping a conscience sensitive to the Holy Spirit.
5. A life of love as a true child of God.

Word Meanings Essential to Interpretation

v. 25   *Therefore* refers to the basis of Christian doctrine in the preceding sections. This doctrine prepares the way for the Christian ethics that follows. Abstinence from sin and unalloyed zeal for what is right are now introduced. "Saving faith acts both as a solvent and a cement" (Simpson).

Falsehood is the practice of deception and fraud. It heads the list of debased moral standards.

Speak truthfully—a godly principle that counteracts evil.

Members of one body. This phrase introduces the believers' relationship to Christ. His people share a common life.

v. 26- *Anger and do not sin.* This calls for self-restraint. Although we are
27   not always responsible for how we *feel*, we are always responsible for how we *act* on our feelings. Note Psalm 4:4, "Stand in awe, and sin not" (KJV). In any circumstance of provocation, "give no handle to the adversary."

v. 28   *Share with those in need.* The entire verse is a mandate on stewardship. Financial support is to be earned honestly. Theft is always disreputable.

v. 29   *Helpful for building others* refers to the kind of talk that edifies others and that does not grieve the Holy Spirit. It warns against improprieties of speech.

v. 30   *Sealed.* This word is often misinterpreted to guarantee "eternal security." But Paul does not intend to imply irreversible status. The word in the Greek means "to set a mark upon by the impress of a seal, a stamp" (see Thayer). In this case it indicates that the gift of the Holy Spirit indicates who God's people are.

v. 31- *Forgiving each other.* The cross of Christ is set as an example. It "is
32   the sole medium of gospel forgiveness.... "The dimensions of sovereign grace overlap our aggregate inequities" (Simpson).

v. 5:1- *Imitators of God.* We are to walk in love as God loved us. This is a
2

characteristic of Christian living.

As Christ gave himself. The "offering" he gave was his incarnate life and atoning death. His sacrifice was a "slain offering."

Alternate Outline

This outline has two distinctions compared with sermon 20. First, this is a "running" commentary in which the points are made in consecutive divisions. Attention is given to each major ethical item with an accumulating effect. Second, the word *integrity* is conceived as a corporate virtue, an element that obtains in the church.

This illustrates the importance of determining a sermon's purpose. The interpretations are basically the same but the focuses are different. In the first, the purpose is to sensitize the church to the importance of maintaining integrity in moral choices. In this second approach, the purpose focuses on the necessity of exercising integrity in all areas of moral choice. Both are legitimate purposes; neither does violence to the meaning of the text.

Sermon 20-A
The Church Witnesses with Integrity
Ephesians 4:25—5:2

Introduction

New Testament ethics finds its application in the believer's daily life. No moral issue is exempt from the careful scrutiny of the church. The details of the Christian lifestyle are all subject to moral discipline. This message focuses on the personal practices that contribute to the integrity of the church. They have deep implications for an effective witness from the community of faith.

Theme: The church strengthens its witness with Christian **integrity.**
    A. The **integrity** of the church is supported by *truthfulness.*
       Christianity calls for living that is true.
       1. Speaking *truthfully* affects internal relationships.
       2. Speaking *truthfully* affects community relationships.
    B. The **integrity** of the church is supported by *self-control.*
       Christianity calls for control of the temper.
       1. *Uncontrolled* anger makes room for satanic control.
       2. *Uncontrolled* anger makes room for sinful conduct.

C. The **integrity** of the church is enhanced by *honesty*.
    Christianity calls for negotiations that are fair.
  1. *Honesty* permits no stealing.
  2. *Honesty* looks for dutiful employment.
  3. *Honesty* shares income with the needy.
D. The **integrity** of the church is confirmed by purity of *speech*.
    Christianity calls for clean speech.
  1. *Speech* expresses the quality of life.
  2. *Speech* expresses the quality of thought.
  3. *Speech* expresses the quality of influence.
E. The **integrity** of the church is upheld by positive *disposition*.
    Christianity calls for positive attitudes.
    A *positive* disposition deals with:
  1. Bitterness as a sinful attitude.
  2. Wrath as an evil passion.
  3. Anger as a sinful impulse.
  4. Clamor (brawling) as disreputable speech.
  5. Slander (railing) as a violation of peace.
  6. Malice as an evil disposition.
F. The **integrity** of the church is sustained by *compassion*.
    Christianity calls for the exercise of love.
  1. *Compassion* provides the context for kindness.
  2. *Compassion* provides a basis for forgiveness.
  3. *Compassion* provides the motivation for self-sacrifice.

Conclusion
    Our motivations are found in:
  1. Goodwill toward others.
  2. Determination to "resist the devil."
  3. Stewardship of caring.
  4. Sensitivity to the Holy Spirit.
  5. Cultivation of good feelings.
  6. Commitment to a life of love.

PART VI

Ephesians 5

Preaching Christian Ethics

Guidelines for Preaching Christian Ethics

The grace of God that brings salvation is available to all people. It teaches us to say no to ungodliness and worldly passions. It calls us to live with self-control, to be upright, to live godly lives in this present age. Redemption is designed to redeem us from all wickedness and to purify us for Christ to be a people that are his very own, eager to do what is good. These then are the things you should teach and preach. Encourage and rebuke with all authority.[1]

> Christianity has a distinctive ethic as well as theology, and the preacher can not escape a twofold responsibility. First, he must make clear the moral principles that are basic to Christian living. Second, he must guide his people in the application of these principles to personal and social problems.[2]

The gospel has ethical implications. The New Testament writers emphasized the meaning of salvation but not without reference to subsequent moral behavior. Some passages, like the one under consideration, speak to moral issues in specific human relationships. The outline that follows sustains biblical standards of sexual morality.

> We have a responsibility to expound God's standards with clarity and courage, and without compromise; and to exhort our own congregations to maintain and exhibit these standards with joyful faithfulness; also, to go on to commend them to the secular community.[3]

An essential factor on the preaching agenda is to help Christians know how to live with the pagan nature of contemporary society. The long list of evils that dominate current culture is a perennial challenge to our Christian witness. The most convincing testimony to the reality of Christian faith is the life of consistent morality.

There is a common tendency to preach in generalities. To become specific about certain evils requires a sound basis of biblical authority derived from eternal principles. The morality of daily life stems from the primary principles of faith and practice. "The New Testament epistles go into exact detail about morality because the first Christians needed to know how their love of Christ should affect their daily living. So do we. We need preachers who will help us see in specific terms what a Christian is"[4] and how a Christian behaves.

A major task in preaching is to relate the Word to human need and personal behavior.

> When we proclaim the gospel we must go on to unfold its ethical implications, and when we teach Christian behavior we must lay its gospel foundations. Christians need to grasp both that their faith in Christ has practical consequences and that the main incentive is actually personified in our moral teacher.[5]

In reference to the role of giving ethical advice, Chief Justice Earl Warren is quoted as saying that "that belongs to ministers of religion and is one of their greatest responsibilities."[6]

Christians are often confronted with the need to make responsible decisions on many matters affecting behavior. We need a Christian perspective with which to make our choices. We must remember that our bodies are the temple of the Holy Spirit. Human relationships and personal indulgences are open for constant review and discipline. Such matters as drinking alcohol, the use of tobacco, questionable amusements, styles of clothing, striving for affluence, and wasteful stewardship all have potential for evil. Among these is the challenge to exercise sexual control.

The message of the text under consideration in this chapter has some far-reaching implications upon personal piety and purity. Sexual morality is a major issue calling for an exposition of God's standards with clarity and courage, and without compromise.

"Christian morality releases us from cautious, crabbed ways and sets us free to live life to the full. The whole purpose of morality is to make life rich and joyful for us and for others."[7] This is particularly true of sexual morality. Good behavior in this respect adorns the doctrine of Christian marriage. (See sermon 23.) Domestic ethics affects family relationships.

Introduction to the Outline

Obviously this is one of those texts that requires delicate treatment. It deals with one of the most universal problems in social relationships. It is a subject, however, that needs the kind of proclamation that examines social practices under the light of Christian integrity. We may not bypass the subject simply because our conclusions may be unpopular.

To avoid impropriety in talking about sexual matters in public, it would be wise to approach the subject from a positive perspective. This can be done with the full assurance that one is representing the will of God for the welfare of believers. The frank statements of inspired Scripture here have divine authority.

The church has an obligation to exercise its influence for purity in Christian behavior in all vital human relationships. It may well be assumed that most in the audience want to know what the Scripture has to say about it. One should also represent marital sex as beautiful, honorable, and legitimate. It is the perversion that needs exposure.

Sermon 21
The Church and Christian Morality
Ephesians 5:3-7

Introduction

Fornication and every kind of impurity—let them not even be named among you who belong to Christ. Avoid silliness and indecent and filthy speech—which is unbecoming. Every fornicator or person of insatiable sex is thereby an idolater and does not have inheritance in the kingdom of God.

Let nobody lead you astray with words empty of truth and reason with reference to impurity and illegitimate sexual expression. Because of these things God's wrath is coming on the children of disobedience. [The above is a free translation of the text.]

Theme: The church expresses the will of God regarding *sexual morality.*

  A. *Sexual morality* calls for a **disciplined disposition.**

    1. Saints **witness** against immoral *dispositions.*

      a. A *disposition* that condones illegitimate sexual expressions must be disciplined.

      b. A *disposition* that approves promiscuous sex relations must be corrected.

    2. The church **holds** unclean persons under *censure.*

      a. The *censure* applies to persons who explore illegitimate forms of sexual expression.

      b. The *censure* applies to persons who accept the promiscuous sexual practices of the world.

    3. Believers **submit** covetous persons to **divine judgment.**

      a. God's **wrath** comes on those who are *disobedient.*

        (1) *Disobedience* involves sustained sexual fantasies

        (2) *Disobedience* involves indulgence of lustful desires.

      b. God's **wrath** comes on those who become partners in sexual *dissipation.*

        (1) *Dissipation* follows excessive indulgence of the flesh.

        (2) *Dissipation* involves sexual defilement.

  B. *Sexual morality* calls **holy people** to decency in speech.

    1. God's **holy people** avoid *filthy talk.*

      a. They refuse to engage in morally *degrading conversation.*

      b. They refuse to indulge in talk *offensive to virtue.*

      c. They refuse to hear injurious *remarks against morality.*

    2. God's **holy people** avoid *foolish talk.*

      a. They avoid using *veiled indecencies.*

b. They avoid degrading *references to sex.*
c. They refuse to be involved in *evil-minded chatter.*
3. God's **holy people** avoid *obscene jesting.*
   a. They avoid *offending* one's sense of propriety.
   b. They avoid *stimulating* evil imagery with course wit.
   c. They avoid *language* that turns to base suggestions.
C. **Sexual morality** calls for purity in **social behavior.**
1. Christian **standards** of **social behavior** support the mental *disciplining* of illicit sexual imaginations.
   a. They call for the *control* of daydreaming lustful desires.
   b. They *renounce* sensual greed for sexual indulgence.
   c. They *request abstinence* from imaginary sexual gratification.
2. Christian **standards** of **social behavior** uphold *restraint* in expressions of intimacy in male-female relationships.
   a. They *caution* against physical familiarities that induce sexual excitement.
   b. They *prohibit* social expressions that entertain lustful desires.
   c. They *urge* postponement of a "love-play" that stimulates sexual urges.
3. Christian **standards** of **social behavior** gives credence to sex within marriage.
   a. They protect the sacred function of *marital sex* from perversion.
   b. They preserve the sanctity of *marital sexual* intercourse.
   c. They promote the purity of *marital sexuality.*

Conclusion
    Sexual immorality misrepresents Christ in any profession of faith because it
   a. Debases spiritual aspects of legitimate sexual experience.
   b. Defiles social relationships that are intended to be wholesome.
   c. Destroys the nobility of pure interchange among males and females.

Word Meanings Essential to Interpretation

3 *Sexual immorality* refers to practices outside of wedlock which debase the nobler functions of sex. All forms of social sin involving sexual experience are contrary to Christian ideals and are opposed to life in the kingdom of God.
Greed (or *covetousness*) involves expressions of lustful desires and urges.

v. 4   *Obscenity* pertains to filthiness and evil-minded chatter.

Foolish talk is both folly and sinful.

Jesting refers to polished and witty speech, such as sly questions, smart answers, shrewd intimations, and acute nonsense.

v. 5   *Such a person is an idolater*, one who puts sex before moral values.

v. 6   *Empty* [or *vain*] *words* which condone heathen practices stem from thinking lightly of sexual offenses. Such things are brought under the judgment (wrath) of God.

Disobedient is a descriptive word that describes persons indulging in illicit sex experiences.

v. 7   *Partners* is a word that defines the association of persons who disregard the standards of Christian sexual morality.

Integrity in preaching

Preachers, of all people, must be sincere. They must mean what they say, and practice what they preach. Jesus warned his disciples against duplicity in believing one thing but doing something else. He condemned the Pharisees as persons who "tie up heavy loads and put them on men's shoulders, but they themselves are not willing to lift a finger to move them. They do not practice what they preach."[8] Any person who proclaims the gospel must have embraced it personally first. The one who preaches Christ must know Christ by experience. As Spurgeon once said, "A man can not only preach, he must also live."

Authentic preaching relates particularly to the use of Scripture. When one discovers the meaning of a passage, one is under obligation to convey that meaning to the audience. If in the course of one's study one finds that the passage does not express the intended message one should find another passage, one that supports the intended purpose. Or if the passage has been assigned, the nature of the message can be changed to conform to the meaning of the text.

In the use of Scripture the preacher's integrity is at stake. We may never make a passage support an idea that does not represent the meaning of the text.

People expect in the preacher high standards of morality. They also have a right to expect evidence of Holy Spirit's anointing. We cannot hide what we are. They expect to see in the preacher a model of spiritual maturity and moral integrity.

We admit that in being human we depend on God's forgiving and liberating grace. He knows that we are subject to frailty. He knows we are vulnerable to temptation and suffering. But there is a strangely fascinating power of influence emanating from those who are utterly sincere in performing their pulpit functions.

The apostle Paul allowed no room for deception. In his testimony to the Corinthian church he said, "We have renounced secret and shameful ways; we do not use deception, nor do we distort the Word of God. On the contrary, by setting forth the truth plainly, we commend ourselves to every man's conscience in the sight of God."[9] Personal conviction, consistency of conduct, and rejection of deceitful disguise are standards that apply to the whole preaching ministry. "There was nothing in Paul's lifestyle which hindered his hearers from believing.... They believed him because he was believable. What he said and what he was were all of a piece."[10] The positive influence of being a thoroughly Christian person in and out of the pulpit goes beyond human measure. As Stott put it, "Hypocrisy always repels, but integrity or authenticity always attracts."

Authenticity has particular application to the message. A strict honesty in the use of Scripture commends the message to an audience with divine authority. In the case of preaching on sexual morality, as in the outline above, more is involved than mere human opinion. Many pagan voices in the world undermine commitment to moral standards of purity. These can be answered by proclamation of truth from the Word of God.

Phillip Brooks once said, "A preacher is in some degree, a reproduction of the truth in personal form." The preacher is a channel of divine truth to express the will of God and should preach with a sanctified enthusiasm. The preacher should model, for instance, control over sex urges. In addition to the sermons' warning against immorality, the preacher's life can serve as a model for the beauty and strength of moral integrity.

There is no need to fear criticism for preaching about private practices in such matters as sexual behavior. As Stott says, "To teach the standards of moral conduct which adorn the gospel is neither legalism nor pharisaism but plain apostolic Christianity."[11] As such we are under obligation to preach the whole truth and nothing but the truth. Being taught how to live does not mean salvation can be "earned" by good behavior. On the contrary, being saved makes a significant difference in human behavior. The children of God are called to a life of purity. We live and serve for the glory of God.

CHAPTER 26

Communication

Guidelines to Communication

The secret of successful preaching is in communication. We must remind ourselves again and again of the perpetual question, "What does the preacher mean?" We must remember that we have not communicated effectively until people in the audience have understood.

Ineffectiveness in communication can sometimes be traced to an improper attitude in the speaker. Just as communication with God depends upon right relationship with him, so communication with an audience is effected by that relationship. Love *(agapē)* is the key to establishing open relationships with God and with people.

The church is a place for understanding the truth and identifying with it. The community of faith offers healing for broken relationships. Its loyal commitment to Christ in preaching and practice removes a primary barrier to communication. The text for this chapter focuses on living as children of light. That light shining upon the "fruitless deeds of darkness" opens the way for people to understand "what pleases the Lord."

The gospel message to be communicated is by its very nature spiritual. These texts in Ephesians with their moral implications speak to our union with Christ. They clearly reflect the context of Christian brotherhood. They are positive in their pronouncements and imperative in their address regarding moral issues. The challenge to the preacher is to communicate their meanings clearly and in the power of the Spirit.

Expository sermons can reflect the same variety that exists in the Bible itself. In the course of this sermon series from Ephesians, we are challenged to communicate ideas, doctrines, emotions, propositions, values, commands, appeals, and expressions of encouragement.

The communication of biblical truth goes beyond the territory of verbal expression. It relies upon the effects of regeneration. The new life in Christ makes the mind amenable to divine truth. Ultimately, this depends on forces outside the human ability to communicate. "The primary author of an effective transmission of the message is the Holy Spirit."[1] The Spirit operates both in the preacher and in the audience. By preaching the Word we bring people into a confrontation with Christ so the Spirit can work in them an awareness and conviction of sin, righteousness, and judgment.

> Communication is . . . the lifeblood of the church. It is inherent in the message. Persuasive, convicing communication is its great task under all circumstances and situations. The reason that communication has become a great problem is that the church is experiencing the evident lack of persuasive and convincing power. . . . The search is on for a more effective presentation and communication.[2]

In the proclamation of divine truth we must be prepared to face unsympathetic reaction. The gospel is a scandal to self-confident human wisdom. It goes against the natural person. But it has power to change the believing soul who responds to the Spirit's call.

Even though the best communication of the Word does not guarantee success, we must continue to proclaim its message. It promises eternal life to all who receive and believe it. It also declares judgment against those who reject it. When that attitude persists, the heart becomes hardened.

This means we must recognize the active forces of evil. We are confronted with the influences of "principalities and powers" as well as the direct interventions of Satan himself. But we should do all within our reach to communicate the will of God in the most persuasive form.

Introduction to the Outline

This outline covers various aspects of the Christian influence upon the non-Christian society. It presents a challenge to expose the "fruitless deeds of darkness" by living as children of light. It affirms the standards Jesus expressed in his Sermon on the Mount. As John R. W. Stott says, "If the church realistically accepted his standards and values as there set forth, and lived by them, it would be the alternative society he always intended it to be, and would offer to the world an authentic Christian counter-culture."[3]

One recent author has stated in sharp relief the gospel call of this passage:

> Are we prepared to live as Christ's distinctively called out community? We have much to gain by allowing the Holy Spirit to develop in us a Christ-centered life-style. If true believers fail to offer a positive and constructive resistance to the modern mindset and life-style, we will continue to see the breakdown of our families and ... will compromise our ethical conduct and morality.[4]

This text offers an opportunity to undergird a Christian faith that makes a difference in moral behavior. Observe the theme which asserts that social purity in the church expresses moral light. That light is needed today. Let this sermon do its part in promoting the "fruit of the light" to make Christianity visible.

Sermon 22
The Church and Its Moral Witness
Ephesians 5:8-14

Introduction

W. O. Carver's paraphrase of Ephesians 5:6-7 brings out the essence of its message:

Let nobody lead you astray with words empty of truth and reason with reference to all this category of impurity and sex expression [vv. 3-7] for it is just because of these things that the very wrath of God comes upon sons of disobedience, persons who in selfish and fleshly abandon are so ready to disobey all moral and religious restraints [and thus are] called children of disobedience. Do not then permit yourselves to become partners in their shame and sharers in their doom.

Theme: Social purity expresses *moral light.*
A. *Moral light* defines the Christian **way.**
   1. It is a **way** of *goodness.*
      a. *Goodness* counteracts evil desires.
      b. *Goodness* respects the consequences of behavior.
   2. It is a **way** of *righteousness.*
      a. *Righteousness* means conforming to the will of God.
      b. *Righteousness* means adhering to principles of moral purity.
      c. *Righteousness* means avoiding evil associates.
   3. It is a **way of** *truth.*
      a. The way of *truth* applies principles of purity.
      b. The way of *truth* establishes patterns of self-control.
B. *Moral light* reproves the works of **darkness.**
   1. Works of **darkness** are reproved by *moral practices.*
      a. *Moral practices* expose social evils.
      b. *Moral practices* condemn immoral conduct.
   2. Works of **darkness** are reproved by *purity of life.*
      a. *Purity of life* reflects light on evil intentions.
      b. *Purity of life* throws light on secret behavior.
C. *Moral light* emanates from **Christ.**
   1. The light of **Christ** shines through the *believer.*
      a. The *believer* seeks to know the Lord's will.
      b. The *believer* seeks to do the Lord's will.
   2. The light of **Christ** shines in the *church.*
      a. The *church* respects the headship of Christ in moral discrimination.
      b. The *church* observes the lordship of Christ in moral decisions.

D. *Moral light* makes visible **God's pleasure.**
1. **God's pleasure** is seen in the *believer's behavior.*
   a. The *believer's behavior* promotes principles of purity.
   b. The *believer's behavior* practices principles of purity.
2. **God's pleasure** is conveyed through a *believer's understanding.*
   a. *Believers understand* moral issues.
   b. *Believers understand* moral controls.
3. **God's pleasure** is expressed through a *believer's influence.*
   a. The believer's moral *influence* is regulated by divine truth.
   b. The believer's moral *influence* is effected by divine power.

Conclusion

You are light in the Lord. Live as children of light. The light makes everything visible. Moral light manifests purity. Christ will shine on you.

Word Meanings Essential to Interpretation

8   *Darkness.* Refer to John 1:5 for this and for the word *light.* It characterizes the status of the unbeliever. This has implications for social influence.

   Light. This designation of the believer is a signal of relationship with Christ who is "the light of the world" (John 8:12). It is the dominant concept of this text.

9   *The fruit of the light* is expressed in terms of personal character (goodness), social dealings (righteousness), and principles of behavior (truth). They mark obligations to self, to our neighbors, and to God.

10   *What pleases the Lord.* The phrase encapsules the ultimate fulfillment of faith, the focal point of moral investigation.

11   *Fruitless deeds* are those which yield no blessings. Self-originated sinful deeds have no "fruit," although they have consequences. Christians must not only avoid evil; they are to expose them (cf. John 3:20).

12   The offenses of *disobedience* are to be exposed. Shameful behavior is condemned.

13   *Everything.* All the secret sins—when they are shown to be what they really are—are to be reproved. Darkness perishes in the presence of light, which in itself is a purifying force. The person who receives the light of Christ reflects it (cf. John 3:20-21).

14   *Rise from the dead* appears to be a free rendering of Isaiah 26:19. It

conveys the idea of awaking from sleep to rise to action. The relation of the believer to Christ engages the light of eternal life.

Entrusted with the Gospel

A particular responsibility rests on all who are engaged in preaching. Being entrusted with the gospel means being a guardian of the truth and appealing to believers to apply Scripture to their daily lives. This word is to be communicated under God's anointing.

God trusts the preacher to deliver his word. He trusted his Son to provide the *means* of redemption. Now he trusts his messengers to deliver the *message* of redemption. With this consideration we use the example of the apostle Paul as reflected in his first letter to the Thessalonians.

Preaching calls for *courage* and *care*.

> You know, brothers, that our visit to you was not a failure. We had previously suffered and been insulted in Philippi, as you know, but with the help of our God we dared to tell you his gospel in spite of strong opposition. For the appeal we make does not spring from error or impure motives, nor are we trying to trick you. On the contrary, we speak as men approved by God to be entrusted with the gospel. We are not trying to please men but God, who tests our hearts.[5]

Paul preached with boldness. That required courage from him that was refined by the spirit of caring. He was determined to tell the good news in spite of opposition. Suffering and insult did not deter him from his commission.

We, too, are required to proclaim the truth regardless of circumstances. Where there is opposition, whether assumed or declared, we are entrusted with the gospel. Its message must be delivered without apology. When confronted with a sensitive message or delicate contemporary issues, we need to speak with courage and care. Even with sermons that deal with "private" matters like sexual morality, we are expected to be courageous and appropriate.

Preaching calls for *confidence* and *concern*. We have confidence in the Word. Our concern is directed toward the common good. Back of the need to be informed is the need to be inspired by the truth of moral benefits. Purity of motive in dealing with such matters is essential to effectiveness in communication. The urge to preach must not derive from any form of deceit or of uncleanness. The sermon is not an occasion for craftiness or human eloquence. It is to be given in the power of the Holy Spirit with a conscious effort to please God and to accomplish his purposes. The confidence in the Scriptures rests on the assurance that faithful proclamation of the Word will accomplish some purpose for the glory of God. We are entrusted with this divine instrument to achieve spiritual realities.

Preaching is to be done with divine *power* and Christian *piety* (see vv. 5-6). Paul renounced the use of flattery and worldly devices to manipulate human reaction. Preaching must derive its force from plainness of speech and clarity of thought. The gospel with which the preacher is endowed can be communicated only as it is communicated with pious intentions. The Word of God invades the moral realm of human choices. So we use it to stir up the minds of committed people to reach a higher level of faith. Sincerity in this resolution is based on a genuine desire to please God and to glorify the name of Jesus.

Preaching requires expressions of *love* and consistency of *life* (see vv. 7-8). Paul had a sympathetic and self-sacrificing love for people. He was a man of tenderness and tears, an outgoing person. For us, when we preach, a tender regard for the audience conditions the spirit of the message. When offering the benefits of the gospel, an affectionate desire imparts the soul along with the message. The effectiveness of the sermon depends a great deal upon the effectiveness of the person who delivers it. Much rests on self-giving out of love, making the message convey an authentic appeal. Meeting human need has always impressed people when they sense the motivation of love behind it. Serving in the name of Christ is the key.

Preaching involves spiritual *insight* and moral *integrity* (see vv. 9-10). There has to be a demonstration of the message we preach. Referring to his own life and practice Paul said, "Surely you remember, brothers, our toil and hardship; we worked night and day in order not to be a burden to anyone while we preached the gospel of God to you. You are witnesses, and so is God, of how holy, righteous and blameless we were among you who believed." The stress here is on the divine nature of the message and the supporting character of his own life.

"We communicate by life more than we communicate by language." To live in holiness is to have a deep religious motivation, preaching out of a sense of call and a desire to do the will of God. Righteousness (justice) means living and serving in conformity to God's will. To be blameless is to perform our duties without cause for reproach. Transparency of life is a convincing witness.

Persons who preach with both *word* and *work* reflect the anointing of God. Paul said, "You know that we dealt with each of you as a father deals with his own children, encouraging, comforting and urging you to live lives worthy of God, who calls you into his kingdom and glory" (vv. 11-12). To carry out his commission, he exhorted persons, comforting them and charging them to faithfulness in their commitment to Christ. Without a commission, preaching becomes a mere propaganda. The risen Christ commissioned the apostles to be witnesses of his resurrection to the ends of the earth. Inner compulsion mixed with the Spirit's anointing makes preaching a dynamic event. God has trusted us to declare his offer to forgive and to transform all who repent and believe. This is an urgent call. "Woe is me, if I preach not the gospel."

Finding the Message

Guidelines to Finding the Message

Every biblical text contains a fact or principle that has relevance to human behavior. After choosing a text, one needs to identify the crucial issue identified by that particular passage.

Since this series of sermon outlines is taken from the book of Ephesians, we are already committed to using its focus on the church. Next we must focus an issue more sharply. This particular passage speaks to Christian morality.

After having determined these two factors, we must identify which existing moral needs this sermon answers. That will help to determine what elements of truth exist in this passage that throw light on moral behavior in the church.

Preaching requires a sensitive awareness of needs among the

people. To be able to communicate the Word effectively, one must know something of the background and circumstances of people in the audience. If one is not informed of the nature of the anticipated audience, one must project an audience image that represents general and specific needs. The text will then be addressed to an average group of assembled people. The average audience is made up of diverse interests and varied spiritual experiences. Therefore the major emphasis will be determined by the content of the text.

In the outline that follows, most of the main concepts are drawn directly from the text. Even the subordinate elements are taken from the wording in the Scripture. Thus the biblical material forms the basis of the message. The crucial task is to relate these meanings to the assumed needs of the audience.

The reverse approach is also valid. One can take the anticipated needs of the people and find the elements of truth in the text that speak to those specific needs.

During this process of analysis and arrangement of material, the purpose of the sermon becomes more clear. Once it is sharply defined, the development of the message can move forward. At the same time we must work toward achieving unity by developing a distinctive line of thought. In this outline it is designated as "moral wisdom."

The nature of the message is communicated through the title, the theme, or both. The use of both is illustrated in the outline that follows. The title "The Church and Moral Wisdom" and the theme "the church exercises wisdom in moral issues" both carry the dominant thought combining morality with wisdom. These are used as descriptive elements of the church.

Besides suggesting what the sermon is about, the title should attract interest. For that reason it is designed for public announcement. It also serves as a guide in preparing the sermon. Generally the purpose is more fully stated in the theme (proposition). In any case, the title should be stated in few words. It should not promise more than the sermon can deliver.

The nature of a particular sermon is determined by two factors: the content of the text and the needs of the audience. After linking the needs of the church with the counsel of Scripture, the preacher can deliver the resulting message with confidence. The preacher's purpose must reflect a balance in matching the interpretation of Scripture and the needs of the congregation.

Introduction to the Outline

This portion of Scripture is rich in its breadth of interest. Observe the contrast it contains:

wise and unwise
evil days and opportunities for good
foolishness and God's will
drunkenness and Spirit fullness

Additional phrases suggest other foci for a sermon:

group unity for interchange
music in the heart
gratitude to the Father
in the name of Jesus
reverence for Christ

Among these we have chosen a message about the church and its moral wisdom. In order to unify the message, other great concepts are incorporated regarding moral integrity in the church. This is another illustration of selecting a theme to fit into the series on the church.

While analyzing this text, it is good to keep in mind the context which speaks to the point of sexual morality. This passage extends our previous discussion about ethical values. It also emphasizes domestic purity.

Sermon 23
The Church and Moral Wisdom
Ephesians 5:15-21

Introduction

The call to carefulness in living involves moral discernment. It helps to shape and walk in the light of sound ethical principles. It affects attitudes, behavior, and personal responsibility. It requires a search for resources with which to make moral decisions.

The standards of Christian conduct need visibility. The application of truth needs spiritual courage. This passage throws light on both truth and commitment in the Christian walk. It lays a foundation of faith for victorious living.

Theme: The church exercises ***wisdom*** in moral decisions.
  A. ***Wisdom*** uses opportunities to exert **moral influence.** (v. 16)
     1. **Moral influence** counteracts *current evils.*
        a. *Current evils* are identified by spiritual discernment.
        b. *Current evils* are overcome by consistent living.
     2. **Moral influence** supports religious *reform.*
        a. The *reform* is directed to practicing social ethics.
        b. The *reform* is directed to adopting ethical standards.
  B. ***Wisdom*** exercises diligence in applying **moral standards.** (v. 17)
     1. **Moral standards** are set by the *will of God.*
        a. The *will of God* measures the dangers of world standards.
        b. The *will of God* sets the order of moral behavior.
     2. **Moral standards** are expressed in the *Word* of God.
        a. The *Word* is a handbook for moral guidance.
        b. The *Word* is the authority for ethical distinctions.
  C. ***Wisdom*** finds resources to activate **moral dynamics.** (v. 18)
     1. **Moral dynamics** are sustained by *self-discipline.*
        a. *Self-discipline* controls evil tendencies.
        b. *Self-discipline* supports moral ideals.
     2. **Moral dynamics** are released by the *Holy Spirit.*
        a. The *Spirit* prompts righteous judgments in moral decisions.
        b. The *Spirit* gives power to resist temptations.
     3. **Moral dynamics** are vitalized by devotional *experience.*
        a. *Experience* with God sensitizes the conscience.
        b. *Experience* with Scripture provides moral wisdom.
  D. ***Wisdom*** uses group unity to celebrate **moral integrity.** (vv. 19-20)
     1. **Moral integrity** is affirmed by *spiritual interchange.*
        a. *Spiritual interchange* expresses psalms of faith.
        b. *Spiritual interchange* expresses songs of joy.
        c. *Spiritual interchange* expresses hymns of adoration.
     2. **Moral integrity** releases feelings of *gratitude.*
        a. *Gratitude* covers appreciation for divine grace.
        b. *Gratitude* covers appreciation for divine wisdom.
     3. **Moral integrity** is maintained in the *name of Christ.*
        a. The *name of Christ* represents divine power.
        b. The *name of Christ* authorizes divine witness.

E. **Wisdom** engages corporate submission in **moral commitment.** (v. 21)
  1. **Moral commitments** are supported by the interaction of the *believing community.*
    a. The *believing community* creates a context for moral support.
    b. The *believing community* offers lines of corrective influence.
  2. **Moral commitment** is clarified by the interaction of the *believing community.*
    a. The *believing community* interaction develops moral consensus.
    b. The *believing community* interaction affirms moral decisions.

Conclusion
  Morality in the church is seen in the character and conduct of its members.
  Moral integrity is evidence of the Spirit's presence and power.
  Respect for Christ determines the wisdom of moral choices.

Word Meanings Essential to Interpretation

. 15   *Be very careful.* The seriousness of their circumstance made it urgent that the Ephesian Christians "watch their steps." Their walk demanded exactitude.

  How you live (walk) pertains to the witness Christians give in a misguided world.

  Wise, unwise. These modifiers refer to the meaning of living.

. 16   *Make the most of opportunity* (redeem the time). This phrase carries the concept of "buying up opportunity." *This is the time to act.* "Make the most of every opportunity" (cf. Col. 4:15) because there is only a limited time for service and the times are precariously evil.

. 17   *Foolish, understand.* This calls for prudence in behavior and witness. Instead of an intellectual exercise, it calls for faithful stewardship of time (cf. Matt. 11:25).

  Will of the Lord. The supreme consideration in life is *God's will.*

. 18   *Drunk with wine* deplores licentious behavior and warns against such indulgence.

  Filled with the Spirit is discussed under the final section of this chapter. Christianity is a counterculture that exposes the futility of riotous living.

. 19   *Speak to one another* refers to joyful interchange within the church. E. K. Simpson says, "The first title suggests the Davidic Psalter, the second, effusions of praise, the third, lyrics of a general description."[1] This reflects the fervor of Christians being filled with the Spirit. See the treatment of the phrase *in the heart* in the guidelines section above. "Hearts must be in harmony with their words."

v. 20   *Giving thanks to God.* Westcott says, "The intense quickening of the higher life shows itself in many ways: in the joy of [interpersonal relations], in personal feeling, in thanksgiving to God, in mutual consideration."[2] Gratitude deserves a major emphasis in the sermon.

v. 21   *Submit.* Personal rights give way to the rights of others. Even secular rights are to be subordinated out of "reverence for Christ." In this mutual subjection there is a corporate suggestion that the church stands with moral integrity and operates with Christian motives.

Alternate Outline

To develop a message from a given text, one needs to make a preliminary analysis of the passage. The outline above illustrates how the message took shape around the significance of wisdom in coping with ethical issues. On another occasion one might develop a sermon around the phrase "Understanding the Will of God." Another approach to this same passage could emphasize the "Fullness of the Spirit."

The phrase "sing and make music in your heart" stands out in this passage. The following sermon carries the title "The Secret of a Singing Heart." The theme is "the secret of a singing heart is in knowing God's will." The main divisions and first subpoints are as follows:

Sermon 23-A
The Secret of a Singing Heart

A. Live with discernment. (vv. 15-17)
   1. Keep a sharp lookout on how you relate to society.
   2. Buy up opportunities to challenge evil.
   3. Understand God's will.
B. Live by the Spirit. (v. 18)
   1. The need for stimulation is fulfilled by the Spirit.
   2. The need for inspiration is supplied by the Spirit.

3. The need for security is achieved by the Spirit.
4. The need for expression is satisfied by the Spirit.
  a. Speaking to ourselves in group unity is discipling.
  b. Singing among ourselves is edifying.
C. Live in submission. (v. 21)
1. The spirit of submission upholds church welfare.
2. The spirit of submission conditions corporate witness.
3. The spirit of submission supports ethical values.

Conclusion
  "The joy of the Lord is your strength" (Neh. 8:10)
  Reverence for Christ is in your purpose.
  Gratitude to God is included in your benevolence.

The Fullness of the Spirit

To be filled by the Spirit is to be dominated by divine wisdom and power. It means to be controlled by God's will. In all matters of choice we are to be directed by the Holy Spirit. Living in the Spirit is essential to fulfilling the will of God. It is a normal expectation of God's messengers.

Spirit fullness is supernatural in its origin. It is achieved by divine action. The human elements are conditions that open the channels of Spirit action. It begins with the desire for a fuller and richer life. Fullness of the Spirit vitalizes our profession of faith in Jesus Christ and requires our renunciation of the world. It brings the believer into a position where the fullness of divine blessing can be received. The will must be brought to the point of yieldedness to God.

Being filled by the Spirit is normative for Christian experience. Although receiving the Spirit is a definite and completed act, the infillings become habitual. One must keep on abiding in Christ. We trust him for a perpetual intercession at God's throne. Requests for fresh infillings are requested in the name of Jesus. God's response is power to serve. It enables the believer to cope with evil forces that stand in the way of an effective witness.

The evidences of the Spirit are many. It is expressed in the kind of spiritual fervor that emanates from an inner experience with God. The outward effect is realized in demonstrations of obedience. It is expressed in a spirit of mutual submission among the believers. Bearing with one another and sharing together in the common cause lifts the gospel to a level of attraction. Collective living and serving is characterized by this mutual loyalty in loving and being loved.

In the preacher this fullness is to be manifested in the suppression of self-assertions. It opens the way for counsel and cooperation. It involves a denial of selfish interests to give priority to the spiritual needs of others.

We are called to lose our lives in the larger concerns for the spiritual health of the faith community. Our brothers and sisters must be regarded as having more importance in the kingdom than ourselves. This kind of self-giving makes room for the fullness of the Spirit to flow through human relationships. Ours is a caring ministry.

The cultivation of fullness follows dedication to Christ. "Do this out of reverence for Christ" (v. 21). Spirit-fullness finds itself activated by mutual fellowship among the believers. Submission to one another is prompted by submission to God. Obedience is the key to finding favor with him, and faith is the act of appropriating his grace.

The whole of life must be brought under the constraint of divine control. In that position we can realize the Spirit's wisdom and power. In prayer we find the power to cope with the forces of evil.

Messages like the one outlined above, along with sermons (numbers 21 and 22) from this same context, call for sharp sensitivity to today's moral needs. As we put the fullness of the Spirit into action, we may expect to see an improvement in the purity of the church.

In writing to the Ephesians, Paul makes some weighty remarks about the unique relationship between the believer and the divine will. We become children of God "in accordance with his pleasure and will, to the praise of his glorious grace" (1:5). We are advised of the mystery of his will according to his good pleasure (1:9). He will "gather together all things in Christ" (2:21). We were chosen in Christ "who works out everything in conformity with the purpose of his will" (2:11). His inheritance will be shared with those who hope in Christ (1:14).

The purpose of God's will is "to show the exceeding riches of his grace through Christ" (2:7). The wisdom of that will is now made known in the church according to his eternal purpose in Christ (3:9-10). The intent of this holy will is to shape the believer after the character of God, "in true righteousness and holiness" (4:24).

This brings us to the privilege of living (or walking) with God to make the most of every opportunity to witness for him (5:15). Knowing God's will in this regard calls for consistent living. Understanding the will of God calls for appropriate action. Redeeming the time involves the exercise of gifts, the circumstances of vocation, and the opportunities for worship. The urgency to act is prescribed by "evil days."

CHAPTER 28

Sermon Objectives

> *Guidelines*
> *Introduction to the Outline*
> *Outline:* The Church and Marital Harmony
>   Ephesians 5:22-33 (Sermon 24)
> *Word Meanings Essential to Interpretation*
> *General Objectives*

Guidelines to Sermon Objectives

In a previous discussion of guidelines (chap. 6), attention was given to "purpose" in preaching. There, an emphasis was placed on choosing a purpose early, since it affects the selection and treatment of material for the sermon. The section also refers to the influence this selection has upon the progression of thought in the message. In this discussion the focus is on what happens *after* the sermon is delivered. Therefore we turn to a consideration of the ultimate objective.

A preacher enters the pulpit to meet an evident need, not just to explain a passage of Scripture. While this explanation is essential to preaching, the major task is to use the Word to accomplish a practical spiritual objective. Sermons are intended to have results, especially in meeting human needs.

Whatever explanation is given about the meaning of the text, it serves to form a basis of conviction about some aspect of human behavior. The sermon makes proposals about what to do with the meaning of Scripture and how to go about achieving its goal. The purpose has to be to convince the mind and heart of truth, and to move the will to action.

Often preaching is designed, not so much to inform people about what they do not know, but to motivate response to what they do know. This does not negate the importance of knowing the truth. Rather, it underscores the importance of change in persons. It aims to prod the will to make application of truth to personal needs.

The needs of a congregation are diverse, arising as they do from individual circumstances and a variety of personal experiences. For that reason it is difficult to establish priorities in determining current needs. We must rely upon promptings from the Holy Spirit to determine the most essential factors to be included in the sermon. Even though we may project an opinion about what the sermon should accomplish, we need to be open to other possibilities that may emerge during the process of preparation.

When a series of sermons is drawn from a single book in the Bible, the text is predetermined by its location in the chosen series. The text must then be matched to specific needs in the congregation. Conversely, elements of truth in the text can be compiled to meet a general (or even a specific) need in the congregation. In either case, the meaning of the text should speak to a need in the congregation.

The homiletical purpose is a major concern in developing the message. The purpose may be determined by the awareness of a specific need, or it may be found in the text itself. In either case the sermon is designed to meet a need.

For the sake of coherence, a choice of purpose will need to be made from among several dominant ideas in a passage. That element of truth best suited to meet the specific need will provide the theme.

A single passage of Scripture may be the seedbed of several themes. A particular need observed in the community may determine which idea becomes the focal point. It is not necessary to use all of these ideas—only those that contribute to the meeting of the identified need.

When one identifies a specific objective for a sermon, one also identifies the expected results. The ultimate goal of the sermon relates to what can be accomplished in the life of the hearers.

It is always helpful to determine as nearly as possible what the writer's intention was by including the context of a chosen passage. The writer's intention may have been to meet a particular need of that time, one which is not duplicated in form in our day. In that case we must discover the principle involved and apply it to our current culture.

This is illustrated in the particular passage under consideration in this chapter. Although cultural patterns of the Ephesians are not currently duplicated in form, the principles expressed in the epistle are applicable in today's marital relationships. For that reason we take seriously the pattern of marital harmony for the church and family today.

The procedure for this aspect of sermon preparation is as follows:

1. Select a text suited to a specific purpose. (In this case the text is determined by the series.)

2. Ascertain what purpose it served originally.

3. Identify what need it can meet today.

4. Select material that achieves that purpose.

5. Arrange the material according to an adopted aim.

6. Embody an appeal in line with the purpose.

It is important to remember that the sermon is intended to bring an answer to some specific human need. The preacher stands between what the Bible has to offer in achieving a particular purpose and the particular need identified in human experience. As we stand behind the pulpit to proclaim divine truth, we are under a commission to declare what God has to say about human need.

Introduction to the Outline

This particular passage appears to have a simple structure. It has been divided into two parts, the "submission of the wife" and the "love of the husband." But other elements of truth are intermingled with these two phrases. Observe the prominence of Christ, whose name occurs five times, and that of the church, which is mentioned six times. And, of course, the concept of marriage is related to all four of the above—wife, husband, Christ, and church. Since all five are so intricately interwoven throughout the passage, the order of thoughts does not follow in direct succession within the text.

Because these themes are so closely related, it is hard to put them into a consistent sermon structure. Finding a coherent pattern, such as we seek to obtain in this sermon, is a repeated challenge.

A further complication in this text is the fact that each concept can be expanded into a full sermon. This puts us back to the starting point to decide what objective is to be achieved. The purpose will determine which concept to use as the point of emphasis. For illustrative purposes we submit the following possible titles: (1) Christ Loves the Church, (2) The Church Is the Body of Christ, (3) The Role of the Wife, (4) The Responsibilities of the Husband, (5) Two Become One Flesh, and (6) The Church and Marital Harmony.

I have chosen the latter for three reasons: (1) this is one message in a series on the church, (2) the immediate context is devoted to domestic realities, and (3) it offers an enriched backdrop for the consideration of marital harmony.

The closing statement of the text for sermon 23 sets the stage for consideration of the family relationships promoted in this text. The call for members of the church to submit to one another introduces the particular nature of conjugal relationships. Here the foundation of an ordered community of faith rests on a vital relationship with Christ in the marriage union. In this text we see the true significance, order, and symmetry of the family in a Christian society. With this sermon we commend Christian ideals and standards worthy of our profession of faith.

Sermon 24
The Church and Marital Harmony
Ephesians 5:22-33

Introduction

Marriage provides for the fulfillment of divine purpose. God has designed this means of propagation for the human race. Marriage also provides for the fulfillment of legitimate human desires. In this relationship husband and wife can share in life's deepest secrets. When harmony prevails they heal each other's wounds, meet each other's needs, and enrich each other's lives.

Theme: Marital harmony is enriched through living **in Christ.**

A. **In Christ** the wife is conditioned for **submission.**

   1. **Submission** is motivated by regard for *Christ.*

     a. *Christ* demonstrates trustworthiness for submission.

     b. *Christ* identifies the blessedness of submission.

   2. **Submission** is demonstrated in the relation of the *church* to Christ.

     a. The *church* is made holy through the Word.

     b. The *church* is made radiant through divine grace.

   3. **Submission** is based on the husband's *fidelity.*

     a. *Fidelity* is expressed in conjugal faithfulness.

     b. *Fidelity* is expressed in conjugal intimacy.

B. **In Christ** the husband finds a pattern of **loving.**

   1. **Love** is manifested in *self-giving.*

     a. *Self-giving* finds ways of caring.

     b. *Self-giving* finds ways of sharing.

   2. **Love** is manifested in *self-sacrifice.*

     a. *Self-sacrifice* is expressed in domestic support.

     b. *Self-sacrifice* is expressed in moral support.

   3. **Love** is motivated by strength of the wife's *character.*

     a. Strength of *character* induces moral confidence.

     b. Strength of *character* offers marital stability.

     c. Strength of *character* supports emotional security.

C. **In Christ** marriage constitutes a **marital union.**

   1. A **marital union** involves physical *intimacy.*

     a. Physical *intimacy* involves mutual attraction.

     b. Physical *intimacy* involves mutual possession.

     c. Physical *intimacy* involves mutual appreciation.

   2. A **marital union** involves social *understandings.*

     a. Social *understandings* develop mutual interests.

     b. Social *understandings* develop mutual affection.

     c. Social *understandings* develop mutual aspirations.

   3. A **marital union** involves spiritual *commitments.*

     a. *Commitments* to mutual loyalty become fixed.

     b. *Commitments* to common ideals become deeper.

     c. *Commitments* to mutual exaltation of Christ establishes vocation.

D. **In Christ** marriage **symbolizes** spiritual realities.

   1. Marriage **symbolizes** Christ's headship in the *church.*

     a. The *church* functions as Christ's body of truth.

     b. The *church* functions as Christ's mission of redemption.

   2. Marriage **symbolizes** Christ's *love* for the church.

     a. *Love* reflects a profound mystery.

    b. *Love* establishes a permanent covenant.

    c. *Love* expresses itself in tender caring.

  3. Marriage **symbolizes** Christ's *commitment* to the church.

    a. *Commitment* engages reciprocal duties.

    b. *Commitment* engages reciprocal devotion.

Conclusion

    Marital harmony is achieved and sustained by simple rules of domestic interaction:

  1. Demonstrate mutual affection.

  2. Express mutual appreciation.

  3. Share common interests.

  4. Pursue common aspirations.

  5. Show concern for each other's spirituality.

Word Meanings Essential to Interpretation

22   *Submit.* This is the same word used in the preceding verse. There it identifies all members of the Christian community who are to live and act on the principle of "submission to one another out of reverence to Christ." Since it is addressed to the point of interrelationship "to one another," it leaves each person "autonomous and responsible." This submission is to be voluntary and personal. Here in the relationship between wife and husband the wife is not "commanded" to be in subjection. She is rather permitted to take the initiative in subjecting herself.

  As to the Lord. All authority resides in the Lord. When the wife is subject to her husband, she recognizes the divine order in marriage. Equality in worth, in grace, and in spiritual privilege does not interfere with the principle of domestic order. Wives have autonomous responsibility for their own conduct "to the Lord."

23   *Husband is head.* This is God's plan for the family. It finds its illustration in the church's recognition of Christ's headship. The comparison breaks down at the point of Christ's saviorhood. The application refers only to the order of creation.

24   *Church submits to Christ.* This parallels the principle of the wife's subordination to the husband. The church voluntarily submits to Christ.

25   *Love your wives.* Whereas the admonition to wives puts them into a

voluntary position, husbands receive unqualified imperatives. It is their duty to live with a self-sacrificing devotion.

v. 26   *To make her [the church] holy.* The instrument by which this is accomplished is the Word. This is not regarded as a sacrament but as a cleansing agent in the process of exercising faith.

v. 27   *A radiant church.* The hidden imagery looks upon the church as Christ's bride. His sacrifice (atonement) prepared her with fitness and beauty so that she could be presented to Christ as his bride.

v. 28   *So ought husbands.* The love and action of Christ is the "pattern and measure" of the husband's love. Christ advanced his love to make the church holy. The husband's love must bear the same test, and overcome the wife's failings. The wife deserves the same affection as Christ bestows on the church.

vv. 29-
30   *Caring for elementary needs.* As Christ cares for the church, the husband's responsibility is to his wife. He is to care for her as much as he cares for his own body.

v. 31   *Leaving father and mother* emphasizes the total devotion and commitment that constitutes a one-flesh union.

v. 32   *Profound mystery* refers to God's revealed ideal. The perfect relation of Christ and the church is the ideal and standard of the marriage relationship.

v. 33   *However.* It remains for each couple to put these principles into practice.

General Objectives

In previous chapters we examined the use of explanation and application in achieving one's sermon objectives. Each sermon is expected to accomplish at least one specific goal.

Here we will take a brief look at some general objectives. Each of these represents a different objective in preaching. The following speaks directly to the content of the sermon from different angles.

Some sermons are designed to achieve *evangelistic goals.* They make a direct appeal to persons in need of being converted. God is pleased through the foolishness of what is preached to save those who believe. (See 1 Cor. 1:21b.) Salvation comes through hearing the gospel and responding to its call to repent and believe. Sermons designed to achieve that goal are called evangelistic. (See sermon 12.)

Another type of sermon may be characterized as having a *doctrinal* objective. This type of message is designed to help people understand the teachings of the Bible. It is intended to build respect for biblical truth. It is used frequently to establish new Christians in the faith. It concentrates on biblical meaning and encourages commitment to its implications. (See sermon 16.)

A third general objective pertains to *ethics*. Sermon 21 is an example of that objective. Such sermons are concerned with Christian conduct. And as we see in the sermon above (sermon 24), Christian ethics is concerned also with the proper relationship between husbands and wives. In the next chapter we will find ethical concerns expressed in relationships between parents and children and between other members of the household. In all of these there is an overall concern for right relationship to God. Christian conduct is controlled and inspired by Christian principles. (See sermons 19 and 21.)

Another type of sermon might be identified as having a *consecration* objective. This refers to sermons designed to enlist Christians for service in the church and its witness. It employs spiritual means to induce believers to dedicate their talents and time to kingdom causes. It capitalizes on those elements of appeal for the consecration of the total person to serve Jesus Christ. It employs such language as "I urge you . . . to offer your bodies as living sacrifices, holy and pleasing to God—which is your spiritual worship [or reasonable service]" (Rom. 12:1). (See also sermon 17.)

Many problems in society are more or less universal. Sermons designed to meet the needs of persons with troubles or problems have *supportive* objectives. They are aimed at helping people to rely on the grace of God to meet whatever suffering has occurred. The preacher should be able to use God's Word to bring solace to people with any form of personal distress. The supportive purpose seeks to encourage and undergird those who need divine strength and wisdom to meet recurring difficulties. (See sermon 15.)

There is one more common experience that needs a repeated voice from the Lord, namely, devotional growth. These sermons will have a *devotional* objective. This puts the focus on worship, piety, and faith. These sermons stress the value of devotional experience—the benefits of prayer and Bible study. Preaching that helps people to understand how spiritual growth takes place contributes to Christian maturity. (See sermon 18.)

As H. C. Brown, Jr., has said,

Purpose is that which the preacher attempts to accomplish through the preaching of his sermon. An attempt to accomplish something through a sermon lends concreteness to the thrust of the message, creates a vivid sense of expectancy in the mind and heart of the preacher, tends to stimulate the congregation, and casts light upon the entire sermon.[1]

PART VII

Ephesians 6

CHAPTER 29

Sermon Preparation

Guidelines
Introduction to the Outline
Outline: The Church and Domestic Order
Ephesians 6:1-9 (Sermon 25)
Word Meanings Essential to Interpretation
Reflections on Expository Preaching

Guidelines to Sermon Preparation

Certain characteristics should be common to every sermon. The prominence of each will vary from sermon to sermon, of course, but each sermon should:

Inform the intellect.
Kindle the imagination.
Move the emotions.
Convince judgment.
Clarify ethical duty.
Give impulse to the will.
Induce response in worship.

People come to the sermon time with a wide variety of specific expectations. The preaching mission achieves its goals with a major emphasis on proclamation. It proclaims the:

Power of God's forgiving love.
Potential of life's fullness.
Purpose of God's will.
Practice of Christian community.
Prospect of spiritual growth.
Prominence of servanthood action.
Pilgrimage toward eternal habitation.

Some specific concerns deserve special attention. Occasionally some crisis in the community creates an awareness of a specific need to be addressed. Among them are to:

Explain the nature and implications of faith.
Find consolation in a time of tragedy and grief.
Establish priorities in human values.
Bring judgment against an overt sinful practice.
Identify solutions to a human predicament.
Express the practical meanings of eternal life.
Address involvement in a specific moral issue.

Some needs relate to personal spiritual health. Preaching offers an opportunity to identify crucial issues and to address them with affirmation of Scripture. Sermons are intended to help people:

Resolve their problems of guilt.
Gain reassurance from fear and distress.
Overcome feelings of loneliness.
Resolve feelings of anger.
Conquer the grip of injurious habits.
Find peace in the midst of tensions.
Establish security in Christ.

There are some powerful influences in modern society that can be destructive. These are direct challenges for the pulpit ministry. The elements of evil are often mixed with legitimate forces of good. With careful discrimination one can use Scripture to frustrate the impact of pagan philosophy and sensual practices. The church encounters such forces as:

Inroads of worldliness
Erosion from secularism
Reliance upon technology
Toleration of evil cultural practices
Individualism in the religious profession
Infiltration of cultism
Obsession with materialism
Influence of liberation theology
Sexual promiscuity

The preaching mission has an opportunity and an obligation to reinforce "the things that remain." That calls for preaching on such subjects as:

Radical discipleship
Consistent stewardship
Support of the brotherhood
Sanctity of marriage
Principles of peace
Respect for authority
Vocational integrity
Christian counter culture

Introduction to the Outline

Preaching requires a sympathetic awareness of the life context of the people in the pew. This applies to their home environment and their daily work relationships. There is danger in the overuse of theological issues in the pulpit at the expense of "operational theology" (how faith works in the home and in vocation). The challenge to translate biblical meanings into the language of the household and the language of the street remains a constant task of the preacher. People want to know what the grace of God has to do with homelife and the daily rounds of vocational duty. This text is well suited for that purpose.

Average church members are subject to the influence of secular society and diverse working conditions. They want to know how to practice the truth they have heard from the pulpit. They must hear some practical ways in which the gospel can be applied to daily human relationships.

The most convincing argument for Christianity is the demonstration of Christian living at home and on the job. This sermon text has the ingredients to nurture faith for family living. In the course of delivering this sermon one should focus on the "how" of achieving a consistent witness of divine grace.

Sermon 25
The Church and Domestic Order
Ephesians 6:1-9

Introduction

In addition to the strength of marital relationships, the church is made strong when the households composing its membership live and work in harmony. This passage projects the moral and spiritual benefits that are realized when the household is Christian in its profession and practice. It again underscores the centrality of Christ as the point of common ground for social action.

Theme: The church receives **strength** through household harmony.

    A. Parents contribute **strength** by **wholesome attitudes.**

        1. **Wholesome attitudes** are cultivated by exercising *consideration.*

          a. Consideration exercises courtesy and respect.

          b. *Consideration* exercises authority with restraint.

        2. **Wholesome attitudes** are expressed in *positive discipline.*

          a. *Positive discipline* follows proper training.

          b. *Positive discipline* relies on loving relationship.

        3. **Wholesome attitudes** are conditioned by *Christian experience.*

          a. *Christian experience* develops a sense of responsibility.

          b. *Christian experience* develops trust and expectation.

        4. **Wholesome attitudes** are refined by *self-control.*

          a. *Self-control* suppresses tyranny in demands.

          b. *Self-control* avoids interference with legitimate pleasure.

          c. *Self-control* refrains from imposing unreasonable sacrifices.

    B. Children contribute **strength** through **respectful** attitudes.

        1. **Respect** is shown in *obedience to parents.*

          a. *Obedience to parents* is a divine obligation.

          b. *Obedience to parents* is a primary human duty.

          c. *Obedience to parents* is the first lesson in submission.

          d. *Obedience to parents* is regulated by regard for Christ.

        2. **Respect** is shown in *honoring* parents.

          a. To *honor parents* is a divine principle.

b. To *honor parents* has a promise of well-being.

c. To *honor parents* qualifies for long life.

C. Laborers contribute **strength** through **positive attitudes.**

1. **Positive attitudes** are expressed in *acceptable service.* (v. 5)

a. *Acceptable service* is performed as to Christ.

b. *Acceptable service* is performed with honesty.

c. *Acceptable service* is performed with sincerity.

2. **Positive attitudes** are expressed in *spiritual service.* (v. 6)

a. *Spiritual service* is modeled by obedience to Christ.

b. *Spiritual service* is patterned after the will of God.

c. *Spiritual service* is motivated in the heart.

3. **Positive attitudes** are expressed in *wholehearted service.* (vv. 7-8)

a. *Wholehearted service* is viewed as serving the Lord.

b. *Wholehearted service* is motivated by love.

D. Employers contribute **strength** through **compassionate attitudes.**

1. **Compassion** holds a *high regard* for persons.
It deals with persons on the basis of *brotherhood.*

2. **Compassion** gives *credit* to honest performance.
It gives employees due *recognition* for work done.

3. **Compassion** *withholds threatening* in discipline.
It respects employees with *sympathetic understanding.*

4. **Compassion** acts *without partiality.*
It acts on the *basis of principle.*

5. **Compassion** is exercised by *divine grace.*
It finds expression through *imitation of Christ.*

Conclusion

Brotherhood considerations are essential in maintaining Christian relationships.

Loyalty to Christ is the supreme factor in preserving a Christian household order.

Word Meanings Essential to Interpretation

1   *In the Lord.* In addition to their natural affection for parents, children are to be influenced by religious duty. Children are under the same obligation as adults to do what is right.

2   *Honor* (see Exod. 20:12; Deut. 5:16). This divine ordinance has long stood as a standard for filial relationships. Honor expresses the frame of mind from which obedience proceeds.

. 2-3   *First commandment with a promise.* This phrase could mean that it was first in the sense of primary importance. Or that it was the first to have with it a promise. The two phrases *well with thee* and *have long life* both have to do with human welfare. The promise of God to reward obedience still holds.

v. 4   *Do not exasperate* by giving a feeling of injustice, by leaving an impression of being inconsiderate, or by provoking a child.

In training carries the concept of discipline, answering to the mind of the Lord. It includes the force of *correcting* or *chastisement*.

Admonition. This word carries the concept of training to the point of "warning" (cf. Rom. 10:11). Its distinctive feature is training by word of mouth, in terms of exhortation. Admonition is a mode of discipline, a special means of warning and correction.

Of the Lord. This kind of nurture is prescribed by the Lord. It is administered in his name. It carries a positive and negative element, a blend of firmness and gentle treatment. Religious households constitute the nurseries of freedom and docility, and amenability to being taught. Obedience is met by loving education.

v. 5   *Slaves* or servants—persons serving in subjection to masters. The emphasis is on an obedience that includes respect, singleness, and sincerity of heart. Comparison with one's attitude toward Christ puts the relationship to the "masters" into the religious category.

v. 6   *Slaves of Christ* lifts the direction above the level of secular inducements. The principle is reliability in service. It puts a premium on Christian behavior in labor relations. It involves inner attitude.

v. 7   *Reward you.* Respect for Christ shows up in service. We are to keep the eternal benefits in mind while fulfilling an earthly contract.

v. 8   "*Masters*" have an obligation to exercise the same respect expected of "employees." This refers particularly to respect for personality. Treat them as you want to be treated.

v. 9   *Both theirs and yours.* The reference to the Christian spirit pertains to both the employer and employee. There is no partiality with God. Both are under the same mandate to be faithful stewards of opportunity, time, and position.

Reflections on Expository Preaching

Chapter 2 (an "Introduction to Expository Preaching") focused on four primary aspects of this method of preaching. The last section of chapter 15 focused on "Principles of Expository Preaching." This chapter summarizes the various factors involved in the use of this method.

John R. W. Stott says, "All true preaching is expository preaching." By this he means the dual purpose of exposing the meaning of Scripture and of applying that meaning to current issues. "Our responsibility as expositors is to open it [the text] in such a way that it speaks its message clearly, plainly, accurately, relevantly, without addition, subtraction, or falsification."[1]

In expository preaching, as in other methods, each preacher must be author of the pattern of construction. The outline of the sermon has the basic elements of introduction, body, and conclusion. Within that framework we seek to achieve unity of thought, order of presentation, and proportion of ideas in a progressive line of truth.

Forms take their shapes under the influence of personal factors. The speaker's manner of thinking will be reflected in the outline. One's awareness of audience need and expectations will have a bearing on the approach. The adopted purpose of the sermon will affect one's selection of material. And a keen understanding of the message embodied in the original text will determine much of the thrust of the sermon.

The outlines in this book are intended for the reader's evaluation and imitation. A variety of themes has emerged from the Scripture. A studied attempt has been made to make clear statements (incomplete sentences) of biblical truth. The study of the text was begun in the section on "Word Meanings." These are not intended to cover all that is involved. Depth studies from evangelical resources are needed to enrich and correct the understandings that appear on the surface.

The following series of homiletical principles may serve as further review and extension of applied homiletics:

The expositor's task includes the following procedures:

1. Discover the main theme, or at least some theme, in the passage. Take time to formulate a clear sentence.
2. Identify a valid use of the passage, or find a passage that promotes a desired purpose. It is important to pinpoint an aim to be accomplished.
3. After analyzing the constituent parts of the passage, find the unify-

ing elements that relate to the adopted purpose.

4. After organizing the selected thoughts, look for the essential relationships they have to contemporary life.

During the construction of an outline, one should be aware of some general elements of sermon preparation needed to enhance its effectiveness:

1. Interpret the passage with care, exposing its unique meanings with confidence.

2. Explain the implications of extracted meanings for our understanding of God's will.

3. Amplify the importance of the truth in its support of the stated theme.

4. Apply the meanings of Scripture to human need.

5. Use illustrations sparingly and appropriately to illuminate truth for immediate acceptance.

Keep in mind the following general objectives of the pulpit ministry:

1. To inform the intellect of spiritual truth.

2. To convince the judgment of ethical principles.

3. To move the heart to Christian devotion.

4. To crystallize conviction for religious duty.

5. To move the will to act in personal commitment.

6. To nurture Christians with spiritual resources.

7. To build the church for worship and mission.

CHAPTER 30

Preaching the Gospel

Guidelines for Preaching the Gospel

On the occasion of Jesus' ascension farewell he said to his disciples, "This is what I told you while I was still with you: Everything must be fulfilled that is written about me in the Law of Moses, the Prophets and the Psalms."

Then he opened their minds so they could understand the Scriptures. He told them,

> This is what is written: The Christ will suffer and rise from the dead on the third day, and repentance and forgiveness of sins will be preached in his name to all nations, beginning at Jerusalem. You are witnesses of these things. I am going to send you what my Father has promised; but stay in the city until you have been clothed with power from on high. (Luke 24:44-49)

These instructions to the disciples express principles that apply to the current preaching of the gospel. They were given in the context of the resurrection. The gospel message always reaches its climax in the full bloom of resurrection truth.

The gospel is based on *revealed* truth (v. 44). Jesus appealed to the entire Old Testament as having predictions that must be fulfilled. Since we believe that "God has spoken," preaching the Word can be done with the full confidence of God's authority. Actually what we see in the life and teachings of Jesus is an "enacted revelation."

The gospel is understood as *spiritual* truth (v. 45). On this occasion of Jesus' farewell speech he "opened their minds so they could understand the Scriptures." In like manner the person in the pulpit is called upon to interpret the Scriptures so the people can understand its spiritual implications. The applications we draw from it are designed to meet spiritual needs. We come to know the truth which we preach through faith in the risen Christ and by the illumination of his Holy Spirit. In order to communicate its meaning the message needs to be translated into contemporary terms.

The gospel is composed of *redemptive* truth (v. 46). The core of saving truth is the death and resurrection of Jesus Christ. His sufferings are related to deliverance from the guilt of sin. His resurrection forms the basis of victory over sin. An acceptance of these cardinal doctrines leads to a vital spiritual relationship with an assurance of acceptance into the kingdom of God. That opens the way to nurturing believers in Christian discipleship.

The gospel is presented as *decisive* truth (v. 47). Repentance and forgiveness of sin constitute the appeal to be communicated. Repentance decides attitude. Forgiveness decides status. Repentance is the conditioning factor that qualifies for reconciliation. God's act—forgiveness—deals with the human dilemma, the predicament of sin. Our preaching as a message of redemption is designed to elicit the repentance of sinners, to win their devotion, to reshape their wills, and finally to redeem their souls. This must be expressed in the language of real experience.

The gospel is proclaimed as *established* truth (v. 48). We witness not only to established facts but also to established experience. In the crucified and risen Christ, the unique event has happened.

More than that, a new relationship has been established. We are witnesses to the effect of the gospel in turning people from darkness to light, from unbelief to faith, from evil to good, from sin to grace, and from death to life.

The gospel is communicated as *dynamic* truth (v. 49). The power from on high is the fulfillment of a divine promise. It is the dynamic of a divine Person. The Holy Spirit is the enabling power to communicate that message. The Spirit empowers preaching to carry conviction to the hearts of those who hear. The church now vibrates with the power of the resurrection. That is the most practical and decisive spiritual force in the world. The message of the gospel must be proclaimed in the power of the Holy Spirit.

With the words of the ascended Lord addressed to the church, we have an obligation to confront a dissipated world with the gospel. We must make an adequate impact upon our secular age to win people for Christ. For that we will have to draw deliberately and constantly from the values of New Testament truth. The task will be accomplished only as we rely fully and humbly upon the power of the Holy Spirit to convince sinners of their need for salvation. That includes driving home to human hearts both the judgment and the mercy of God.

Introduction to the Outline

This message serves as a climax to the entire series from the book of Ephesians. It makes an appeal to the church to avail itself of the divine resources to overcome the opposition set against it.

The text follows a long line of positive assertions about the nature and mission of the church, declaring the secrets of God's love and grace. The wonders of eternal salvation go beyond description. The beauty of peace and order is revealed, supported by references to the satisfaction of God's leading and the infilling of divine power. The delight of experience in personal holiness is asserted and defined.

These are a few of the great truths that are attached to the cause of the Christian conflict in the world. A note of triumph comes through with full confidence in the power of God to achieve his eternal purpose.

Sermon 26
The Church in Spiritual Conflict
Ephesians 6:10-17

Introduction

The doctrine of redemption and its meaning to the church stands firm in the arena of Christian community. Knowing the implications of that truth for practice in the church is a constant resource with which to confront the opposing forces of evil. The Christian conflict engages divine instruments to overcome superhuman powers.

In this passage recognition is given to the inevitable conflict encountered by living out Christian standards of behavior. It emphasizes the spiritual resources available to overcome evil.

Theme: The Christian conflict engages *divine resources.*

A. Use *divine resources* to withstand **satanic devices.** (vv. 10-11)
   1. **Satan's devices** are detected by divine *wisdom.*
      a. Divine *wisdom* detects unseen adversaries.
      b. Divine *wisdom* detects deceptive intentions.
      c. Divine *wisdom* detects exploitative designs.
   2. **Satan's devices** are frustrated by divine *strength.*
      a. Divine *strength* is needed to face opposition.
      b. Divine *strength* is needed to cope with perversions.
      c. Divine *strength* is needed to overcome subtle temptations.
B. Use *divine resources* to struggle with **evil influences.** (v. 12)
   1. **Evil influences** are overcome by spiritual *resolution.*
      a. Spiritual *resolutions* gain mastery over secularism.
      b. Spiritual *resolutions* gain mastery over fanaticism.
   2. **Evil influences** are overcome by Christian *commitment.*
      a. *Commitment* to Christ counteracts powers of darkness.
      b. *Commitment* to Christ counteracts forces of evil.
C. Use *divine resources* to withstand the **evil day.** (v. 13)
   1. The **evil day** is resolved by resolute *resistance.*
      a. *Resistance* of evil is achieved by consistent faithfulness.
      b. *Resistance* of evil is achieved by deep loyalty to truth.
   2. The **evil day** is resolved by obedient *trust.*
      a. *Trust* in God repels pagan violence.
      b. *Trust* in God repels a hostile world order.
   3. The **evil day** is resolved by firm *conviction.*
      a. Firm *convictions* stand against evil suggestions.
      b. Firm *convictions* stand against seductive elements.
   4. The **evil day** is resolved by "having *done everything.*"

    a. *Thorough accomplishment* puts duty above neglect.

    b. *Thorough accomplishment* puts reality above profession.

    c. *Thorough accomplishment* puts the crisis on hold.

D. Use *divine resources* to combat *spiritual wickedness.* (vv. 14-15)

  1. **Spiritual wickedness** is judged by the "belt of *truth*."

    a. *Truth* promotes loyalty to Christ.

    b. *Truth* promotes faithfulness to God.

  2. **Spiritual wickedness** is resisted by *righteousness.*

    a. *Righteousness* builds strength of character.

    b. *Righteousness* shapes moral practice.

  3. **Spiritual wickedness** is defeated by the gospel of *peace.*

    a. *Peace* gives confidence to engage in conflict.

    b. *Peace* gives strength to conviction for witnessing.

E. Use *divine resources* to quench **satanic attacks.** (vv. 16-17)

  1. **Satanic attacks** are thwarted by *faith.*

    a. *Faith* puts out the fires of criticism.

    b. *Faith* puts out the discouragements of failure.

  2. **Satanic attacks** are withstood by assurance of *salvation.*

    a. *Salvation* opens the strength of divine grace.

    b. *Salvation* gives rest in the conflict.

  3. **Satanic attacks** are nullified by the sword of the *Spirit.*

    a. The *Spirit* uses the Word to answer doubt.

    b. The *Spirit* uses the Word to activate divine promises.

Conclusion

    Ours is a triumphant combat serving with Christ. Let us confront forces of evil with courage and confidence. Let us make use of the armor of God to subdue satanic forces. We rely upon the Spirit and the Word to succeed.

Word Meanings Essential to Interpretation

. 10   *Finally,* in retrospect of previous exhortations. "The thought is turned to special crises of trial."

    Strong in the Lord points to divine resources available to the believer in Christ. It carries the meaning of "be strengthened."

    Power of his might (cf. 1:19). These words, used differently here, describe a resource from God for resisting evil.

. 11   *Armor* is the Christian's spiritual equipment to meet the crises of life, particularly the evil forces around us. Individual pieces of this armor are described in detail.

Able to stand suggests the sense of withstanding against the devil's schemes. Satan's devices are to be detected and overcome. To do so, divine strength is needed.

v. 12   *Struggle* or wrestling. A conflict involving the spiritual realm.

Rulers, authorities, dark world, forces of evil—all represent active influences bent on bringing Christians under bondage. Only spiritual resources can cope with these hostile factors.

v. 13   *Whole armor of God.* The stress is on adequate means of offensive and defensive encounter with pernicious influences.

The evil day is a term indicating crisis circumstances precipitated by evil design.

Having done all, to stand literally refers to thorough accomplishment, particularly with reference to a crisis. It means maintaining a firm stand.

v. 14   *Truth* includes the concept of experience in which the state of the heart answers to God's truth. This element of truth carries the idea of consistency with Christian character. It includes loyalty and faithfulness.

Righteousness pertains to character, to practice, to moral rectitude.

v. 15   *Peace* pertains to a readiness to cope with hostilities, having a firm footing to deal with satanic forces. (cf. Is. 52:17; Eph. 2:17).

v. 16   *Shield of faith.* Saving faith is an effective support in conflict engagements. It is a protective element in the face of disruptive violence.

Fiery darts expresses the concept of shafts of evil. Faith takes away the force of temptation. It sensitizes the will to act on holy impulses in coping with evil suggestions.

v. 17   *Helmet of salvation.* The word *take* is different from that used in verses 13 and 16. Here it means to receive something from God, "the helmet which is salvation" (cf. 1 Thess. 5:8).

Sword of the Spirit. This also is a gift from God. The Word is a revelation given with the initiative from above because the Spirit of God gave it and inspired it.

The Use of Illustrations

Inasmuch as an illustration throws light on something beyond itself, it must be considered as a matter of secondary importance. But that does not mean it has no significance in the process of communication. It is used in a clarifying or supportive function to make the content more effective. As one author says, "It is a form of mental replay." It is a "disguised restatement" of a prose expression of truth. As such it aids the memory of the listener. It "throws light on truth or duty and makes the things of heaven attractive to people on earth."[1]

An appropriate illustration can make the impact of truth more effective and more lasting. If a message is to live and move the audience, it must have enough human interest to hold their attention. But the value of an illustration is not in its intrinsic elements of thought. It must point to a truth outside itself, larger than itself. It must make the point more vivid in terms of concrete human understanding. It is

> valuable only to the degree in which it centers attention on the point being made, not in itself. Consequently a natural illustration, one that does not claim attention for its own sake, one that seems a part of the thought itself, is the most valuable. If it claims attention to itself for its own sake, an illustration disrupts rather than assists the communication of thought.[2]

We generally think of an illustration as consisting of a story, a reference to an event, or a personal experience of the speaker. But there are various other types of illustrative materials. An exclamation, some figure of speech, an allegory, a parable, or a precise quotation can serve as an illustration. Or an anecdote can be drawn from some current event or life situation.

> Actual experiences are probably the most important of all of the speech materials. They enable the audience to share in the events and feelings related to the point the speaker wants to convey. If they are dramatic and well-told, they arouse curiosity and increase interest. If they also include humor they elicit an overt response from the hearers [their laughter] and leave the audience more open to suggestion and to persuasion. The illustration is so important that you are urged to adopt the following rule for all speaking: Any point worth talking about is worth a detailed illustration.[3]

A word of caution is needed. It is possible to overdo a good means of communication. I once listened to a 30-minute sermon in which the preacher used 49 illustrations (my actual count). Obviously, the biblical content was very limited. The audience was spellbound, but to what truth I did not know. Blackwood says, "Limit the number of illustrations. Concentrate on quality, not quanity.... Remember that an illustration occupies a secondary place; so keep a sense of proportion."[4]

The way thoughts are expressed may eliminate the need for illustration of the obvious kind. The sermon structure, with its evident progression in thought, has an intrinsic means of sustaining interest. Properly selected wording can achieve clarity without illustration. The outlines in this book have been subjected to that kind of scrutiny.

The material to be used and the message to be proclaimed needed to be spiced with elements of human interest. Perceived relevance to the listeners' current life situations will sustain attention. The real purpose of a sermon is to bring the audience within the orbit of Holy Spirit action. The Spirit's concrete instrument of influence is the Word of God. That augurs well for the able delivery of biblical sermons, and particularly, the use of expository preaching.

We are called to present biblical truth with the beauty of its holy design. It needs to be conveyed in the language of contemporary thought patterns. As a general rule, we should illustrate how truth is put to use in human experience.

Conviction

Guidelines to Conviction

This element of preaching is directly related to purpose and application, both of which have been discussed in previous chapters (6 and 18). It is also identified with the sermon objective (chapter 28) and the means of achieving it through persuasion (chapter 24). We use the term *conviction* in this section to mean being convinced of the truth and having reached a settled view of its meaning for personal belief and practice. It focuses on the claims of biblical truth to bring about a change of attitude or to achieve a confirmation of faith.

When one shows how the theme applies to the life experience of the audience, one is aiming to convince them of the validity of the message. Subtle suggestions on how to apply the truth in practical living situations helps. By drawing the meaning of one's message down to a specific area of life, one can cultivate conviction about it. Even when the particular application is left to the listeners, the Spirit will use the inherent value of the truth proclaimed to convict them. Often people can more effectively apply a sermon to themselves.

This method of proclamation represents a "calculated risk of losing an opportunity to influence the will to immediate conclusion." Thus, "if truth is not focalized sharply enough to spotlight some particular principle or habit or practice or motive or sentiment or prejudice or disposition or need, it will not be very effective."[1]

Biblical teaching supports the use of persuasion in preaching. When Paul and Silas were in Thessalonica, Paul went into the synagogue. On three Sabbath days he reasoned with them from the Scriptures, explaining and proving that Christ had to suffer and rise from the dead. "This Jesus I am proclaiming to you is the Christ." he said. Some of the Jews were persuaded and joined Paul and Silas.[2] The purpose of their preaching is clear. They asked to have people accept Christ. They relied upon the Scriptures, explaining and proving the validity of their claims.

Later in his epistle to that church he said, "Our gospel came to you not simply with words but also with power in the Holy Spirit and with deep conviction." He recalled how they "turned to God from idols" to serve the "living and true God."[3] In the second chapter Paul thankfully reported the results of their preaching. They became "imitators" of the churches of God.

This letter of Paul to the Thessalonians contains a number of helpful insights for homiletics. "A conscientious preacher, seeking to maintain an ethical ministry, should study these Thessalonian passages to adopt personal ethical standards. They are rich in practical guidelines for persuasive preaching."[4]

Preaching the gospel is neither wholly human nor wholly divine. One must consciously and deliberately dedicate one's powers of communication to the Holy Spirit. For that reason we need to consider methods of influence that will help people adopt Christian values.

Evangelical preaching is designed to change the attitudes, opinions, and behavior of people. It proclaims the Word of God. It confronts the audience with the meaning of divine truth in contemporary living. "The ultimate goal of preaching is not the transmission of information but the transformation of persons, not simply data exchange but behavioral change."[5]

Evangelical preaching calls for spiritual transformation. It affects the wide areas of need involved in personal being and human relationships. In order to achieve a positive response in the listener, the preacher needs to provide motivation for action. A practical formula for sustaining interest employs some simple procedures. "First he must catch the attention of the audience. Second, he must sustain interest. Third, he must make an impression of the subject. Fourth he must motivate response. Fifth, he must direct the action."[6]

Felt needs represent an important motivational key. Curiosity, personal problems, fellowship, worship, respect for traditional authority, desire for information, and help with spiritual needs—all of these can sustain a listener's interest.

But it is not enough to recognize these conditions. The appeal becomes effective through action. Among the personal benefits to be suggested are happiness, peace of mind, social approval, and satisfaction. Some biblical motives to be engaged are: ability to know God's will (Rom. 12:1), to be perfectly united in mind and thought (1 Cor. 1:10), to live lives worthy of God (1 Thess. 2:12), and to lay up treasures as a firm foundation (1 Tim. 6:19).

"The motive power behind effective preaching is love toward God and [for each other]. To love is to live. To preach demands life and love, Christian life and Christian love. In preaching it is especially true, an ounce of love is worth a pound of knowledge."[7] All our persuading is with the solemn fear of God in our minds. (See the J. B. Phillips translation of 2 Cor. 5:11.)

Introduction to the Outline

The preceding description of the believer's armor prepares the way for consideration of the church in spiritual conflict. Prayer and supplication for each other requires a knowledge and understanding of prevailing circumstances. "The body of fellowship which unites the people of God is never more effective than when they are praying for one another." Persistence in prayer is never more urgent than in times of crisis. In the meantime it is important to keep alert to the possible inroads of evil forces.

The strength of the church to cope with satanic opposition is enhanced by spiritual interaction among the believers. The inter-change of concern and support sustains confidence in the witness of the gospel. The conjunction of love and faith puts endurance and courage into Christian perspective. The close association with God the Father and the Lord Jesus Christ puts the church into the position of receiving peace and grace. They are given high priority in Christian experience.

Sermon 26
The Church with Internal Strength
Ephesians 6:18-24

Introduction
    In light of the forces of opposition, the church needs a conscious inner experience of strength for its offensive and defensive action. The channel of that strength is kept open by a continuous flow of prayer for each other. It involves the use of petition on any occasion and watching for it with commitment to act. It is concerned with all the saints. Praying is here defined in respect to its variety and earnestness, its constancy, and its spiritual reality.

Theme: The church is **strengthened** through spiritual interaction.
   A. Believers **strengthen** each other through **supplications.** (v. 18)
      1. **Supplications** are made in *prayers* for the saints.
        a. *Prayers* for saints are a continuous vocation.
        b. *Prayers* for saints address spiritual needs.
      2. **Supplications** are made in the *Spirit.*
        a. The *Spirit* guides in framing such prayers.
        b. The *Spirit* serves as intercessor for such prayers.
      3. **Supplications** are made in persevering *faith.*
        a. *Faith* puts confidence into supplications.
        b. *Faith* puts persistence into supplications.
   B. Believers **strengthen** each other through **intercessions.** (vv. 19-20)
      1. **Intercessions** aid *enlightenment* and utterance for proclamation.
        a. *Enlightenment* and utterance are needed to convince hearers.
        b. *Enlightenment* and utterance are needed to make appeals.
      2. **Intercessions** aid *clarity* and courage in proclamation.
        a. *Clarity* and courage are essential to explain meanings of the gospel.
        b. *Clarity* and courage are essential in validating claims of the gospel.

3. **Intercessions** aid *boldness* and confidence in proclamation.
  a. *Boldness* gives confidence to declare the conditions of salvation.
  b. *Boldness* gives confidence to declare the validity of the gospel.
C. Believers **strengthen** each other through **cooperation.** (vv. 21-22)
  1. **Cooperation** is achieved by reporting *status.*
    a. Knowing the *circumstances* of church leaders provides a subject for prayer.
    b. Knowing the *trials* of church leaders provides motivation for prayer.
  2. **Cooperation** is achieved by *reporting* activities.
    a. *Knowing* the program for action gives direction to prayer.
    b. *Knowing* the opposition it faces gives impetus to prayer.
  3. **Cooperation** is achieved by reporting *relationships.*
    a. Knowing *relationships* aids in identification of need.
    b. Knowing *relationships* aids in identification of purpose.
D. Believers **strengthen** each other through **communication.** (vv. 23-24)
  1. **Greetings** convey concern for *principles of peace.*
    a. *Principles of peace* enhance the spirit of brotherhood.
    b. *Principles of peace* exemplify the spirit of goodwill.
  2. **Greetings** convey concern for the *portrayal of love.*
    a. The *portrayal of love* establishes discipleship.
    b. The *portrayal of love* gives visibility to unity.
  3. **Greetings** convey concern for the *practice of faith.*
    a. The *practice of faith* appropriates divine promises.
    b. The *practice of faith* responds to divine calling.
  4. **Greetings** convey concern for *promotion of grace.*
    a. The *promotion of grace* expresses divine favor.
    b. The *promotion of grace* expresses a divine benediction.

Conclusion

    Prayer and supplication are a great source of spiritual strength in the church. Cooperation and effective intercommunication are channels of grace to all who love the Lord Jesus Christ with sincerity.

Word Meanings Essential to Interpretation

18 *Pray in the Spirit.* This puts a premium on the Christian spirit as well as the Holy Spirit in the exercise of prayer. We are not dealing with form and word only.

Always. On every occasion this spirit should prevail.

With, or through the medium of.

Alertness. Watch with resolute effort to maintain the spirit of prayer.

v. 19   *Mystery* is something hidden in the past that is now revealed. In that sense it denotes a revelation or knowledge only recently understood.

v. 20   *Ambassador in chains* represents a paradox. Paul is a representative of the great King while being held in bondage as a prisoner.

v. 21   *Tychicus,* the beloved brother and faithful servant, was to carry word to the church at Ephesus about Paul's circumstances.

v. 22   *This very purpose.* As a messenger, Tychicus was expected to report faithfully and to alleviate the anxieties of the church there.

v. 23   *Peace, love.* This is a Christian salutation. Peace is God's gift.

v. 24   *Grace* is realized through the believer's cooperation.

Undying love. Free from every element liable to corruption, love is here directed to that which is beyond change.

Personhood in Preaching

The essence of preaching emerges from the personal equation of the preacher's character and life. The preacher's work is done "not on the level where a person acquires a knowledge of technique, rules, and devices, but on the deep levels of self-commitment where he rigorously disciplines his life for the love of Jesus Christ."[8] The minister's task—more than that of any other calling—depends on the quality of life and strength of character that person brings into it.

The Christian ministry is an absorbing life. One who enters it must be prepared to be dominated and controlled by a great enterprise. One must be possessed in heart, mind, and soul with a consuming passion for souls and a burning devotion to Christ. That requires great courage and daring. Indifference blunts the cutting edge of one's preaching.

In one sense the ministry is an exacting life. It calls for faithfulness to duty and intense concentration on one's primary assignment. There is no easy road to success. The minister who is fully committed to the ministry of the gospel often feels physical weariness, the weight of disappointment, and the strain of passion and concern.

Preaching calls for spiritual maturity. We expect to see an unquestioned loyalty to Christ, an expanding demonstration of God's grace, a dynamic overflow in life and testimony, a sense of purpose in living, an acceptance of responsibility for the welfare of others, and an attitude of expectancy for our Lord's return. These are enhanced by the influence of God's Word and the anointing of the Holy Spirit. To achieve true Christian piety one must learn to put first things first. It allows no self-pleasing to interfere with an unreserved consecration to God's will.

Preaching demands vitality in prayer. This is not a professional duty but a means of engaging available spiritual resources. The preacher prays earnestly not because of professional status but because of human limitation. Many times the preacher needs the spiritual and psychological renewal most effectively achieved in the "secret closet." Most failures in the ministry are due to lack of vital prayer.

Effective preaching is done with cultivated humility. Nowhere is self-importance and conscious striving for popularity more offensive than in the pulpit. There is constant need for a discipline that strikes against self-display and all forms of egotism. The call to present every person in Christ Jesus is a momentous task. To function in that role presents a goal beyond the reach of mere human influence. Everything a minister accomplishes is God's work. The visible results that attend one's efforts—like sinners being brought to Christ, saints being built up in faith, and sorrowing persons being comforted—are the ultimate achievements of the Holy Spirit. Thus the nature of the task calls for personal humility.

However, the minister is a person of conviction, a channel for a divine message which carries the authority of heaven. We are living in times that need a note of authority in preaching. We need the discipline of persuasion to convince the audience that God has spoken through the inspired Scripture. The expository method is designed to convey truth with the validity of divine purpose. We need preachers who herald the message of redemption with conviction, who speak with the authority of God's truth, and who deliver it in the power of the Holy Spirit.

Notes

Chapter 1

    1. Romans 10:12-15.

    2. Sweazey, George E., *Preaching the Good News* (Prentice-Hall, 1976), p. 4.

    3. Ibid., p. 4.

    4. Romans 1:16.

    5. Matthew 7:28-29.

    6. Sweazey, p. 18.

    7. See 1 John 2:20-21.

    8. See 1 John 2:24, 26.

    9. See 1 John 2:28.

    10. Stott, John R. W., *Between Two Worlds: The Art of Preaching in the Twentieth Century* (Eerdmans, 1982), p. 56.

    11. Stott, John R. W., *Christian Counter-Culture: The Message of the Sermon on the Mount* (InterVarsity Press, 1978).

    12. Sangster, W. E., *The Craft of Sermon Construction* (Westminster, 1951), p. 22.

Chapter 2

    1. Unger, Merrill F., *Principles of Expository Preaching* (Zondervan, 1955), p. 32.

Chapter 3

    1. Hunter, Archibald M., in *The Layman's Bible Commentary*, Volume 22 (John Knox Press, 1959), p. 45.

Chapter 4

    1. Acts 2:17-21 (cf. Joel 2:28-32).

    2. Staggs, Frank, *The Book of Acts* (Broadman Press, 1955), p. 50.

Chapter 6

    1. Sweazey, George E., *Preaching the Good News* (Prentice-Hall, 1976), p. 18.

    2. Ibid., p. 18.

    3. Stott, John R. W. *Between Two Worlds: The Art of Preaching in the Twentieth Century* (Eerdmans, 1982), p. 93.

    4. Ibid., p. 88.

    5. John 15:26-27.

Chapter 7
1. 1 Timothy 3:16.
2. John 1:14.
3. Hebrews 10:9-10.
4. 1 John 4:9-10.
5. 1 John 1:1-2.
6. Hebrews 2:14-15, 17.
7. Galatians 4:4-5, 7.

Chapter 8
1. Perry, Lloyd M., *A Manual for Biblical Preaching* (Baker, 1965), p. 1.
2. Stott, John R. W., *Between Two Worlds: The Art of Preaching in the Twentieth Century* (Eerdmans, 1982), p. 331.
3. Bauman, J. Daniel, *An Introduction to Contemporary Preaching* (Baker, 1972), p. 284.
4. 1 Thessalonians 1:5.

Chapter 9
1. Carver, William O., *The Glory of God in Christian Calling* (Broadman, 1949), p. 104.
2. Ibid., p. 105.
3. See Westcott, Brook F., *St. Paul's Epistle to the Ephesians*, (Eerdmans, 1950), p. 24.
4. Sterrett, Norton T., *How to Understand Your Bible* (InterVarsity, 1975), p. 74.

Chapter 10
1. Stewart, James S., *Heralds of God* (Scribner's, 1946), p. 156.
2. Bruce, F. F., *The Epistle to the Ephesians* (Revell, 1961), p. 41.
3. Westcott, B. F., *St. Paul's Epistle to the Ephesians* (Eerdmans, 1950), p. 28.
4. Vincent, Marvin R., *Word Studies in the New Testament* (Vol. III, Scribners, 1890; Eerdmans, 1946), p. 219.
5. Godet, Frederick L., *Commentary on First Corinthians* (Kregel, 1977), p. 356.

Chapter 11
1. Kevan, Ernest F., *The Principles of Interpretation in Revelation and the Bible*, edited by Carl F. H. Henry (Baker, 1958), p. 293.

Chapter 13
1. Sterrett, T. Norton, *How to Understand Your Bible* (Intervarsity, 1957), p. 162.
2. Unger, Merrill F., *Principles of Expository Preaching* (Zondervan, 1955), p. 143.
3. Sterrett, *How to Understand Your Bible* (Inter Varsity, 1974), p. 51.
4. Lenski, R. C. H., *The Sermon* (Lutheran Book Concern, 1927), p. 225.

Chapter 15
1. Sterrett, T. Norton, *How to Understand Your Bible* (InterVarsity, 1975), p. 63.
2. Stott, John R. W., *Between Two Worlds: The Art of Preaching in the Twentieth Century* (Eerdmans, 1982), p. 126.
3. 2 Timothy 1:13-14.
4. 1 Corinthians 4:1-2.
5. Bauman, J. Daniel, *An Introduction to Contemporary Preaching* (Baker, 1972), p. 99.
6. Stott, op. cit., p. 133.

Chapter 17
1. Unger, Merrill F., *Principles of Expository Preaching* (Zondervan, 1955), Chapter VI, pp. 48-55.

2. Ibid., p. 52.
3. Ibid., p. 49.
4. Yohn, David W., *The Contemporary Preacher and Biblical Exposition* (Eerdmans, 1969), p. 145.
5. Koller, Charles W., *Expository Preaching Without Notes* (Baker, 1962), p. 108.
6. Ibid, pp. 109-112.
7. Ibid, p. 112.

Chapter 18
1. Brown, H. C., Jr., *A Quest for Reformation in Preaching* (Word Books, 1968), p. 60.
2. Perry, Lloyd M., *Biblical Preaching for Today's World* (Moody, 1973), p. 140.
3. Broadus, John A., *On the Preparation and Delivery of Sermons* (Harper, revised edition by Weatherspoon, 1944), p. 215.
4. Brown, op. cit., p. 61.
5. Bauman, J. Daniel, *An Introduction to Contemporary Preaching* (Baker, 1972), p. 243.
6. Vincent, Marvin B., *Word Studies in the New Testament*, (Eerdmans, 1946).
7. Simpson, E. K., and F. F. Bruce, *Commentary on the Epistles to the Ephesians and Colossians* (Eerdmans, 1957) p. 78.

Chapter 19
1. Lenski, R. C. H., *The Sermon: Its Homiletical Construction* (Lutheran Book Concern, 1927), p. 222.
2. Broadus, John A., *On Preparation and Delivery of Sermons* (Harper, 1944), p. 163.

Chapter 20
1. Sangster, op. cit., p. 137.
2. Sweazy, George E., *Preaching the Good News* (Prentice Hall, 1976), p. 102.
3. Davis, H. Grady, *Design for Preaching* (Fortress Press, 1958), p. 192.
4. Phelps, Austin, *The Theory of Preaching* (Eerdmans, 1947), p. 107.
5. Koller, Charles W., *Expository Preaching Without Notes* (Baker, 1962), p. 41.

Chapter 21
1. Lenski, R. C. H., *The Sermon: Its Homiletical Structure* (Lutheran Book Concern, 1927), p. 131.
2. Blackwood, Andrew W., *The Preparation of Sermons* (Abingdon, 1948), p. 123.
3. Davis, H. Grady, *Design for Preaching* (Fortress, 1958), p. 146.
4. Stott, John R. W., *The Art of Preaching in the Twentieth Century* (Eerdmans, 1982), p. 224.
5. Perry, Lloyd M., *Biblical Preaching for Today's World* (Moody, 1973), p. 47.
6. Jowett, John Henry, *The Preacher, His Life and Work* (Doran, 1912), p. 135.
7. Sanders, J. Oswald, *The Holy Spirit and His Gifts* (Zondervan, 1940), p. 111.

Chapter 22
1. Stott, John R. W., *Between Two Worlds* (Eerdmans, 1982), p. 126.
2. Westcott, B. F., *St. Paul's Epistle to the Ephesians* (Eerdmans, 1950), p. 62.
3. Baird, John E., *Preparing for Platform and Pulpit* (Abingdon, 1968), p. 82.
4. Ibid., p. 88.
5. Koller, Charles W., *Expository Preaching Without Notes* (Baker, 1962), p. 42.

Chapter 24
1. Bauman, J. Daniel, *An Introduction to Contemporary Preaching* (Baker 1972), p. 251.
2. Sangster, W. E., *The Craft of Sermon Construction* (Westminster, 1951), p. 142.
3. Bauman, op. cit., p. 233.

Chapter 25

1. Adapted from Titus 2:11-15.
2. Broadus, John A., *On Preparation and Delivery of Sermons* (Harper, 1944, revised edition), p. 66.
3. Stott, John R. W., *Between Two Worlds: the Art of Preaching in the Twentieth Century* (Eerdmans, 1982), p. 160.
4. Sweazey, George E., *Preaching the Good News*, (Prentice Hall, 1976), p. 239.
5. Stott, op. cit., p. 159.
6. Sweazey, op. cit., p. 138.
7. Sweazey, op. cit., p. 246.
8. Matthew 23:3-4.
9. 2 Cor. 4:2.
10. Stott, op. cit., p. 269.
11. Stott, ibid., p. 158.

Chapter 26

1. Kraemer, Hendrick, *The Communication of the Christian Faith* (Westminster, 1956), p. 28.
2. Ibid., p. 29.
3. Stott, John R. W., *Christian Counter-Culture* (InterVarsity, 1978), p. 10.
4. Webster, Douglas D., *Chritian Living in a Pagan Culture* (Tyndale, 1980), p. 15.
5. 1 Thess. 2:1-4. This "consideration" is based on the text of the first 12 verses of that chapter.

Chapter 27

1. Simpson, E. K., *Commentary on Epistles to the Ephesians and the Colossians* (Eerdmans, 1957), p. 125.
2. Westcott, B. F., *St. Paul's Epistle to the Ephesians* (Eerdman, 1950), p. 81.

Chapter 28

1. Brown, H. C., Jr., *A Quest for Reformation in Preaching* (Word Books, 1968), p. 136.

Chapter 29

1. Stott, John R. W., *Between Two Worlds: The Art of Preaching in the Twentieth Century* (Eerdmans, 1982), p. 126.

Chapter 30

1. Blackwood, Andrew W., *The Preparation of Sermons* (Abingdon-Cokesbury, 1948), p. 152.
2. Davis, Henry G., *Design for Preaching* (Fortress, 1958), p. 255.
3. Baird, John E., *Preparing for Platform and Pulpit* (Abingdon, 1968), p. 114.
4. Blackwood, op. cit., p. 157.

Chapter 31

1. Broadus, John A., *The Preparation and Delivery of Sermons* (Harpers, 1944), p. 212.
2. See Acts 17:1-4.
3. 1 Thess. 1:5, 9.
4. McLaughlin, Raymond W., *The Ethics of Persuasive Preaching* (Baker, 1979), p. 130.
5. Bauman, J. Daniel, *An Introduction to Contemporary Preaching* (Baker, 1972), p. 236.
6. Perry, Lloyd M., *Biblical Preaching for Today's World* (Moody, 1973), p. 174.
7. Lewis, Ralph L., *Speech for Persuasive Preaching* (Lewis, 1968), p. 25.
8. Stewart, James S., *Heralds of God* (Scribners, 1946), p. 191.

Bibliography

On Preaching

Abbey, Merrill R., *Preaching to the Contemporary Mind* (Abingdon, 1963)
————, *Communication in Pulpit and Parish* (Westminster, 1973)
Baird, John E., *Preparing for Platform and Pulpit* (Abingdon, 1968)
Bauman, J. Daniel, *An Introduction to Contemporary Preaching* (Baker, 1972)
Blackwood, Andrew W., *The Preparation of Sermons* (Abingdon, 1948)
————, *Expository Preaching for Today* (Abingdon, 1953)
Bounds, E. M., *Preacher and Prayer* (Zondervan, 1952)
Bridges, Charles, *The Christian Ministry* (Banner of Truth, 1967)
Broadus, John A., *On Preparation and Delivery of Sermons* (Harper, 1944)
Brown, H. C., Jr., *A Quest for Reformation in Preaching* (Word, 1963)
Caemmerer, Richard R., *Preaching for the Church* (Concordia, 1959)
Davis, H. Grady, *Design for Preaching* (Fortress, 1958)
Derrett, J. Duncan, *Jesus' Audience* (Seabury, 1973)
Dewire, Harry A., *The Christian Communicator* (Westminster, 1961)
Eggold, Henry J., *Preaching Is Dialogue* (Baker, 1980)
Fant, Clyde E., *Bonhoeffer: Worldly Preaching* (Nelson, 1975)
Garrison, Webb B., *The Preacher and His Audience* (Revell, 1954)
Griffith, Leonard, *We Have This Ministry* (Word, 1973)
Harrison, Everett F., *The Apostolic Church* (Eerdmans, 1985)
————, *Acts: The Expanding Church* (Moody, 1975)
Hofmann, Hans, Ed., *Making the Ministry Relevant* (Scribners, 1960)
Howe, Reuel L., *The Miracle of Dialogue* (Seabury, 1963)
Jackson, Edgar N., *How to Preach to People's Needs* (Baker, 1956)
Jowett, John Henry, *The Preacher, His Life and Work* (Doran, 1912)

Koller, Charles W., *Expository Preaching Without Notes* (Baker, 1962)

Knox, John, *The Integrity of Preaching* (Abingdon, 1957)

Kraemer, Hendrick, *The Communication of the Christian Faith* (Westminster, 1956)

Lenski, R. C. H., *The Sermon: Its Homiletical Construction* (Lutheran Book Concern, 1927)

Lewis, Ralph L., *Speech for Persuasive Preaching* (Lewis, 1968)

Littorin, Frank T., *How to Preach the Word with Variety* (Baker, 1953)

Massey, James Earl, *The Sermon in Perspective* (Baker, 1976)

McLaughlin, Raymond W., *Communication for the Church* (Zondervan, 1968)

_____, *The Ethics of Persuasive Preaching* (Baker, 1979)

Montgomery, R. Ames, *Expository Preaching* (Revell, 1939)

Nichols, J. Randall, *Building the Word: The Dynamics of Communication and Preaching* (Harper, 1980)

Paul, Robert S., *Ministry* (Eerdmans, 1965)

Perry, Lloyd M., *Biblical Sermon Guide* (Baker, 1970)

_____, *Biblical Preaching for Today's World* (Moody, 1973)

Phelps, Austin, *The Theory of Preaching* (Eerdmans, 1947)

Ray, Jeff D., *Expository Preaching* (Zondervan, 1940)

Sanders, J. Oswald, *Paul the Leader* (Navpress, 1984)

Sangster, W. E., *The Craft of Sermon Construction* (Westminster, 1951)

_____, *The Approach to Preaching* (Westminster, 1952)

Skinner, Craig, *The Teaching Ministry of the Pulpit* (Baker, 1973)

Stewart, James S., *Heralds of God* (Scribners, 1946)

Stevensen, Dwight E., *In the Biblical Preacher's Workshop* (Abingdon, 1967)

Stott, John R. W., *Between Two Worlds: The Art of Preaching in the Twentieth Century* (Eerdmans, 1982)

Thompson, William D., and Bennett, Gordon C., *Dialogue Preaching: A Shared Sermon* (Judson, 1969)

Unger, Merrill F., *Principles of Expository Preaching* (Zondervan, 1955)

Whitesell, Faris D., and Perry, Lloyd M., *Variety in Your Preaching* (Revell, 1954)

Yohn, David W., *The Contemporary Preacher and Biblical Exposition* (Eerdmans, 1969)

On Ephesians

Barclay, William, *The Letters to the Galatians and Ephesians* (Westminster, 1958)

Bruce, F. F., *The Epistle to the Ephesians* (Revell, 1961)

Carver, William O., *The Glory of God in the Christian Calling* (Broadman, 1949)

Erdman, Charles R., *The Epistle of Paul to the Ephesians: An Exposition* (Westminster, 1931)

Griffith, A. Leonard, *Ephesians: A Positive Affirmation* (Word, 1975)

Hendricksen, William, *Exposition of Ephesians in New Testament Commentary* (Baker, 1967)

Hobbs, Hershel H., *New Man in Christ* (Word, 1974)

Hunter, Archibald, M., in *Layman's Bible Commentary*, Volume 22 (John Knox; 1959)

Ironsides, H. A., *In the Heavenlies* (Loizeaux, N.D.)

Makay, John A., *God's Order* (Macmillan, 1957)

Miller, H. S., *Ephesians* (Evangelical Press, 1931)

Moule, H. C. G., *Ephesians Studies* (Hodder & Stoughton-Doran, N.D.)

Simpson, E. K., and Bruce, F. F., *Commentary on the Epistles to Ephesians and Colossians* (Eerdmans, 1957)

Westcott, B. F., *St. Paul's Epistle to the Ephesians* (Eerdmans, 1950)

General Bibliography

Dunn, Charles W., *The Upstream Christian in a Downstream World* (S. P. Publications, 1979)

Galloway, Dale E., *The Fine Art of Getting Along with Others* (Revell, 1975)

Godet, Frederick L., *Commentary on First Corinthians* (Kregel, 1977)

Green, Michael, *The Empty Cross of Jesus* (InterVarsity, 1984)

Henry, Carl F. H., *Revelation and the Bible* (Baker, 1958)

Hogan, Ronald F., *The Glory of God* (Loizeaux, 1984)

Sanders, J. Oswald, *The Holy Spirit and His Gifts* (Zondervan, 1940)

Shriver, Donald W., Jr., *The Lord's Prayer* (John Knox, 1983)

Staggs, Frank, *The Book of Acts* (Broadman, 1955)

Sterrett, Norton F., *How to Understand Your Bible* (InterVarsity, 1975)

Stott, John R. W., *Christian Counter-Culture* (InterVarsity, 1978)

Thayer, Joseph Henry, *Greek-English Lexicon* (American, 1889)

Vincent, Marvin R., *Word Studies in the New Testament* (Eerdmans, 1946)

Webster, Douglas D., *Christian Living in a Pagan Culture* (Tyndale, 1980)

The Author

John R. Mumaw, born in Wayne County, Ohio, and transplanted in Rockingham County, Virginia, was called to serve God and the church in a variety of ways. After having given himself to the cause of Christ for a period of over fifty years, he retired officially from these various callings in missions, evangelism, education, editing, administration, and pastoral leadership. His expository preaching is still in demand.

Mumaw has served in six pastorates, all of which were pursued along with teaching responsibilities. He also found ways of fitting evangelistic services into his schedule, especially during the early years of his ministry which began in 1928.

He began his teaching career in an eight-grade country school. He has taught first-graders, high school pupils, college students, and seminarians. He has had many opportunities to conduct Bible studies, youth activities, marriage seminars, and conference lectures.

Mumaw received his Master's of Religious Education at American Theological Seminary. Longtime president and professor at Eastern Mennonite Seminary, he taught homiletics there for 38 years.

His administration skills have been used in a variety of leadership assignments, such as directing institutes, serving as college president, officiating church functions, organizing service agencies, directing research studies, and performing editorial duties.

Mumaw has consistently used the expository method in his pulpit ministry. His seminary teaching has emphasized the value of the expository use of Scripture. With this method he has used most of the New Testament in pulpit proclamation. He recommends it to all preachers of the Word.

John R. Mumaw and his wife, Evelyn King Mumaw, are members of the Dayton Mennonite Church in Dayton, Virginia. They reside in Harrisonburg.